Beyond Love Trauma

BOOK TWO

P. A. Wagner, Ph.D.

3rd Coast Books
Houston, Texas
2018

Copyright © 2018 by Paul A. Wagner, PhD.

All Rights Reserved

All rights reserved. No part of this book may be reproduced or transmitted in any form or by any means, electronic or mechanical. This includes photocopying or recording by any information storage or retrieval system, without written permission from the publisher.

3rd Coast Books
11111 West Little York Rd., #222
Houston, TX 77041
www.3rdCoastBooks.com

ISBN's

Perfect Binding — 978-1-946743-03-9
eBook/.MOBI — 978-1-946743-04-6
eBook/.ePub — 978-1-946743-05-3

Project Coordinator — Rita Mills
Editor — Faye Walker
Book Design — Deena Rae Schoenfeldt — E-BookBuilders
Cover Design — Ken Fraser

Printed in The United States of America

Dedication

I would like to dedicate this book to my daughters Nicole and Emily. One has married well and raised a fine family. The other will no doubt do the same as she has an inherent, kind and gentle spirit well beyond her years.

Also to my sons Eric and Jason, each of whom I hope will find a spouse meriting their respective capacities for loyalty, honor and unconditional love.

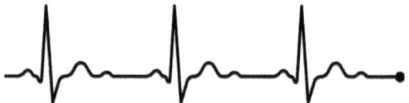

Table of Contents

Dedication iii
Foreword ix
Preface xi
Acknowledgments xiii
Introduction xv

Chapter
1. Your Web 1
2. Finding Dates 15
   Bars 15
   Church Groups 19
   Charities 22
   Exclusive Social Clubs 24
   Hobbyist Clubs 29
   Exercise Clubs 30
   Friends 32
   Grocery Stores 33
   Museums and Theaters 34
   Sports 35
   Spectator Sports 37
   League Sports 38
   Parents Without Partners 38
   Schooling 42
   Self-help Groups 45
   Online Dating 45
   Work 47
3. What do Women Want in a Man? 51
   The Ideal Man 52
   What Men Think Women Want 58
   The Moral of the Story 59

4.	What do Men Want in a Woman?	61
	The Feminist View of the Matter	61
	The Male View of the Matter	64
	The Ideal Woman	68
	Looking for the Ideal Within	69
	Changing Selves	72
	An Assault on Love and the Point of Courtship	74
	Final Note on Attempting to Change the Other	77
5.	What is a Good Date?	81
	Fool's Fancy	83
	The Gold Digger's Delight	88
	Heroes' Homage	94
	Prince's Princess	99
	Romantic Rendezvous	106
	Sadie Hawkins Day	112
	The Essence of a Good First Date	115
6.	Is Marriage a Good Idea?	123
	The Collective Suspicion	124
	Insights of the Few	126
	The Experience of Veterans	133
	Why Marriage is Not for Everyone	136
	Is Marriage Dying?	138
	Children	140
7.	What Choices do I Have?	145
	What Kind of Men are Available?	146
	The Corporate Climber	146
	Embittered Male	148
	The Male Chauvinist Pig	155
	The Patient	156
	Something Else	158
	What Kind of Women are Out there for Me?	159
	Twenty to Twenty-Five Year Old Women	160
	Twenty-Five to Thirty	160

	Thirty to Thirty-Five	162
	Thirty-Five to Forty	165
	Forty and Above	165
	Women	168
	Men	170
8.	Sharing	171
	The Political/Economic Theory of Marriage	171
	Commitment	173
	Saying, Showing, Doing	175
	Failure to Listen; Failure to Watch; Failure to Imagine and Act Conscientiously	180
	Lasting Relationships	181
9.	Intimacy	185
	Sexual Intimacy	185
	Emotional Intimacy	189
	Intellectual Intimacy	193
	The Interdependence of the Intimacies	197
	Intimacy: The Threat to Individuals	198
	Intimacy: The Threat to Relationships	201
	Intimacy: Successfully Exploited	203
	Trust and Patience	204
	Exercise for Nurturing Intimacy	205
	Building a Common Life Project — From Romance to Erotic Love	209

In Conclusion 215
    Reminders for Those Pursuing Erotic Love 216
Epilogue 219
Appendices 221
    About the Author 223
    Appendix A 225
    Appendix B 229
    Rules for Playing the Secret Exchange 230
    The Secret Exchange 231

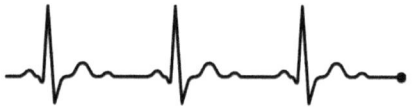

Foreword

This book deals with many personal and sensitive topics as reported by men and women who have experienced the adult dating scene. To protect the identity of certain individuals, I have changed names and occupations as necessary. However, when I have done the latter I substituted occupational descriptions that are as close to the subject's sociocultural and economic role as possible.

When the book deals with women's perceptions or men's perceptions respectively, problems of pronoun reference have been easy to avoid. However, much of what is said affects members of both genders equally. To limit the frequency of "he or she" and "his or her," I used the term *divorcee* as a gender neutral expression. Finally, the title reflects the fact that the concern here is with what is beyond any sort of previous love trauma. This book is intended to serve as a handbook to aid readers in making a success of the adult singles' social life that inevitably follows.

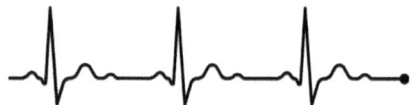

Preface

In a previous book I explain that social scientists do something called action research. This involves getting into the mix of things, observing and then sorting out the experience from the eyes of others most intimately involved. This book too is a report of action research.

Whereas the previous book dealt with the impact of divorce, this book deals with a lighter and more hope-filled topic, adult dating, love and marriage. These topics are a lot more fun to write about.

I use to teach a graduate course, cross-listed for both philosophy and psychology students titled "Philosophy of Sex and Love." So in the book ahead the eye of a trained scholar prevails. But the book is firmly secured to the palpable experience of people dating and sometimes marrying once again.

I have to admit it was fun interviewing people and finding out what they thought of the dating prospects ahead. Whether the stories are happy or disappointing they are nearly all fun to hear. Gender biases and expectations are similarly revealing when learning of them from those who hold the biases and expectations rather than those who studied and interpreted them.

Adult dating can be a lot of fun. Adult dating can also be tedious, unnerving and even depressing at times. To make it fun more often than not you need to find out what type of person you really are and what type of person is likely to find you appealing. More importantly, if appeal is to evolve into something more permanent you have to have the courage to up the ante.

Finding an appealing person and a person to whom you appeal is relatively easy, once you have a grip on Socrates' dictate: "Know yourself." But among those people with whom you share mutual appeal there is a much smaller set of people with whom you can fall truly in love and more challenging yet, marry.

Courage may mean giving up someone you find appealing because when the whistles and bells stop their noise you realize this person isn't for you. It takes courage and an unselfish spirit to walk away from an appealing person before it becomes too late.

Contrary to the self-help books marriage diminishes our sense of autonomy and rightfully so. Contrary to the self-help books marriage necessarily infringes on each person's autonomy in a variety of ways. Marriage involves creating a new social and economic unit that never before existed. The debts of each may be collected from you both. Friends rarely ask Bubbette to a couple's dinner but say "But don't bring Bubba." Marriage is an extraordinary institution. It may not even be a rational institution to become involved in. So before saying or even thinking about saying "I do," you need to think very seriously about what marriage is and what it will cost you.

The rewards of marriage are great for those who understand the institution. For those who do not understand the institution it simply looms ever larger in their lives as an increasing cost they would rather not pay. Understanding marriage and entering into it willfully and knowledgeably can be the most important act of your life ever. Those who have been there will tell you: Take it seriously.

Acknowledgments

To begin, I want to thank the hundreds of people who responded to my very personal and sometimes impertinent questions. In particular, I want to thank the hundreds who shared with me at length the very intimate details of their own divorces. I also want to thank psychologists Zick Rubin and Barbara Herlihy for commenting on the psychological accuracy of the specifically psychological claims made within. Similarly, I want to thank Thomas Stauffer, political scientist and president of the University of Houston-Clear Lake for comments pertaining to the analysis of marriage as a political institution. Also, I want to thank philosophers Richard Grandy, Mitchell Aboulafia and Thomas Gilbert for their advice on bringing the insights of the great masters to bear on mundane concerns of the present social milieu. I also want to thank the Reverend Debra Whisnand, senior chaplain of the Southwest Memorial Hospital System, for her comments on the compatibility of the views espoused with current religious views. Former Olympic medalist, author, and running coach Al Lawrence has also made useful comments on the section pertaining to sports as a social arena for singles. Finally, I wish to thank Marco Portales, professor of literature, for his patience in pointing out to me subtleties of language I hope make this book more readable.

Most especially, I want to thank my editor at 3rd Coast Books for her diligent attention to matters of style and currency. This book is in the end a much better presentation thanks to Faye Walker, Ph.D.

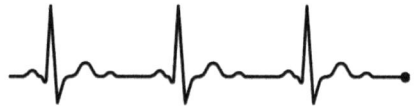

Introduction

In early chapters of this book, I describe how a person should prepare for a new life as an adult single. Each chapter concludes with a summary list of recommendations for making the most of single life. In the middle chapters of this book, I offer a classification, based on the perceptions of hundreds of divorces, of the types of date-mates one is likely to find. I trust the women and men who have shared with me their perceptions of available prospects have, in fact, detected much that is common to urban singles in the United States. In the last section, I discuss divorcees' perception of the institution of marriage, its desirability to them and the elements of commitment they need to acquire to succeed in marriage the next time around.

I do not wish to pretend the categories I offer are so detailed or refined or so rigorous that behavioral scientists can use them for scientific research. I think behavioral and social scientists will find the book raises provocative issues for further study, but I am happy to leave such study to the appropriate scientists. This is a book by and about ordinary persons. It is addressed to the person who is recently divorced and in search of signposts to both the pitfalls against, and the opportunities for, moving on.

In compiling evidence for this book, I began asking friends and dates several questions: what did they think caused their divorce; what is the function of single life; what is the purpose of marriage; what kind of men and women are available for dating; and what makes dating, difficult. From their responses, I discovered there are many parallels among seemingly diverse sorts of people. With my interest piqued, for four years I took every opportunity to interview adult singles further on these matters. For the most part, I used no questionnaires or standardized research protocols (occasions when I did are noted in the text). Rather, I allowed people to tell me their own stories and present their own world views in the most casual and informal manner possible. What I wanted was folk wisdom. I needed to let folks tell their own stories in their own way.

The people I interviewed are middle- and upper-class. Most were white though I did talk with some African-Americans and Hispanics as well. Their stories were similar to their socioeconomic counterparts. This leads me to believe divorce is largely unaffected by race or ethnic background. Nevertheless, I believe it is only fair to alert readers to some of the limitations of my research efforts early on.

My sources are limited to people I felt would communicate their deepest and most private thoughts. I did not talk to every person about every topic discussed in this book. I spoke with a person only as long as a given topic sustained the person's interest. All in all I spoke to well over a thousand people from Boston, Massachusetts; Chicago, Illinois; Columbia, Missouri; Dallas, Texas; Des Moines, Iowa; Fayetteville, Arkansas; Los Angeles, California; New Orleans, Louisiana; New York, New York; Pittsburgh, Pennsylvania; Phoenix, Arizona; San Francisco, California; San Diego, California; Tucson, Arizona; Washington, D.C., and Houston, Texas. Along the way, I also spoke to hundreds of others I met in the above cities but who lived most of their lives somewhere else.

George Gallup and Louis Harris would have gone about this study differently. My models in pursuing this investigation are not the scientific pollsters but skilled social observers like Montaigne, Gail Sheehey, Studs Terkel and the philosophers Aristotle and Ludwig Wittgenstein. I wanted to learn what principles people believe successfully led them through the most difficult aspects of single life. Furthermore, as noted above, I wanted to collect and systematize folk wisdom in a way that makes it less ambiguous and more immediately available to the reader.

Not all readers have equally wise neighbors, friends or confidants. Not all readers have the time or money to travel the country ferreting out the recurring themes of problem-solving and useful folk wisdom. I have attempted to make this wisdom available to the reader in a compact, usable form. As a professional philosopher, I have also added some of my own insights while constructing a single, coherent document, a handbook for the divorced.

Today is the first day of the rest of your life. In the next few pages, you can find something that will show you what YOU can do today to create a wonderful tomorrow.

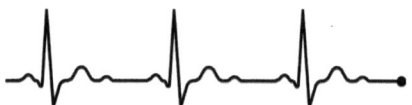

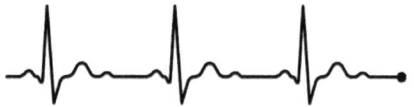

1

Your Web

If you are too scarred by divorce to risk learning and loving again, your social life will be discouraging. If you are too badgered by the furies, you will be too distracted to share with others anything of yourself. Finally, if you have fallen victim to a post-divorce pitfall, a happy social life will elude even your most zealous efforts. On the other hand, if you have passed beyond loneliness and learned to flourish by yourself, if you have developed a sense of wonderment and are exuberant about seeking new adventures, then your prospects for an interesting and exciting social life are good.

People with a sense of security, wonderment and adventure radiate. Associates immediately sense these people are splendid company. To exploit the colloquial, each such person radiates the fact he or she is a "good catch." Anyone lucky enough to match up with such a person will have many good times ahead.

Obviously, persons who are themselves "good catches" will not seek company with those who are not. In contrast to a good catch, a loser is someone who fails to recover from divorce. The point of the first book was to show the reader how to *survive* divorce. Now the discussion turns to showing the divorcee how to move into the winner's circle. That is, how to become the "good catch" everyone else seeks.

People who are good catches are aware others are attracted to them. This attraction is no mere consequence of their wealth, looks, position, power, or any combination thereof. Those who are attracted solely or even primarily by money, looks, position or power generally have little to give of themselves. They are usually uni-dimensional people who hide their own insecurities by associating with, or hiding in the aura created by, others who cast a grand shadow. In short, the "glitz-chasers" will never be considered good catches, certainly not as long as they seek light by hiding in the shadows of others.

To be a winner, a good catch does not require the glitzy trappings portrayed in various television shows. Something much more is necessary. You need to know you have "put it all together." This means you recognize you are good company for others. This alone may make you a good catch. Certainly without their capacity for self-confidence, no one counts as a good catch. For example, consider the following anecdote of a confident and youthful-looking man in his forties.

Bob had reason to fancy himself as something of a playboy. His phone seldom had fewer than two or three messages from young women interested in pursuing a relationship. He had become so confident in the options open to him he arbitrarily restricted himself to dating attractive women no older than thirty. One evening, he approached a woman whom he was shocked to learn was two years older than he. She was delightful company, and he increasingly sensed there was something special about her.

> As time went on, I lost all interest in other women. The other women I dated were lovely people. They were young and quite attractive. But somehow none of them had, for me, what this woman had. Each week, I found myself increasingly attracted to her as a person. She even started getting better looking to me. Now, objectively, I just knew that an attractive woman in her forties couldn't look as good as an attractive woman in her twenties. Still, the longer I was with this woman the more I found myself falling in love with her, the more I found myself, literally, seeing her as more attractive than women much younger. She just seemed right in my life.

The self-proclaimed playboy in this case found himself "snowed" by an older and ("objectively-speaking") less attractive woman than the others he had dated. Her charisma is what made her irresistible. Her sense of herself as a winner made her one. The playboy admitted he expected his love life to center around the young and beautiful. Nevertheless, much to his surprise and delight, he discovered, as Plato long ago noticed, beauty is far more than skin deep. So much for the myth women must be young and pretty or men rich and powerful to find truly beautiful partners. So much, too, for the myth women over forty had best give up any hope of finding a love and marrying again.

Confident, well-adjusted adults are not distracted by the superficial traits the media leads people to believe are essential for success of any kind. They know in addition to a pleasant, accepting personality, and a well-developed sense of decency, what makes them attractive is the *unique array* of experiences and interests which constitute their life histories. Good catches do not *sell* themselves to anyone. Their uniqueness *attracts* others.

Being a good catch does not mean you can go home and just wait for your power of attraction to work. "Good catches" know to attract others you have to go places. To attract other good catches they go to places where others such as themselves are likely to congregate.

If you do not see yourself as a good catch, it is unlikely anyone else will. For example, if you are a woman over forty and you believe all the statistics indicating your chances for marrying again are negligible, then you are unlikely to see yourself as a good catch. "I'm too old!" you complain.

The statistics describe groups. They do not describe an individual. There is no reason to believe you will not be one of the over-forty women who marries and happily so. This realization alone may be sufficient to help you evaluate and recognize you are a good catch just as you are. If that happens to you, the numbers about your age *group* mean little for you as a *person*.

The older you are the greater the number and the greater the variety of the experiences you are likely to have acquired. In general, with age, each person becomes more complex, more intriguing, more richly endowed with insight into the world.

In other words, with age there is reason to believe your chance of becoming a good catch will increase. With age, people also become more idiosyncratic in their selection of close companions and the array of activities they find pleasing. At twenty, a person's range of experience is so limited that most any activity, conversation or companion is easily tolerated. As one gets older, one learns while some activities things or persons have become more exciting, others have become merely tolerable while still others are simply unquestionably objectionable. Attending a new art opening may become even more interesting, visiting your doctor tolerable and toga parties written off altogether as stupid.

So what counts as a good catch? At first glance, it may seem as people age they become more close-minded. Perhaps people become more discriminating, more sophisticated. With wisdom, a hoped-for by-product of age, people realize there are too few years to do all that is truly worth doing. This recognition makes one less likely to waste precious time. "Time is money," declares the businessman. Time is also the receptacle into which we pour our life. As the receptacle fills, self-fulfilled people become cautious not to spill or fumble any of life's valuable experiences yet to come. For those who are not good catches, the relentless pouring out of life becomes a source of fear; it signals the beginning of the middle-aged crazies and betrays their future.

Youth, well-balanced or not, is unlikely to realize the preciousness of time. The aspiring model, athlete, or writer, the kid out to make his or her first million, may each pursue life with a sense of urgency, trying to fill relatively short-range goals as quickly as possible. Curiously, these people seem most vulnerable to the "middle-aged crazies" when the goals of youth have been achieved or have receded in importance. For most young people, time is not an issue. When compared to the middle-aged, they are indeed rich in time though short on experience.

Young women are the first to sense the value of a life rich in experience. This may be the reason they find older men attractive. The older man is enriched far beyond most of her male age-mates. Of course, there are limits. May/December romances draw the younger person vicariously close to the throes of old age and death and this may be a discouraging consideration.

Men in their sunset years will still find a disproportionate number of available women, but they are well advised to seek partners of similar age, even more so than in their youth. Only companions of similar age can share dated anecdotes, appreciation for a diminishing future, acceptance of an aging body and joy at sustaining a youthful mind. These considerations perhaps help explain the irony and truth that causes audiences of late night television to laugh at Jay Leno's cryptic line, "You know what it's like to look into the eyes of a nineteen-year-old girl? It's like looking into the eyes of a chicken!" I trust Leno's humor is not just a nasty bit of chauvinism. Surely, Leno's point is understood as applying to male and female alike. At nineteen, regardless of one's maturity and intelligence, time sharply limits acquired experience. Neither intelligence nor zeal can substitute for experience. The narrowness and modesty of a nineteen-year-old's experience is perhaps best testified to by the conviction of many of them that they have already experienced much of the world. And, with a little luck, they expect to experience the rest of it in just a few more years.

Middle-age, that period of life which serves as home to most divorcees, is a period when people become more conscientious about filling their lives with experiences that really "fit." This concern for not wasting time, for learning how to make the most of each minute, can cause some to lose their sense of adventure and wonderment and to avoid taking risks. For others, recognition of the value of time motivates them to find new experiences, expand their horizons as did their most valued experiences of the past. To accomplish this ambitious task requires people to heed the old Socratic dictum, "Know thyself." People who know themselves always seem to stand out in crowds no matter how retiring they may be at the moment.

Coming to "Know thyself" at any age is a difficult task. Most make some effort in this direction while in high school or college. With so little acquired experience, however, the goal is often much too lofty. For many people, the attempt to construct a systematic sense of self is set aside not to be revived until shortly before death (if even then). For others, the goal to construct what psychologist Jerome Bruner calls a "life narrative" is revived following a traumatic event such as the death of a family member, a serious personal illness, divorce or even an attack of the "middle-aged crazies." While never complete, the successful attempt at constructing a life narrative leads to the recognition that selecting a range of activities and people will likely complement the narrative's further development.

A life narrative is a story. Like most stories, with each additional chapter, a whole range of events become improbable additions to the following chapters. For example, the onset of menopause eliminates the possibility of child birth. Turning fifty marks the end of a man's chances he will win an Olympic gold in track. By diminishing the likelihood of certain events, a person's life narrative advances in ever more predictable fashion. And with each advance, one's life falls increasingly under one's own control. The self-control increases because the individual who knows him or herself seeks out new experiences that make sense *in light of* his or her current life narrative.

Consider the story of a thirty-one-year old insurance agent. All her life this dark-haired and wiry sportswoman felt she had a special affinity with nature. Her ex-husband had no such sense. As she laments, the disparity between them was too much to overcome and, she assured me, in any subsequent relationships she would be sure to associate with men more her ilk.

> He was a nice enough guy. Really, he was. He was a lawyer and worked all the time. His idea of relaxation was to go to the most expensive restaurants to see people and to be seen. His idea of vacation was to fly to some "Yuppie-approved hideaway," see the sites (in air-conditioned luxury), throw around as much money as possible and then return home with bragging rights to all we had done.
>
> Don't get me wrong. I like to go out to a lavish dinner as much as the next person, but I think there's got to be more to life than that. I love nature. I love to go horseback riding, camping, backpacking, and hiking. He thought you only did that sort of thing if you were poor. After our divorce, when I decided it was time to start dating again, I joined the local Sierra Club. I've met a couple of nice guys, though no one special. That's okay. I've got time to wait. What I won't ever do again is marry someone with so little respect or interest in nature. That's just too important to me to ever again marry someone who has no overlapping interests with me about nature.

Is this woman narrow-minded, egocentric or unable to mature? Probably not. Rather, she learned she needs to share with a loved one her love for nature. Her husband was not available for that type of sharing. This doesn't make him bad, but it does make it impossible for them to *share* their lives with each other.

For this woman, loving nature is one of those things I will describe later as a life-locating principle. In the present context, this life-locating principle is the guiding beam of her unfolding narrative light. Without the organizing principle of this theme, much of her subsequent life experience will not make sense. In coming to understand this about herself, the woman made a giant stride forward in knowing herself and hence in knowing what must be edited from the future.

"Why does this sort of thing happen?" Typically it happens because people marry too quickly and at too early an age. On the surface, it may seem by marrying young, the task of knowing thyself as well as the other is lightened since neither has much experience to sort through. It's also the case people lack sufficient focus in their early twenties. Admittedly, young people ask searching questions of one another. Still, most are too easily satisfied with the allure of a good tale. Flashpoints are sought, not subtlety, comprehensiveness, the ordinary or the peculiar.

Young people give even less attention to their own life stories than they do to a beloved's. As a result, however woeful may be their understanding of others, their understanding of themselves is virtually non-existent. This claim is pointedly made in the following recollection of a twenty-five-year old divorcee:

> I guess we were too young when we got married. I was nineteen and he was twenty-two. He was a law student and loved to read. I hate reading. I got railroaded into college by my parents. They never even went to college themselves! Still, they were sure it was a good idea. Anyway, all my girlfriends thought Jared was just the cutest thing. So when he asked me to marry him, I said yes. I never knew how much I hated to be around somebody who reads all the time, not until I had been married to Jared for two years. Actually, six weeks was enough. I'm just not that kind of person and I can't see throwing my life away with that kind.

Without self-knowledge or shared understanding of a prospective spouse, people cannot effectively assume responsibility for a common project such as marriage. The ill-defined narratives of youth leave people adrift, likely to repeat the most self-destructive patterns of their own past. A woman medical doctor makes this point clearly:

> My ex-husband thought my first duty was to have his kids and keep food on the table. My parents kept forcing that on me, too. I was valedictorian of my little high school senior class. I had some scholarship opportunities from some really first-rate universities. I wanted to be a doctor. My parents convinced me that was stupid. They sent me to the local university. I got a biology degree and kept my eye open for an *MRS*. After marriage, he and my parents decided I needed a job, not a career, a job. I went back to school and became a medical technologist. My first job as a med tech turned my life around. The more I was around doctors the more I realized they weren't that smart. I knew I really liked working in a

hospital and remembered as a kid how much I wanted to become a doctor. So I decided to apply to medical school. If my husband and family didn't want to support me, then so be it. That's where I belonged! The rest is simple. I went back. They all objected. I am now divorced, but I am also a doctor. There are men out there with whom I am compatible. My life before was a sham. Now, I am who I am supposed to be. And I am confident I will marry again. This time with someone who will love me for who I am and not for what he thinks I'm supposed to be.

As people mature emotionally, they become more discerning. They exploit experience systematically to make sense of an evolving life narrative. The doctor's experience as a medical technologist reminded her of a deep running theme in her life narrative which was poorly scripted. This extraordinary self-knowing individual refused to destroy what had all along been life-locating principles. She knew her life, her story, would only make sense if she took control and began penning the next chapter herself. Today she is a doctor and she is living a life which fits her. Moreover, for the first time in her life, she sees herself as a good catch for the right man.

People who are incompatible are not necessarily bad; they are just bad for each other. Being a "good catch" in the eyes of your partner will not allow the two of you to elude the destructive effects of holding incompatible life-locating principles. No matter how good of a catch you are, you should know you cannot sustain a relationship with someone who is fundamentally different from you. If two people are fundamentally compatible at the level of core, life-locating principles then they can make a go of it. Each may have lived a richly-textured and complex life and as a result, there may be numerous occasions which elicit differences of opinion between the two. Considerable effort may have to be exerted to bring them substantially closer in the pursuit of a common life project. But this is not impossible. And as debate refreshes the intellect, they may even find the experience enjoyable. Compatibility is a matter not of how many ideas people agree on but on the commensurability of a few basic principles lying at the core of each person's world view.

Self-awareness has advantages as well as disadvantages. When one is confident in the dating world ("I'm in no hurry. I can take my time"), others are quick to notice. This is clearly an advantage for self-confident people. On the other hand, people with dynamic and complex histories know there are few people compatibly unique. *With every half decade, the life of each adult becomes more intricately woven, the ruts become deeper and the distinctly new is delicately patched onto the edges of an ever more elaborate belief system.* An experienced, self-knowing individual is admired and valued and difficult to match with an appropriate other.

The American philosopher Willard Quine has made an extensive study of how people weave their belief systems together. His most accessible book on this subject, which he co-authored with Joseph Ullian, is *The Web of Belief*. As the title hints, Quine thinks our belief systems evolve into something like a spider's web. Those strands farthest from the center are the most fragile and subject to change by even the slightest shift in wind or nearby movement. Those strands closest to the center are the hardiest and most resistant to change. If one were to press the web analogy further, the larger the web, the stauncher the inner threads must become. To adapt Quine's work to the issue at hand, consider the following. As we age, the center of our web of beliefs form a hierarchy of beliefs and interests very nearly unshakable. They are unshakable because they are at the heart of who we seem to be. Those beliefs further out towards the edge are many in number, and these we hold only tentatively until we feel we have learned more (spun more supporting fiber) and thus are on sounder footing.

When new people catch our fancy, we begin inquiring into their view of the world. We want to know if their way of viewing the world meshes with our own. Disagreements on small issues have no effect on interpersonal compatibility nor pose any threat to a budding romance. In fact, disagreements on small matters tend to enhance romance since they invite debate in a non-threatening manner. Disagreements of a more substantial sort require careful thinking, patience, unrelenting tolerance, and a deliberate rearranging of previously held beliefs. Disagreements which resound at the very core of how each sees the world are generally insurmountable. Core beliefs are not held on the basis of evidence or sound reasoning. Rather, core beliefs determine what one will allow to count as evidence or as sound reasoning. There is nothing else to appeal to if these determinations are questioned. There is nothing further back or outside the web which can be retrieved to settle dispute. By definition, these determine how one defines one's place in the world and what shall count as the world.

When there is conflict between people on how these matters should be viewed, there is little hope for a settlement. These disputes cannot be resolved by reference to more fundamental principles or to an objective third party. There are no more fundamental principles that matter and nothing to be objective about. This is the stuff about which it makes sense to say, "That's how I am and I can't change." Such beliefs and interests are what I referred to above as "life-locating" principles. They give us a center from which we begin to understand ourselves and the world in which we live. Without them, there would be no way to make sense of any experience, past or present, near and dear, or remote and abstract.

As one accumulates additional experience, the life-locating principles become even more embedded. Wait a minute. Shouldn't a life rich in experience produce greater tolerance and the ability to work within a wide range of competing claims? Yes and, in fact, it does. But this is not at the expense of the life-locating principles. Rather, it is because of them.

Again, consider the web analogy. The increasing stability and strength of the central strands (principles) make it possible for the web to extend outward, accommodating increasingly vast domains of novelty. Tear at the edge of the web and it can easily be repaired. It can even be reconstructed and made to cover more territory than before. Tear out the center and the web is destroyed.

There are a few basic principles at the core of a person's web of belief. To ask a person to change one of these is to ask the impossible. To change any of these principles requires adjustment to nearly everything else one believes. The principles at the core are self-defining of one's perspective. They locate the person in the midst of all he or she has experienced. Without these, there would be no sense to be made of experience, no sense of life as constituting an organized whole. Imagine, for example, someone asks another to give up his/her belief in the regularity of cause and effect (a notion Quine believes is at the core for most of us) or imagine an individual who previously believed him or herself to be a lovable person is convinced otherwise. Would this not be sufficient provocation for some to lapse into severe distress?

The further away a belief or interest is from the center, the easier it is to change it. This is done either through self-reflection or through the persuasive techniques of others. But to attempt to change a person's life-locating principles is to deny the person the very core of his or her personhood.

The sportswoman who said she could never be with another person who didn't share or, at least respect, her love of nature, is on to something very profound. If love of nature is at her core, there really is no way she can ignore it. This does not mean that love of nature is a higher value than those of her ex-mate, it just means the apparent orientations of each is incompatible with that of the other. If two people hold such incompatible life-locating principles, there is no way of sustaining a relationship. Wise people recognize this and make it a point to learn the nature of their own life-locating principles as well as those of prospective mates before marriage.

The Unfolding Plot of a Life Narrative

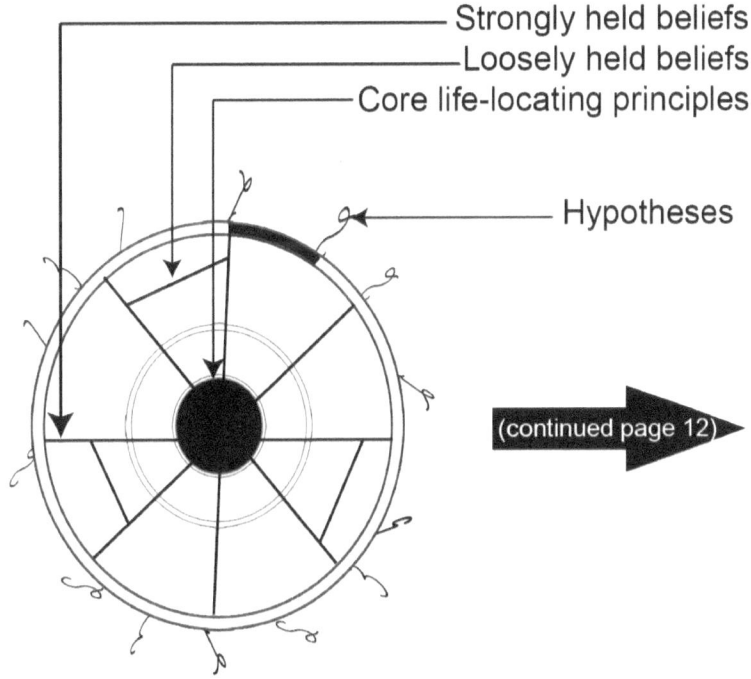

At 5 years old your life locating principles form a a core that guides your interpretation of all other experiences. The life-locating principles closest to the core are strongly held but not irrevocable. The principles at the edge of the core are loosely held and open to immediate revision. The dangling threads are hypotheses about new experiences and may or may not get woven into the web of belief.

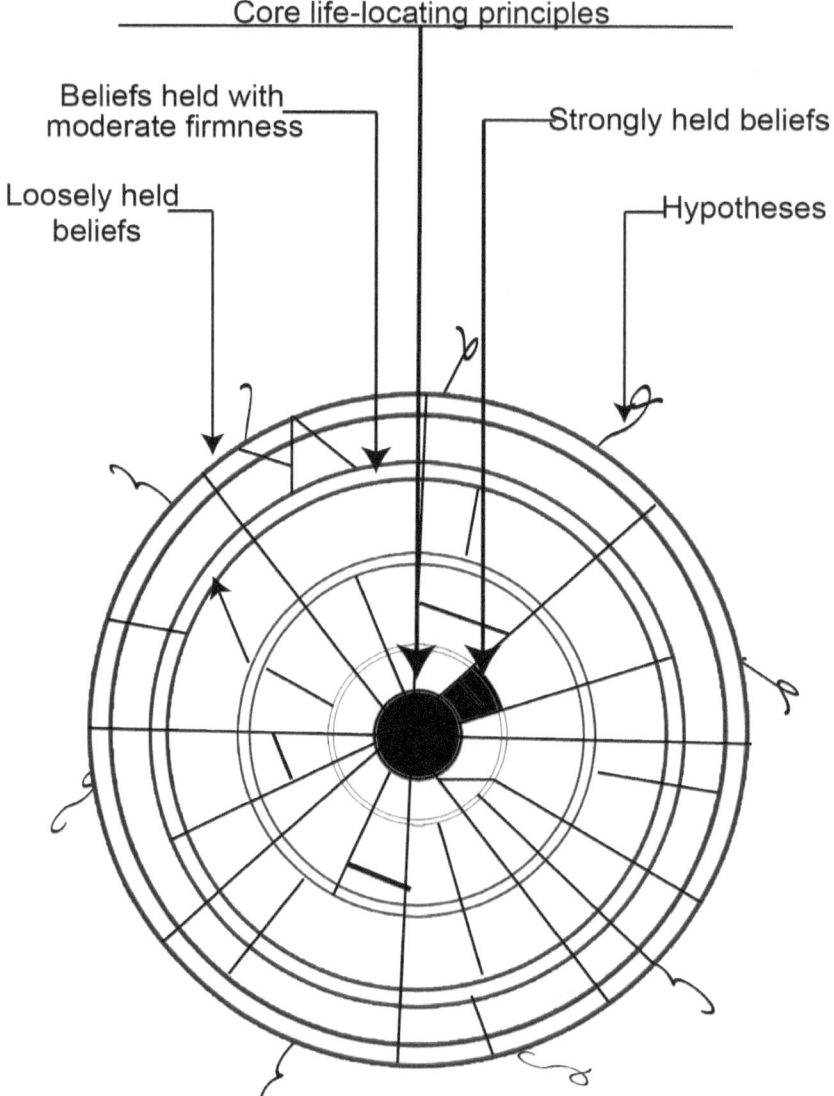

At 40 years old you have carried with you an unadulterated set of core beliefs. You still retain most of your strongly held beliefs and have added new ones. You hold many beliefs moderately and if you have lived a richly textured life, the range of events covered by loosely-held beliefs is positively enormous. If you are a good catch there are a number of hypotheses you entertain and share with others covering a vast number of topics. (Instead of a web, you might also imagine an intricate set of gears with the drive shaft located at the core with hypotheses powering no other gears.

Summary

People whom others see as a good catch will have many opportunities for socializing with others. Part of what makes a person a good catch is he or she possesses a certain common sense wisdom. Pleasant people of common sense know they can get along with most anyone. Such people can anticipate an active and varied social life. Still, there is no guarantee, even for a good catch, he or she ever will meet Mr. or Ms. Right. The very complexity which enriches the person make it increasingly difficult to find promising candidates for a lifetime project of togetherness. Meshing two complex personalities is not unlike matching together an intricate system of gears in a piece of complicated machinery. This is not to say it cannot be done, but it will require the expense of much emotional and intellectual energy. In saying this, I do not intend to sound a pessimistic note for those hoping to re-marry one day. The point is to warn against establishing marriage as the culminating experience of a successful social life. The success of a person's post-divorce social life should not be measured by the proficiency with which one engages another spouse. Social life is best measured by its ability to enrich the person's unfolding life-narrative.

If you should chance upon another whose very presence in your life enriches and develops you, then, by all means, go ahead and marry if that is what the two of you want. On the other hand, there is no need for dismay if you do not feel the prickly darts of Cupid's best arrows. Social life can be just as enriching with or without marriage. To know what is best for you, know yourself as you have never known yourself before. And learn about any prospective mate as you have never learned about any other person—before you set off for the altar! To make the best of post-divorce social life you will find it advantageous to remain mindful of the following:

1. Think of yourself as a winner, a "good catch." Remember, if you do not think of yourself this way, no one else will either.

2. Know thyself: If you have not already done so, it's time to take inventory. What sorts of beliefs, interests and attitudes do you hold tentatively or weakly? Which do you hold strongly? Which are at the very core of your existence?

3. Learn the details of your lover's life narrative before letting cupid run off with your heart. **Do not** be distracted and subsequently satisfied by what you find at the *edge* of his or her *web of belief*. **Do** all you can to determine if the *life-locating principles* of the other are compatible with your own.

4. Do not make the prospect for marriage the sole criteria of a successful social life. Instead, measure your social life by its contribution to your world-view. If your world-view is becoming more optimistic, expansive and healthy, your social life is a success.

5. Remember, if your life-locating principles are not compatible with those of another that does not mean either of you are bad. It does mean the two of you are not good for each other and attempts to pursue the relationship will only end in hurt and injury to you both.

2

Finding Dates

All right, you say, my divorce is long since behind me. The experience of loneliness and the attacks of the furies have abated. I have waxed philosophical. I am full of wonderment. I *truly believe* I am a good catch. In short, I have done all folk wisdom recommends. So here I am. Where should I go to find appropriate dates and, if the fates are generous, my own good catch?

If you have already begun taking an active role in hobbyist clubs, charities and sports as suggested, you have discovered several sources for meeting like-minded people. Let's discuss popularly recognized venues for meeting available people.

Bars

Divorced or not, nearly all singles over the age of twenty-five condemn bars and nightclubs as places to meet interesting men and women. One curious fact about this universal condemnation is people seem to make the judgment on the basis of their own past experience. This suggests at one time or another the vast majority of all singles show up at these places. If night spots are so despised, why does nearly everyone make a periodic trek to them? Why is it that when you travel to a new city you can ask almost any single person where the action is and hear the name of a bar or two?

The numbers reinforce the single's proclivity for socializing at bars. On the other hand, folk wisdom is seldom entirely without support. We might hazard the suggestion it is merely a matter of fashion to condemn bars. Disparaging the scene verbally is different from foregoing participation. Even the person who makes nightly rounds is reluctant to admit bars constitute the center of his or her social life. Maybe that is why, for most night club regulars, the standard response to the question, "Do you come here often?" is "Not often, but sometimes." On the other hand, there *are* many singles (self-reports suggest most singles) who do the night club scene only rarely. When they do, they claim their prejudices against such places are confirmed.

Then why return to such places, even only once or twice a year? A jocular thirty-seven-year old banker confessed, "Because you might have nothing else to do. Who wants to stay home alone? Besides, sometimes you do meet a decent girl at a bar. Such encounters may be rare, but it happens. When you're lonely, it's your recollection of the exception that lures you back." Similarly, a small, business-like CPA named Ann admitted:

> I just go after work on Wednesdays and Fridays if I have nothing else to do. When you work all day in a job like I do, you see the same old faces. You go home to your apartment, and it's more of the same. If you're going to meet anybody new, you've got to go out. I never stay past eight o'clock. Should anyone ask, your excuse for going is to eat from the buffet most clubs offer as an enticement to get you in. After eight o'clock, you get the regulars. The crowd seems to change completely. The professional types, like myself, use the excuse of the buffet and then get out before the hard-liners show up. It's unlikely you're going to meet anybody you like, even in the early evening. Guys who get in the habit of going for the buffet seem to shortly extend their stay into the late evening hours, usually because they have too much to drink. Also, a lot of the men you meet in the early evening are trying to find a sure thing. If they think they've found one, they call home and tell their wives that they are working late or going out with a customer. If they find no prospects for the evening, they leave by seven and the wives are none the wiser. Anyway, in answer to your question, sometimes it's just better than doing nothing.

That last remark is common among singles excusing their visits to taverns. They may also add, "And, besides, I like the music and the atmosphere helps me wind down."

The bar scene is no gala affair. Except for couples out on dates, bars expose lonely people to their collective loneliness. Consider the account by Morris, an articulate doorman, working at a posh nightclub in the heart of a big Midwestern city. Morris was twenty-eight-years old at the time. He had already completed his law degree from a major state university, a divinity degree from an Ivy League school and was currently a full-time graduate student in philosophy. He had been moonlighting at the club for just over a year. The customers regarded Morris as amiable, well-informed and very sensitive. Morris described his insights:

> Bars are lonely places. Really, it's just the opposite of what you would think. When I was in college and law school, I always thought of bars as happy places. You hoisted a few mugs, chased skirts, and sang songs. You just partied. But these places that cater to the yuppie and well-to-do crowd are the pits. The guys come in wearing six-hundred-dollar suits, fifty-dollar ties, heavy gold rings and throw their money around, grandly tipping and boasting of their successes. The women look pretty good, too. They're trim, and some are downright sexy-looking. Most of the ones I've talked to have fairly decent jobs. Before I started working here, I always thought this place was hopping. The parking lot was always full, and the valets were always rushing about. Some nights, there were even lines of people standing outside waiting to get in. I came once or twice as a law student and later as a graduate student. I figured I just didn't have the money to play with these people. When I started working here, I was stunned by what I found. Most of the crowd each night are regulars. They come one to four times each week. There is a lot of whooping it up—but that seems to be on the surface. Underneath, these people seem to be terribly lonely. The guys brag about expensive things they are buying, and they appear to be riding the crest of success. On the other hand, they all seem to look at least ten years older than their actual age. Their skin gets deeply wrinkled, their eyes blood-shot and discolored. A lot of them are starting to get those broken blood vessels in their face and a gleaming red nose—you know, the signs of too much booze over too many years. Each one prides himself on being something of a lady's man, but you can tell from what they say they'd like a more permanent relationship with someone. Or at least that's how it seems to me.
>
> The men claim they just can't find a decent girl because the women of today are [he shrugged] . . . they cite a variety of excuses. In fact, what happens is that they try to rush each girl to bed. Even with the AIDS scare, most of these guys haven't slowed down. Occasionally, one of them will meet up with a girl who hasn't been

here before. They dance a few times and then they retreat to talk at length in some quiet corner. Things seem to be going fine. Then suddenly his "I've got to drink her into bed" switch gets flipped on, and he starts ordering drinks more rapidly and tries to get her to drink more. Inevitably, the girl will get mad and go back to her friends or leave.

Occasionally, the girl will stop and talk to me. The story is always the same. She asks if I noticed the guy she was talking to. She goes on to say, "He seemed so nice at first. All of a sudden, he starts drinking more and starts alluding to getting me to bed. What's wrong with men? Is sex all they think about?" From the girl's description, you can tell this has happened to her before. She'll probably be back at another bar in a few days, weeks, or months still looking for that rare Mr. Right. As long as she's at a bar she'll probably find the same scene repeated.

The guys come up and talk to you, too. They complain that women are so unpredictable, "Like that girl I was just speaking with. Things were going fine. All of a sudden, she decides it's time to go and leaves. What the hell? If she weren't interested, why did she waste so much of my time and her time?"

Actually, more often than not the girl was interested. But the guy interprets every display of interest as an invitation to bed. For some of the girls here, it is. Of course, that's not the kind of girl the guy is looking for. And so it goes, night after night, men and women looking around, hoping to find someone different, but always with the same results.

Another thing that's causing change is that the women who use to be so free-spirited seem to be a little more careful now because of the AIDS fuss. The guys, well, you can't really tell. Some talk as if they're concerned, for example, about the relative value of rubbers. Other guys just stress the statistical odds against getting AIDS, and they seem to continue with business as usual. The girls who remain free-spirited seem to be more popular than ever.

> Since working here, I've pretty much lost all interest in bars. I'm starting to feel too old for the college bars, and these places are depressing. Do I ever go to bars anymore? Occasionally, I've come here. I mean, I know everyone and [he laughs] I only do it when I have nothing else to do.

As Ann commented, people go to bars only "when there is nothing else to do." Echoing the doorman, Julie Smith, in her award-winning mystery *Axeman's Jazz,* has her protagonist Skip Langdon observe, "Where would I go if I were new in town, didn't know anyone and wanted a drink?. . . Home. . . If guys, then what? A quick and dirty lay? True Love! Who'd go to a bar to find true love? But the answer was all too obvious. Someone with no place else to go. Someone with no other ideas and very little imagination, someone stupid!"

Even the most vibrant people are typically depressed when at a bar. In addition, since they do not *expect* to meet an interesting person, it is unlikely they will. The prejudices singles have about bars irreparably impair their ability to recognize a good catch even on the rare occasion they meet one. Night club experience may become yet more discouraging if you are not approached or are rejected by people you approach.

It is not impossible to meet a good catch at a bar. If you have no other way of meeting people, the night club is always available: no invitations are required, no memberships need be purchased, you come and go as you choose, and you can always while away the hours looking at those presumably less fortunate than you.

Church Groups

Churches, synagogues, and other religious groups have long attempted to provide for the need of teenagers to meet and socialize in an informal and comfortable setting. However, only in the past twenty years or so have churches begun to respond to the same sort of need for people over twenty-five. Most churches today sponsor young adult clubs, older singles' clubs, thirty-plus clubs, post-divorce groups and so on. Some church groups struggle to keep a dozen or more people involved while others enjoy the participation of hundreds.

Big or small, *church groups tend to attract a limited range of personalities.* Some groups may be composed principally of the religious zealot while other groups contain nearly every sort of non-atheist. People in church groups tend to share conservative values though some in the more charismatic congregations tend to be quite liberal. Generally, the people ooze with tolerance towards one another though a few of the more fundamentalist groups are suspicious of strangers and generally hostile to the outsiders. There is an over-abundance of pollyann-ish regard for each participant. For those not comfortable with the competitiveness of much of single life, the church group brings a welcome relief. Also, church groups tend to be very relaxed and supportive of the *needs* of the divorced and older singles. In fact, they can be so relaxed they are often boring, so concerned with the needs of the lonely, they are saccharine.

For most people, church single's clubs do not hold much promise for finding Mr. or Ms. Right. This has nothing to do with whether or not religious types count as good catches. Most church singles' groups contain participants who are only lukewarm believers and many may be joining in several groups of different faiths in their quest to find friends of the opposite sex. No doubt, many good catches are very religious. Yet good catches are likely to pass through the church groups and move on to other avenues for meeting singles. The singles who remain are too often those who lack confidence to venture out to other events.

One extraordinarily gifted young advertising executive with an enchanting personality and broad educational background who had studied at universities in the Far East, explained:

> I think of myself as a religious person, but I would never advise anyone to go to a church singles function. You just can't expect to meet anyone really interesting there or at least not my type. I say this having to admit that I met my husband at a church group. Several weeks after I broke my leg, I was starting to get bored, unable to go anywhere. A couple of my friends suggested we go to a local church Friday night social. It was just a matter of a pot luck dinner, some board games and conversation. It didn't sound like a whole lot of fun, but it was obvious I couldn't do much else so I went. I met a lawyer there who later became my husband. That was the first time I had been to the Friday night affair in over a year. He grew up in that area and had gone to the church all his life. Every year or two, he might show up at a meeting just to catch up on stories of old friends. For the most part, he thought most of the people attending the meetings were nerds—and they were.
>
> We often chuckle about how we met. I doubt I would have ever gone back. In fact, now that we are married, I am interested in going back sometime just to see the people and place where we met. My husband still thinks it would all be too boring, so we don't.

From a quite different part of the country, a thirty-three-year old systems analyst decried:

> I must have gone to seven different church groups, and they are all the same. The people are bland, boring, usually still hurting from a previous divorce and eager to play nursemaid to each new visitor. Everyone I met was a real decent sort. But plain decency can be real boring. I would be glad to have them all around my death bed. But I can't imagine dating any of them. You can tell they all see dating as a step away from marriage.

Churches don't run the hottest singles' events in town, but they do help people get started again *as* singles. Beverly, a statuesque nursing administrator said:

> In my own life, I sat around home for about four months after my divorce and did nothing. I think I went to a bar once with friends, but you know what kind of places those are. Anyway, I decided to go to my church adult singles' group. I liked it. They really helped. Everybody was really friendly and supportive. It gave me something to look forward to once a week. Also, they used to do some interesting things like go to ball games, bowl, meet for happy hour at different night spots. I never dated anyone from the group. The guys were nice, but they just weren't my type. The club did get me to check out different activities so that later on I would return to some of my favorites with friends from work. I guess what the church group did was show me where and how to start building my own social agenda.

Beverly went on to say she has recommended the church group scene to several of her friends, and they had the same reaction. Few singles feel church groups can be sustained as the center of their social life. They agree the groups help many people learn ". . .where and how to start building a social agenda." Newcomers to the singles world should not neglect church groups. It may also turn out *your* "good catch," the "love of *your* life," *your* true "soul mate" may show up at the function you attend. Because church single's groups are generally low-key organizations, they nurture your self-confidence when you most need it.

Charities

Take an active interest in charity work. First, by working with people in real and obvious need, divorcees learn to take heart in their own prospects for a rewarding life. Second, charity work involves collective social action. By engaging in such activities, divorcees become less susceptible to the pitfall of reclusiveness. A third reason is it may just be one of the hottest things going for today's singles!

Before rushing to the office of the nearest charity, be advised that not all charities are equally promising. For example, the Humane Society provides little opportunity for social life while the American Cancer Society, the American Heart Association and the Muscular Dystrophy Associations are three outstanding examples of charities that have become central to the social life of many upper-middle-class singles.

In the not too distant past, charities were viewed as the private domain of rich old dowagers and elegantly dressed corporate wives. In the wake of the baby boom's graduation from college, the competition for jobs, clients, patients, and customers became enormously intense. Young doctors, lawyers, accountants and stockbrokers, essentially anyone with a product to sell to a limited and well-heeled market, sought ways to introduce themselves to those who could advance their business or professional interests. Previously enterprising young male professionals sought business connections through participation in such service organizations as Kiwanis, Rotary and Optimists' Clubs and the Junior Chamber of Commerce. As competition for business increased, a number of young men and young women professionals sought alternative roots for enhancing their business opportunities. Charities represented a novel and largely untapped source of business. The moneyed interests dominating the charities early on were older women so what better place for young women professionals to establish themselves?

The rest of the scenario is easy to imagine. Young men and women met in an atmosphere of beneficence. The cordiality required subdued what was otherwise an intensely competitive situation. Charities became the single most promising settings for baby-boomers from the professions to mix and mingle.

Unlike the night-club scene, there is no "meat-market" atmosphere. On the surface, everyone is there to bring about some humanitarian good. Like the business world, people must meet and relate to each other in cordial fashion to get a job done. Unlike the business world, there is no taboo or expectations that co-workers are not to date. In fact, the prospects for enhancing one's social life is a primary if not the sole reason many people continue with charity work year after year. As tawny-haired, shoe store manager Connie observed:

> At charity meetings, you are expected to introduce yourself to each other. If you find someone interesting, you can talk to them at some length. It's a way of singles' scenes. There is no pressure to act impulsively, revealing how you feel about the other as a member of the opposite sex. You get to watch how a person gets along with others and how he sets about getting a job done. You can talk about common interests, offer to share a ride, meet before or after the meeting for a drink to talk about charity work, life or the possibility of dating. When someone calls you up that you met at a charity you know something about him. You don't expect to find Jack the Ripper in a business suit as you might in a night club. Usually, if someone asks you out, or you ask a person out, you both know you want to see each other socially before the offer is made. I think the work we do is important, but I surely wouldn't be doing this for three years just to do good! I mean, I care that we do good but since this is my own time, I see no reason why this shouldn't be rewarding to my social life, too!

Limit yourself to active participation in one or, at most, two charities. To maximize the benefits a charity has to offer, you must become highly visible for at least a year or so. You meet people through serious work efforts, not by hanging around. In other words, to play the game well you must play by the rules. In the case of charity work, the rules dictate you advance the interests of the charity.

Major political campaigns also attract singles in large numbers. Be advised political parties remain active all year long, year after year. If you find you are a political idealist or an opportunist seeking suitable patronage, you may want to remain active in political affairs as a matter of course. On the other hand, if your principal reason in associating with a political cause is to enhance your social life, it is probably best to wait until a major campaign begins to enter full swing before committing yourself.

Political campaigns can be exhausting. As the campaign nears culmination, you are expected to work harder and longer with fewer opportunities for socializing. Unless you are a person of boundless energy, the pace can be exhausting. As Mark, a shaggy-haired, and apparently much beleaguered, attorney put it:

> I got wrapped up in this campaign as a kind of lark. My best friend's Dad was running for the U. S. Congress. When I first showed up at a couple of meetings, it seemed there were young, college age women everywhere. I immediately assumed, or at least hoped, that I was about to get involved in one long party. Some nights we didn't have anything to do. But instead of socializing, people either sat around—bored out of their minds—or gossiped about the opposition. Most of the time, however, we did real work—phone calls, stuffing envelopes, driving people around, arranging for groups to meet the candidate, people to carry posters etc. To make matters worse, the work is usually work you do by yourself. Because I'm an attorney, I'll probably get involved in the fringe of a campaign or two in the future; at least I'll make a financial contribution. But never again will I get involved to the extent I did this last time. It was just more work. And during the whole campaign, I went out with only one girl associated with the campaign. All she talked about was politics. All I could think was "So this must have been the way things were in the sixties!"

Not all singles' accounts of political campaigns are quite dispiriting. But few people—even the most active politicos—see campaign work as a Mecca for socializing. Also, a few women warn political work gives rise to the same meat market atmosphere permeating the much maligned night club. So the final word on charities and political campaigns seems to be charity work really can become an act of love but politics merits a surgeon general's warning: "Buyer Beware! This May Not Be Beneficial to the Health of Your Social Life!"

Exclusive Social Clubs

Country clubs, yacht clubs, expensive private spas, members-only night clubs and restaurants have a certain allure for status seekers in quest of money, power and potential dates willing to share their riches. These are generally not places to find the love of your life. If your life plays to the theme of Tina Turner's "What's Love Got to do with It?" you may find these places exciting.

While most exclusive clubs were originally designed for married people and families, the dramatic increase in divorce rates from the late sixties to the early eighties caused these businesses to adjust to accommodate more singles. With the recent increase in marriage rates and the accompanying decrease in divorce rates, these establishments can be expected to cater once again to a family oriented membership. With the prospect for future change, the reader should treat the following as more a commentary on recent history than an assessment of what to expect.

At present, the singles' scene at these places still centers around the older man and what Barbara Gordon, in her book *Jennifer Fever*, calls the "Jennifer." For Gordon, a Jennifer is a woman dating or desiring to date a man much older than she. Gordon's examples indicate she has in mind an age difference of fifteen to thirty or more years.

The clever Jennifer will go to great lengths to get herself invited to the right club. While there, she makes all the connections she can, ensuring a ready battery of future invitations. She tries (perhaps desperately) to establish herself with the "country club" set. Older men believe these Jennifers will dote on them and so find the Jennifers an interesting source of flattery. Because there are generally many other Jennifers in attendance at these clubs, the competition can become intense—all to the delight of the older men.

Divorced women who are club members, and the most natural age group companions for the male members, tend to avoid the singles' activities at the club. For example, Margaret, a deeply-tanned and trim forty-eight-year old with exquisite taste explains:

> These guys are all just like my former husband. They want you to be young and pretty in order to make them feel young and virile. When you can no longer do that for them, they pay-off your option, as it were, and look for another. If I ever get married again, it will be to someone interested in me as a person and not as an accessory. These girls really don't know what they are getting themselves into. But I suppose most of them have to learn through experience just as I did.

Rita, a woman in her early- to mid-forties, with long dark hair and a youthful resiliency resembling that of someone in her late twenties, assessed the reception her club was holding for a visiting celebrity:

> These receptions are not just for singles. But I suppose most people here are working at seeing and being seen. There are a lot of unstable marriages around here and a number of successful singles. So if you're available, it just makes good sense to attend. By the way, there are a lot of happily married people here, too. But, for the most part, they will come just to meet (the celebrity) and go home, or to circulate to prepare the road for potential business contacts later. My ex and I used to attend these things to help build up his practice. During the last couple of years, he claimed he just got tired of it all and left this sort of thing to his junior partners. Of course, after we got divorced, the old goat started showing up at these things with his brother's secretary. He's fifty-two and she's twenty-nine. It's no big deal, that's just the way things are. He can have his twenty-nine year old. To men in their late fifties or early sixties, I'm still a sweet young thing so I'm happy with the way things are.

The moral of this story seems to be: once a Jennifer always a Jennifer. Gordon confirms this is often the case. Sooner or later though most women, including Gordon herself, realize, she says, that the richness of companionship is the most important consideration of all and is best experienced with someone close to your own age. Unfortunately, as Gail Sheehy's book *Passages* suggests, women learn to value stability and intimacy at an earlier age than do men. Middle-aged women will be frustrated by the fact that most middle-aged men may not see the light until they are in their late fifties.

Gordon devotes one chapter to relationships in which the women are older—what she calls the "Jeffrey" phenomenon and what the press dubs the "boy toy" phenomena. Gordon's examples of Jeffery relationships are typical of couples much closer in age than in the case of the typical Jennifer/older man scenario. Gordon notes while there is much talk about the alleged benefits of Jeffery relationships, in reality the public has not accepted the phenomenon. Men may date or marry a Jennifer attracting little more than a wink or a smile from friends or onlookers. The comparatively few women involved with a Jeffery often feel other women are looking to them with disapproval. Gordon warns keepers of Jeffries or, boy toys, not to take the relationship too seriously because much of the social fabric is set against sustaining these romances. If a woman does enter such a relationship, she must accept the good times while they are available and move on when it's all over. This inevitability was hauntingly detected over a hundred years ago and immortalized by Richard Strauss in his opera, *Der Rosenkavalier*.

A dignified-looking woman in her fifties, Betsy, observes:

> You know it's really not fair. These Jennifers, as people now call them, haunt the clubs fairly regularly and no one really thinks twice about it. There is, I'm sure, some resentment among women my age that these women seem to take up with all the available men our age, but no one really thinks of them as sluts or prostitutes. On the other hand, if a woman were to show up with a man only ten years her junior, she would immediately become laughable even to other women. They would immediately think he was a gigolo or just after her money. Her friends may tell her "Bravo" for dating a younger man, but behind her back they'll subject her to the most inconsiderate gossip.
>
> Even without such social stigmas I don't think women, at least women my age, would have much interest in younger men. We learned long ago that even men our own age tend to be immature so you can imagine the problems a woman would have with someone significantly her junior.

Let's consider the perspective of the Jennifer's ideal quarry. Ralph, a recently married man of about fifty-five, graying at the temples, an active marathoner, and an established corporate executive, summed up the singles scene at his club:

> It's boring. . .and embarrassing! My first wife died of cancer five years ago. We had been married for twenty-four years. It wasn't a perfect marriage by any means, but if I had it to do all over, would I marry her again? You bet. I got into the single's scene at our racquet club a couple of years after her death. My friends would fix me up with children, well, girls barely thirty. I couldn't believe they would want to have anything to do with me. But they did. Then, of course, I started worrying that they were just after my wallet. Eventually, I became convinced I was quite a dandy. I started dating frequently and trading stories with my other single friends just as we did in school. Then it struck me: I was looking awfully foolish—

foolish to myself. Here I was planning retirement in five to ten years and these women had no business thinking about such things for twenty years. What did they think they were going to get out of a relationship with me? I'm far healthier than most people my age, but, still, things are slowing down and breaking and it will get worse in the future. I intend to be as active as possible, right up to the very end, but I will age and the effects will show more rapidly each year. I certainly did not want to marry someone and feel her pity as I aged or fear her dissatisfaction with my deterioration or envy her youth.

The woman I'm married to now is three years younger than me. We met at a race. She pulled a muscle just before the finish line, and I helped her across. Right away, we knew we could be friends. We dated occasionally at first, sometimes just going to races together and so on. Over the next year, we just started seeing each other more and more frequently. It was probably five months before we had our first intimate encounter. When we're with each other, we each feel right about our age and happy with our time together. It just made sense that we should get married. We did, and we're very happy. I look at my friends, still at the tennis club, still trying to fight off Father Time by chasing the girls. I don't know what the answer is. Maybe some people just aren't suited for marriage and some are. My wife and I still play tennis and go out to dinner on occasion. But our friends now are married and live lives very similar to ours and quite different from the singles. I see little of my single male friends anymore. They have a different sense of what's important in life than do I. I hope they're as happy as I have become now—but I doubt it.

Exclusive clubs attract a certain-type of singles and repel others. As with bars, the majority of the singles present seem to be in search of a product more than a person.

A bar is a bar. Regardless of the number of limousines parked in front, regardless of the number of expensively dressed patrons passing through the front door, a bar is still just a bar. As the clock approaches midnight, there are few Cinderellas discovering their Prince Charmings in the recesses of an expensively appointed lounge. More than anything else, the late night hours reveal how little difference there is between the corporate executive's efforts to woo a willing model and the local union organizer's efforts to woo a willing welder. Only the cost of the surroundings differ. The next afternoon, nearly everyone once again agrees, bars are not the place to go to meet a good catch.

You may happen to get lucky, but the folk wisdom is not encouraging. There is no reason to believe the prospects for finding long-term happiness increases because the price of the drinks increases or because there is an expensive membership fee involved. The costs involved may deter participation by certain cultural/economic classes, but the social and psychological characteristics of "bar types" remain generally inveterate.

Hobbyist Clubs

Passion extends beyond love for another. Chess, camping, hiking, gourmet-cooking, bridge, square-dancing, ballroom dancing, numismatics, traveling, stamp collecting to name but a few, can also induce feelings approximating romantic passion in some. Recall the story of the woman who loved nature, but her husband did not. The disparity in their life-locating principles eventuated in divorce. It is all too easy to limit the concept of passion to romantic encounters, but as psychologist Mihaly Csikszentmihalyi points out in his book *Flow*, the optimal experience people seek through the serious pursuit of a hobby is a passion. People can be wholly self-absorbed in any optimal experience be it with a romantic interest, work or a hobby. As the term optimal experience suggests, there is no room for outside considerations. The experience is truly a jealous mistress. Few people can sustain a relationship with a person who objects to the other person's passionate pursuit of a hobby. True soul-mates must be accommodating to one another's respective quests for optimal experiences.

For the intensely passionate hobbyist, a club or association is a fine source for meeting compatible companions. This does not mean people who are intensely passionate about a hobby can only "connect" with other hobbyists. It simply means the more intense a person's interest, the more important it is to meet others who can respect the *intensity* of those interests.

For the casual hobbyist, a club or association may not be as appealing. Most hobbyist groups, at least outside the athletic domain, are populated by married people and not by singles. Single people do participate, but not in the kind of numbers that make the hobby club a good idea for someone whose principal interest is in meeting potential dates. As one twenty-three-year old woman noted:

> For some reason I was always good at chess. So when a chess club opened in my community, I decided to join. I don't really like chess that much, but I'm good enough that I'm able to bluff people into thinking I know something about the game. My real reason for joining was to meet guys. Chess players tend to be intelligent, serious, lots of the things I like to find in a guy. Also, I knew enough about who likes chess to know that I would probably be one of the few girls there in a room full of guys. I went for about three months. The number of people that showed up ranged from about six to twenty. Every week except one, I was the only female there, and most of the guys were single. You would think I would have had a field day! In reality, it was awful. These guys really came to play chess. In fact, I think the first couple of weeks, they were suspicious about my participation. But after I beat a couple of them they accepted me—as one of the boys! All we ever talked about was chess. One of the guys did ask me out once, but it was just more chess. A couple of interesting guys showed up on one occasion, but they never returned. I just figured this was too much work for too little reward.

If you have a hobby you are passionate about, the hobbyist association is definitely for you. If you don't, then you're probably better off investing your efforts elsewhere.

Exercise Clubs

In the nineties, exercise clubs were "discovered" as THE place for singles to meet. Rhonda, a former social worker explains:

> I remember in 1976 I was finishing my M.S.W. I was too old for the college bar scene and getting tired of Saturday nights eating popcorn and watching TV with the girls. I REALLY hated the bar scene. You always seemed to meet the same kind of person. And in the case of the more adult bars, more often than not that person was married. You knew there had to be neat guys out there, but where were they? Were they home eating popcorn and watching

> TV, too? We used to laugh, saying that maybe we should put an ad in the paper saying we usually had more than enough popcorn to share in our apartment with interesting and lonely men.
>
> One of my roommates took a golf class just as a lark. After the first couple of weeks she came home and exclaimed, "I've found them!" She said the indoor track at the University field house was just full of runners at lunch hour. Doctors and lawyers from the community, professors and graduate students from the university. Lots of them, unmarried, smart and conscientious about maintaining their health. These were the kind of guys who didn't go to bars and now we had found them.
>
> It seemed that in just a couple of years, exercise clubs were popping up all over the country and everyone knew that was the place to meet. Of course, things have all changed now. The best-looking guys in the clubs all seem to be more concerned with watching their own bodies than talking to women, while the pot-bellied guys on the prowl just do curls and join aerobics class to leer at the girls in their spandex outfits.

Rhonda's opinion of exercise clubs is guaranteed to produce ire in club owners, yet she is not alone. Many women throughout the country now echo similar sentiments.

Men seem equally dissatisfied with exercise clubs. James, an extremely muscular commercial airline pilot (with no evident pot-belly) laments:

> I have always tried to keep myself in shape. But I hate things like running, and I'm too old to play baseball three or four times each week. I also knew that a lot of girls went to the club I'm now a member of. So I figured I could combine getting in shape with meeting girls who care about taking care of their bodies. At first, it was a good idea. I met lots of girls and used to hang around the club whenever I was home. Now I just go to exercise and then go home. The women are *real* serious about their exercising. So much so they evidently don't want to be bothered. About the only time to make contact is as you and a woman are both leaving the club. If you are joining a club just to meet women, you would be better off putting your money into a fancy car, park outside and meet them as they leave.

Exercise clubs are no longer a place for socializing—they really are for exercising! Many clubs still go to great lengths to organize co-ed activities such as racquetball and tennis tournaments, but as James notes, the emphasis of participants is on the activities and not the other sex.

Friends

The thought of a friend arranging a meeting for you with a prospective date may conjure up images of yentas and tasteless jokes about the appeal of a blind date. As a youth, you may remember agreeing to a date with your best friend's cousin from Duluth. The cousin had all the appeal of Freddy Krueger from the movie *Nightmare on Elm Street*.

Now you are divorced, and friends are trying to engineer your social life. They arrange a dinner party and invite you and, conspicuously, one other single person. If your counterpart is appealing, you may be flattered your friends think so highly of you. If your counterpart could be cast as Quasimodo, you conclude your friends think so little of you. Finally, you risk being embarrassed if your pre-selected counterpart finds you disagreeable. Clearly, the prospect of friends selecting potential dates for you is fraught with many small dangers.

On the other hand, some of your friends know you well. A friend loyal equally to both parties has given due consideration to whether or not the two of you can sustain an interesting conversation with one another. Under such circumstances it is unlikely the encounter will be anything like the "cousin from Duluth" experience.

When meeting someone through the intercession of a mutual friend, try to schedule an informal afternoon, one that has established time limits, lunch, a drink after work or an early dinner. This allows both parties an opportunity to meet without imposing on either an obligation to be charming for a whole evening. If there is chemistry, you can suggest another more date-like meeting.

If friends arrange dates for you, always be gracious. Remember, your friend's reputation has become entangled with yours. If you are impolite to your date, you make yourself look bad as well as your friends. You may rid yourself of further contact with an unattractive date but you may lose your friends as well. No divorcee gains by offending a friend.

Grocery Stores

If you have not kept up with the latest in self-help books and talk show wisdom, you may be surprised to find the neighborhood grocery store listed as a place to cruise. Actually, there are a few grocery stores in major cities catering to singles. They sponsor special events for singles, sell gourmet food and play trendy music. Next time you're in New York, visit Zafar's! With these exceptions, however, the grocery store scene is largely a myth. Customers, married and single alike, go to grocery stores to purchase groceries and nothing more.

The grocery store idea stems more from media-created imagery than from any evident social trend. It must be admitted there is a simple beauty to the idea two people may inadvertently reach for the same head of lettuce, notice the coincidence, and then, while apologizing, realize they are standing face to face with the love of their lives. Obviously, lettuce is not essential to the scenario any more than any other grocery item. The outline and essential features of the story are equally pleasing (and equally likely) in a book store, a coin store or most any other retail outlet.

It is a lovely thought two people can meet quite by accident and from that point on explore a relationship that will one day become their common life project. However, one would have to spend many hours in the grocery store to meet even a few suitable prospects for dating. In fact, the very idea of pursuing such a tact is not only humorous to imagine but also paradoxical. Who, for example, is likely to be charmed by a man or a woman hanging around the yogurt and bean curd looking for a date?

If, while shopping in a retail outlet you notice someone, it might be worth the effort to introduce yourself and see how things go. This is not something you should do as a matter of routine. There are times when people are more approachable than others. If a person is hurriedly shopping, it is probably best to leave him or her alone. On the other hand, if the person is moving at a leisurely pace he or she is more likely to be receptive to your presentation. The best time to find people in an approachable state is during off hours. As Grady, a fifty-ish businessman explains:

I really started looking forward to shopping in the large department stores at the mall. My interest started on Secretary's Day. I had forgotten to get my secretary anything so I rushed to Neiman Marcus Department Store. I was wandering around looking for some ideas and a sales lady approached. There was nothing unusual about this, but in a few minutes she had learned that I was divorced, had no girlfriend, a decent job and no kids. She told me she was divorced, offered me her phone number and suggested we get together sometime for lunch. Later, in the same store, and on the same day, I had the same thing happen. Since then I have had a similar experience at different mall stores always between say ten and eleven in the morning. When you think about it, it makes sense. There are mostly women employees around, a handful of women customers and one or two men—not bad odds.

While Grady was struck by the fact the "odds were in his favor," note the atmosphere in stores at that time of day is generally relaxed and unhurried. It is not a church social or community picnic, but it may be the closest we have in today's modern world.

Museums and Theaters

This is the Rolls-Royce of the singles' scene. In nearly every major city, museums (particularly art museums), operas and ballet companies, symphonies, and many theater groups have put together a variety of sponsoring societies. People join these societies for fees ranging from a few dollars to thousands of dollars per year. Membership to the societies is open and includes several formal opportunities to mix with other "cultured" singles. In addition, these organizations occasionally sponsor a "Singles Night" to entice new audiences to their art.

The museums and theater events offer the best of everything. Large numbers of singles, all fairly educated (certainly educated enough to figure out the city's cultural events are a promising place to meet a good catch) and mingling in an environment that has almost none of the meat market qualities of a bar.

Ostensibly, everyone present at an arts event is there to view an exhibit, watch a performance or merely show support for the arts. One need not be an aficionado to initiate a conversation or respond to the remarks of another. The attractive, stylishly dressed people in attendance often know little of the arts. And, if they do, they are too polite to embarrass someone else who does not. There will be some authentic aficionados in attendance, but they are easy to spot and even easier to avoid. The enthusiasts speak in obviously affected ways and dress in a disheveled manner. They have a distinct proclivity for standing about in groups loudly sharing erudite criticism of various artist's products, styles and methods. If you've never been to one of these events but are familiar with Woody Allen movies, you're already well-acquainted with the repertoire of art devotees.

In contrast to the dire enthusiasts, most other people are there, in part at least, to see and be seen and to meet new faces. The new faces you are likely to meet will be well-groomed, and their dress will be in keeping with a stylish sense of fashion. Many are financially secure and may be downright wealthy. The point in mentioning this is not to alert the gold diggers to a new site for prospecting but to show there is an obvious business interest drawing many to arts events as well.

Arts events are an invaluable opportunity for establishing business contacts. Indeed, the late J. Paul Getty once observed, "The biggest deals in business almost always originate, in some fashion, at art events." If there is promise in a meeting for either business or social purposes, the common etiquette is to exchange business cards and promise to call.

Do not go to an art event to "pick someone up." The expected sense of social decorum is entrenched. People feel relaxed when responding to a stranger's solicitations at these events since the solicitations are properly subdued and often business-oriented. Don't worry about opening lines. Any comment on the purpose of the occasion is in order. These receptions are not a place where you try to "make it happen." They are for networking, and sometimes, they can be a staging area for your next romance.

Sports

This is a broad category. The first category consists of life-long co-ed sports like running, bicycling, tennis, racquetball and skiing. The second category includes spectator sports attracting large crowds, including basketball, baseball, football, and hockey. The third category is for sports similar in many ways to hobbyist activities, things such as sky-diving, scuba diving, square or ballroom dancing, fencing, mountain climbing and swimming. These skill-intensive activities do not accommodate casual participation so think carefully about how much time and effort you want to invest in trying out an activity from this category. The fourth category is league sports which include such things as bowling, softball, flag football and volleyball. The final category is miscellaneous and includes exotic participatory sports such as the triathlon and crew as well as spectator sports such as gymnastics. None of these sports attract a substantial following of singles, but collectively, they comprise a realm of opportunity you at least ought to know about, particularly if you're a serious athlete yourself.

Aerobic athletics: Most singles think about the life-long co-ed sports. It takes only a moment's reflection for even the non-runner to realize that in, for example, San Francisco's Bay to Breakers Run, Houston's Symphony Run, Atlanta's Peach Tree Run, Chicago's Classic 20K, Boston's Marathon, and New York's Jingle Bell Run there are thousands and thousands of single men and women who care enough about their bodies and social life to engage in these activities. Sociological and physiological research indicates "The more educated you are the more likely you are to run or engage in some other aerobic sport," and "Runners have more sexual appetite as evidenced by average weekly episodes of intercourse." Hanging out with runners can be fun. Of course, the easiest and most comfortable way to hang out with runners is to become one yourself.

If you do begin a running program, you will increase your physical fitness and hence your attractiveness to others. On the other hand, if you are dead-set against running, volunteer to work at a major race. You may not feel as much a part of the race as a runner, but you are. The runners know it. And no one will shy away from you because you don't run. A major race is a social event, and most runners treat it that way. Also, in nearly every major city, there is a popular running course frequented by singles. If you don't run, walk the course. You will quickly be absorbed into the running crowd. Nearly every day of the week can turn into a social event for single runners and their groupies. If there is any drawback, it is in the disproportion of available women to available men. Gary, a thirty-two-year old inveterate runner insists, "There's five of us to every three women!"

The lifestyles of bicyclers is becoming more like that of runners. With a variety of races and well-known biking courses, the biker's world increasingly offers the social advantages of the runner's world. The same can be said for skiing.

If racquet sports are more to your liking, every city has a variety of racquet clubs and public courts affording even a novice opportunity for participation. These events do not provide access to as many people as running, biking and skiing events, but they are substantial and can adequately fulfill the social needs of most people.

To meet someone, the best opening lines are those which pertain to the weather or other conditions affecting the event. If a person is interested in you, she or he will encourage you to speak further. If not, you can expect a pleasant nod and then he or she will continue on alone. There is rarely any sign of rejection on such occasions because, for all intents and purposes, the person approached could be so immersed in the event he or she is unwilling to allow any distractions. Egos are thus shielded from possible feelings of rejection by the knowledge the athlete may have an intense commitment to the sport and is not in the right frame of mind for welcoming *any* new person into his or her life.

Adults who care about fitness are generally doing well in life and pleased with the results. They engage in aerobic activities to get as much out of life as possible, making them a population likely to harbor many good catches.

Spectator Sports

All too often spectator sports are dismissed as male-dominated domains. However, more women have freely pursued interests in spectator sports. Many women have also undertaken the pursuit of men, much the way men pursued women only a generation or two ago. If a certain sport is known for attracting a broad range of eligible bachelors, one can expect women have discovered the sport.

The spectator sports providing the greatest opportunity for the adult singles vary from region to geographic region. There are two reasons for this. First, given differences in climate and socio/cultural traditions, some sports have long had more appeal in a given region than other newly initiated sports. Second, a sport's appeal to adult singles is, in part, determined by the arena's proximity to the business or finance center of the city. The sport of choice for many businessmen, lawyers and financiers is simply the one they can easily get to after work.

In the Northeast, hockey and basketball dominate the scene, in the South, football, in the West, basketball and in the Midwest, baseball and basketball. This rough taxonomy is not wholly accurate for every city. Obviously, in a midwestern city such as Lexington, Kentucky, horse-racing dominates, as does car racing in Indianapolis and in the South, greyhound racing in Pensacola. If you're considering attending a spectator sport, look to your own city for sports which offer the most hospitable surroundings to people you think might appeal to you.

Making contact with possible dates at such events can be problematic. If an attractive person is sitting near you, it is a simple matter to comment on a play or a performance. On the other hand, if it is a matter of meeting someone during intermission or at a concession stand, things get more complicated. Your solicitation is immediately recognized as a come-on. That does not mean you should not introduce yourself, but rejection will be part of the game from time to time.

League Sports

League play provides a ready forum for opening lines of communication. As with spectator sports, one can always attempt to begin a conversation by commenting on a play. If the person you address is unresponsive, your ego assumes he or she is preoccupied with the thrill of the game. League sports are particularly satisfying to evening and night shift workers because these sports may be one of the few opportunities they have to socialize with others who appreciate the stress of shift work. On the other hand, since leagues often form around work or church groups, you may duplicate associations already in your life and thus add little to your dating opportunities.

Parents Without Partners

Divorced parents go through both the dissolution of a marriage and the dissolution of a family and many regard the latter as much more devastating. For example, Jean, a dental hygienist, tearfully exclaimed:

The first time I got married, I expected it to be forever. We had one child and were hoping to have a couple more when things started falling apart. I don't know whose fault it was. But when we divorced, we were both sure we were doing the right thing.

I got custody of Brooke. At first, Guy kept close contact, exercised his visitation rights and always paid his child support. Later, he started seeing Brooke less and less. He always pays his child support, but he is out of our life altogether now. Christmas and birthdays are miserable. Brooke was only four when we divorced so it hasn't been as rough on her as it has on me. You can survive as a single parent, but given the way I was raised, there is something strange about living a life as a half a family.

I know it was rough on my ex, too. I think his own unhappiness in visiting Brooke was a consequence of his feeling that it was no longer a family affair. It was just a bit of play-acting. How do you make a broken family look like an 'unbroken' family?

I got married again five years after the divorce. That marriage lasted only a year. That divorce was difficult, but it was not as bad as the first one. The first one destroyed a family. The second one only destroyed a romance. Brooke was upset by the second divorce, probably, in part, because she was older and understood it more. Still, she seemed upset because of the effect it had on me and not because of the effect it had on her. She got along with my second ex just fine. But she's a bit jaded. She's never really known family life the way I have. She just saw my second husband as a sort of friend, and friends part ways. I wonder what we are teaching our children about relationships and commitment?

I sometimes wonder if I would do things differently if I had it to do all over again. I know the answer I'm supposed to give, at least the answer that's always given on television: "No." I'm not so sure that's the right, or even a very truthful, answer. I've talked to several of my divorced single-parent girlfriends about this. There was something awfully nice about growing up in a family. Everyone's parents fight. Yet they always stayed together. As a child you just knew they would. I think in many cases, both the child and the parents are happier in the long run when they know that despite any fights or problems, each member of the family is unquestionably committed to supporting the others "til death do us part."

Could my first ex and I have made it if we tried harder? Probably. But, you know, it just wasn't the thing to do then. Wherever you looked, television, the movies, your friends, everyone was getting divorced. If marriage wasn't all it was supposed to be or you weren't being fulfilled because of it, you just divorced your partner and you started again. But when you're a parent, you just can't start again. Divorced or not, you remain a *piece of a broken family*. Even if you get married again, your new family contains pieces of the old. I'm not saying you can't be happy this way, but your life is. . .well, lopsided. Am I making myself clear?

Divorced baby boomers, particularly those with children, find themselves anguishing over their earlier purchase of an ill-fated ideology. In pre-baby boomer days, marriage and family were seen as harboring the fruits of Eden. Adults were presumed happy only when safely nested in a marriage and one hoped it produced many adoring and well-behaved offspring. In the late sixties and early seventies, this image was challenged. Instead, marriage and family became products. One bought into marriage only if it contributed to one's personal joy and self-fulfillment. If the price proved too high, that is, if the cost in terms of time and effort purchased too little in the way of immediate happiness, it was all right to discard the defective product and look for a better buy.

Historian Christopher Lasch describes the seventies as the Age of Narcissism, a time when satisfaction of personal interests became the Holy Grail, a time when self-sacrifice and commitment to others were decried as oppressive and unreasonable. Now, baby boomers who married and divorced are reviewing their lives and expressing concern their life narratives are infected with some bad ideology, "some bad dope" in the rhetoric of the sixties. In short, many harbor the haunting thought Jean confessed, ". . . you remain a piece of a broken family."

Family life requires self-sacrifice and regard for others—particularly the family's children. Divorce confounds the exercise of these virtues. The recovering divorced parent faces twice the challenge of other divorcees, laboring under the consequences of a broken family for a decade, a score of years or more. Whatever difficulties the divorcee faces as a single, the divorcee's problems are compounded dramatically if he or she has a child.

Baby boomers themselves do not understand the history their generation has produced thus far. Many are suspicious that earlier free-wheeling attitudes toward sex, marriage, family and commitments were misguided, and they have become increasingly conservative. While some precariously attempt to maintain a wait and see attitude before abandoning an old ideology or adopt a new one, others have unhesitatingly pursued traditional family values, values that only a few decades ago were an object of derision. Regardless of the single parent's attitudes on these matters, there is much uncertainty. No other generation has created so many bits and pieces of family. No other generation has enticed so many parents to set out on a life of their own without the benefit of suitable role models. Single parents then are left to look to each other for advice and support. As the British say, they are left to "muddle through as best they can."

Those who never shared the responsibility for raising children may sharply and deliberately change the course of their life narratives following a divorce. In contrast, those who live as a "...piece of a family" are denied many of the options available to others. Parenthood limits the autonomy of the parent in ways analogous to childhood's limitations on the child. There are roles to be fulfilled, regardless of the pulls and tugs of one's natural inclinations.

Parents Without Partners provides an ideal opportunity for the single parent to associate with and learn from others who are doing the best they can to muddle through. Divorced parents, men and women alike, with or without custody, learn from each other how to deal with the daily trauma of helping a child cope with what is left of the family. Parents Without Partners is not just a support group for divorced parents, it is also a singles' group. Parents with custody of their children often find they are social pariahs to the opposite sex. As Tom, a thirty-seven-year old medical supplies salesman reports, "On the second date I had with Karla (a beautiful twenty-seven-year old nurse), she found out I had custody of my kids. She told me we shouldn't see each other again. She pointedly told me she likes kids, but her own—not those of others." This reaction is typical. Many singles look forward to having children someday. Others look forward to life unfettered by the responsibilities of parenthood. Few look forward to a life where they are asked to be a stepmother or a stepfather to someone else's children. When one person marries another with custody of children, he or she does so despite the other's parental obligations.

Men are especially loathe to tie their fate to what one union leader dismissively described as "...some other man's cast-off family." Similarly, Ann, a thirty-two-year old, never-married clinical child psychologist admits, "I love children and one day I want to have my own. I don't want to have anything to do with someone else's children. I see the complications this creates in families every day. I think I deserve my own family. I don't want to become a part of the remnants of someone else's mistake." Finally, an attractive thirty-year-old lawyer declared simply, "As soon as men find out you've got a couple of kids, they're gone!"

At Parents Without Partners' events, everyone has parental responsibilities. People there are generally comfortable with the idea a prospective mate's life is complicated by children from a previous marriage.

Parents Without Partners is not for everyone. Any single parent will readily admit personal freedom is compromised by parenthood. And for that very reason, he or she may not want to risk any further loss by creating a mixed family.

When it comes to intimate associations, society insists people be allowed to affiliate as they like and for whatever reason they choose. Parents Without Partners treats this population very specially and whether a match is to be found there or not, all have grounds for sharing a common sense of empathy with one another.

Schooling

Post-secondary education was once the exclusive domain of eighteen to twenty-six-year olds. All that has changed, however. Nearly all divorcees work. With shifting career opportunities, financial misfortunes, and family responsibilities, many people in their thirties and even up through their fifties return to school for some form of re-training. Others return to school to learn a new social skill, begin a new hobby or study a subject that interests them.

Junior and community colleges, vocational schools, museums, libraries, and organizations such as the YMCA all offer vocational and hobbyist courses covering a variety of topics. What may begin as a quest for career enhancement or personal development can become an opportunity for romance. The courses people select reveal they share something of a common goal or interest.

Particularly in urban areas, colleges and universities offer expanded night and weekend curriculums leading to a degree. And colleges now offer a number of non-credit courses to students as well as babysitting services to boot.

MBA programs and graduate programs in law, education and engineering dominate the night school scene. Most of the people enrolled in these programs work full-time during the day and are pursuing advanced degrees at night.

Some adults re-enter college after the successful completion of one career in order to pursue another one, albeit less lucrative but more ennobling. For example, two engineers, both with MBAs, had recently completed careers as administrators with the NASA Space Center. Their homes were paid for, their children in college, so they decided to get certified as public school teachers and, in their words, "do some real good for the country." Kenny, a forty-nine-year old divorced lawyer who also returned to college to get certified as a public school teacher explained:

> I had a heart attack at forty-four. I couldn't believe it. I was lean, ate well, didn't smoke. I drank in moderation and played vigorous tennis. Heart attacks were supposed to happen to those other guys. I was in an unhappy marriage and had a thriving but stress-filled law practice. Our children were grown so I didn't think it would be a big deal to get divorced. I was wrong. I nearly had another heart attack. Anyway, the law practice was still getting me down. I was making lots of money, but what did I need it for? I decided to go back to school and become a teacher. I thought this way I could do some good and be happy with myself. I met the most delightful woman in one of my classes. She had recently divorced her husband and was becoming a teacher to support herself and ten-year old son.
>
> We have much in common. Her ex-husband provided her with most of the material niceties. But, like me, she discovered that one thing money can't buy is love and happiness. As teachers, we plan to enjoy long automobile trips in the summer. I've never been happier.
>
> We eat at the salad bar at McDonald's because we have to be careful with our money. There is always so much to talk about, so much to plan, so much interest on both our parts to search out all the simple joys in life. My blood pressure has gone down, and my doctor assures me I'll be around for her son to grow up.
>
> When I decided to go back to college, I never thought I would meet a woman my age in one of my classes (his fiancée is thirty-

eight) much less one that shared so many of my same goals and similar interests.

The arts, social studies and humanities are each finding a greater demand for their course offerings in the evenings as well. There is only so much television and so many pop novels or self-help books any reasonably intelligent person can handle. Consequently, many adults both married and single are looking to the local university as a source of challenge and new insights. For example, in a graduate evening course I teach entitled "Philosophy of Sex and Love," no one who enrolls for the course needs it to satisfy a particular degree requirement. Many are not even enrolled in a degree program at all. They take the course for credit or as an audit simply because the topic interests them. Many are divorced. Most are between the age of twenty-five and fifty. It is not uncommon for students to occasionally strike a bond of friendship with one another. Courses in poetry, foreign language, music history, art history, and psychology are all likely meeting places for singles looking to fill their lives with new and deeper meaning.

As an academic, I am loathe to encourage people to return to college to find dates. College is for study and learning; it is not the single's club of the future. Still, adults are finding in college a comfortable and non-threatening environment in which they can meet others with similar interests and intentions.

Do not try to "psych out" the curriculum, selecting a course you think is likely to attract members of the opposite sex. If you do not like the course subject matter, you will look bored and, worse yet, be boring. You will not attract the kind of attention you want. Choose a course that animates you. This leads others to see you as exciting, thoughtful and dynamic.

Colleges limit enrollment and thus screen the type of person likely to sit next to you. A person who ten years ago flunked out of his or her freshman year of college cannot enroll for a graduate course in medical ethics and human experimentation. Similarly, a person who barely graduated from college with a degree in physical education will not be allowed to enroll in an advanced course in tax law. A person working as a bank clerk or gas station attendant is unlikely to set aside the sum required to take a three-hour course in international affairs at a prestigious private school such as Georgetown University. The forces of selection tend to ensure your classmates will have backgrounds similar to your own.

Self-help Groups

In her novel *Axeman's Jazz,* Julie Smith explores the world of self-help junkies and twelve-step programs in New Orleans. On the West coast and throughout the South, self-help groups and twelve-step programs are "evolving into favored locales for single neurotics to cruise for other neurotics." This observation of Smith's detective O'Rourke is not far from the mark. Before I risk offending anyone, let me note in one way or another everyone is neurotic—even happily married people who never divorced! It may well be people confronting the challenges of more severe neurosis can meet the challenge better while at the same time help another meet the challenge through a romantic liaison.

However, before turning to a self-help group closely aligned to your most mischievous neurosis, consider watching the movie *Days of Wine and Roses* with Lee Remick and Jack Lemmon as two alcoholics trying to kick their addiction. I tried to find a more current movie, but this particular one says it all. You may just conclude treatment for addictions and neurosis are not to be confused with quest for romance. One thing you will find in every self-help group is tolerance and acceptance. Be careful that the security afforded by the group does not become debilitating of your efforts to live a free and autonomous existence.

Online Dating

Divorce increased the ranks of the adult single population dramatically throughout the seventies. Prior to the sixties, people graduated from high school, college or professional school and, within a couple of years, married. The term "adult single" conjured up the image of a widow or widower, typically fifty years of age or older.

Today, the term adult single identifies millions of Americans between the ages of twenty-five to fifty-five. Dating and searching for dates occupies the leisure time of many an adult single. In fact, the quest to meet that "good catch" has become an avocation for some. With literally millions of adult singles on the market, the more frenzied lament, "There must be at least one out there for me. But how do I find that person?"

Capitalizing on the zeal with which singles pursue dating, entrepreneurs have assembled a variety of gimmicks for introducing singles to Ms. or Mr. Right. An increasingly common venture is computer dating services. The client fills out a questionnaire identifying a set of ideal physical and psychological attributes and the company "scientifically" matches these with those listed by other clients and then gives the client access to the individuals through an online service.

But before rushing to your computer, consider the observation of those who have been online a year or more. Gary, a ruggedly-handsome thirty-one-year old systems analyst spoke for dozens:

> When I first joined, it was wonderful. You could always get a date and you met people from all over the city. After a while, you start realizing that all the people you meet are somehow messed-up. They are either recently divorced or have just broken up a long time relationship. The ones that are not on the rebound have a biological clock ringing in their ears. I guess I was that way, too. I had just broken up with a girl I had been going with for two years. Other than bars or work, I didn't know how else to meet girls. So it seemed like a good idea.

A vibrant and enthusiastic thirty-four-year old woman, a veterinarian, Angela, complained women had very much the same sort of experience:

> I was skeptical when I first joined. But I figured, 'What the heck, right?' Anyway, I was amazed to find that there really were doctors, lawyers, professors, some fairly big-time engineers, and businessmen online. But then you start going out with these guys and you discover that most of them are still hurting from a recent separation. On the other hand, you also come across a few who are confirmed bachelors and use the service only to ensure that they have a steady source of potential dates on hand.
>
> I got selected a lot. In fact, I never got around to selecting any men. After about three months, I just stopped responding. It was too much. The guys all started seeming alike and the date conversation was disquieting and predictable, "How have you enjoyed your matches?" (Translation: What's my competition?)

"Why did you get divorced?" (Translation: Could you make a compatible mate for me?) I mean, give me a break. This is first date conversation! Even the women who don't often get picked complain about how predictable each seemed to be. The constant undercurrent is always: Can you make a good partner for me?

While online dating might not be a promising source of good catches for you, they do help you get into circulation. They allow people to risk rejection without exposing themselves to personal confrontation. This is reassuring for those who are not yet comfortable with the ups and downs of the dating scene. However, once the divorcee learns the ropes of single life, his or her appetite for people clinging to such dating strategies wanes precipitously.

If the reader has a special interest in meeting people with a certain business background, fear, affiliation with a certain college, culinary interest, or travel interest, such online matches may be just the ticket. Your answer, however, will have to be discovered by experience and not in the pages of this book.

Work

Originally, I had no plans to mention the workplace in this chapter. The common folk wisdom on this matter is entrenched—"Work and play do not mix." However, there have been a spate of articles in the popular media and at least one book touting work as an appropriate place for singles to meet others of like interests and tastes. This may well be the recommendation of a few self-appointed "experts" but people in general still follow the old adage.

Office Casanovas are as disruptive of office decorum as they ever were. In addition, with increased awareness of sexual harassment, office romances are more a liability than ever before. Even when harassment is not at issue, managers and conscientious employers all have an interest in discouraging office romances. When romances fail, the people involved want to avoid contact with each other. If they are expected to work together, this makes their shared emotional travail more difficult. Inevitably each person's work performance is affected detrimentally.

The awkwardness of office dating relationships is captured in the following brief account offered by a confident, twenty-six-year old legal secretary, Colleen:

> I dated one of the lawyers from my firm. We always felt we had to hide our dating. It got to be a real pain. I believed that if the other secretaries found out, they would get jealous and make life difficult for me. He thought that if the senior partners found out, they would think he was not serious enough about his work. Finally, I just switched to another firm. Of course, three months after all that we broke up!

Frank, an insurance officer with a large corporation intimated:

> I started dating my boss about two years after I got there and six months after her divorce. The whole time we felt like we had to sneak around. When we broke up, I transferred to another division. For at least a year afterward whenever we saw each other at work, in a hallway or whatever, it was painful. I won't ever date anyone from work again! I know now why people are adamant in insisting that work and play don't mix.

Summary

There is no list of rules to follow or cautions to heed that can neatly sum up this chapter. Nor are the categories identified of merit for all people. For example, on the surface it would seem charities, museums and theaters, jogging, and education are the best bet. However, if you are a seventy-five-thousand dollar a year general foreman on the night shift of an industrial plant, or a medical resident on evening call, these options may not suit you. What I have done below is construct a chart showing what I take to be the relative merits of the various options; using the following criteria:

1. Accessibility (the ease with which any single can participate;

2. Comfort (the receptiveness of the general social atmosphere);

3. Costs (the expenses likely to be incurred in taking advantage of this option);

4. Effort (the work required to make this a truly viable option. For example, if you are a hundred and fifty pounds overweight, smoke and drink to excess, then the effort required to participate in marathons is inconceivable);

5. Number (the number of people likely to co-participate in any given occurrence) and Yuppie Appeal (This last, a fun criterion, is not entirely tongue-in-cheek. It represents the likelihood for people to meet others intent on raising their social, cultural and economic status to that of at least the upper-middle-class).

Each criterion will have a number from one (1) to five (5) associated with it. One means poor and five means outstanding.

NA will be used to indicate the category does not lend itself well to evaluation using this numerical method. Remember since several of the categories contain subcategories, and since the ratings are necessarily contrived, one should not rely too heavily on the reported evaluation. To discourage over reliance on the summary quality of the chart, I have not included totals under each category. I hope this exclusion will underscore any false impression one can order a set of categories satisfactorily for all readers.

The idea is to encourage the reader to make up his or her own chart and evaluate the various categories according to the reader's own experience, giving a more systematic way of deciding how to spend his or her leisure time. Self-help groups and twelve-step programs have been left off altogether. Their anonymity makes it difficult to collect much good information, and I hesitate to demean the therapeutic good they do some people by evaluating them on criteria wholly irrelevant to their purpose.

Places	Accessible	Comfort	Costs *	Efforts **	Numbers ***
Bars	5	3	4	1	5
Charities	4	4	3	3	4
Churches	4	5	4	5	3
Exclusive Social Clubs	2	2	1	1	3
Exercise Clubs	3	2	2	2	2
Friends	5	4	5	4	3
Grocery Stores (Retail)	5	2	4	2	1
Museum & Theaters	4	4	3	3	4
Parents w/Out Partners	4	4	2	3	5
Schooling	4	4	4	4	3
Singles Groups	4	3	4	4	5
Sports (Participator)	5	5	4	4	4
Sports (Spectator)	5	4	3	2	3
Work	2	3	1	5	2

*1 / Costly — 5 / Inexpensive
**1 / Great Effort — 5 / Little Effort
*** 5 / Many Available Singles — 1 / Few Singles

3

What do Women Want in a Man?

This chapter will not end with a list or a table. Any such list would be misleading. A folk wisdom exists among women regarding the "best" men can offer, but it is in the process of radical change. There was also a traditional folk wisdom among men detailing what they think women *want*, but this body of thought has lapsed into total confusion and outlandish conjecture.

In this chapter, the discussion contrasts what women publicly claim they want with what they privately desire. The discussion then turns to what men once thought women wanted and contrasts this with men's current efforts to become the mythical ideal each woman presumably desires. The chapter concludes by explaining why men and women would both be better off by freeing themselves from the dictates of expert advice and their own second-guessing. The more richly-textured your life, the more vast and complex your web of belief, the more individualistic you will become so what is ultimately appealing to any woman will be an individual matter and not a community prototype. It is inadvisable for a man to become chameleon-like and attempt to capture the fancy of woman-kind. Each woman is an individual. Each looks for an unique range of attributes attracting her to some men and not to others.

People's individualism is a record of their adventures. It also creates something of a conceptual prison. Our individualism makes us aware of some romantic possibilities while distracting us from others. For their part, men do best when they accept their individual life narratives. Then they see that attempting to sculpt an ideal conforming to someone else's specifications will probably be self-defeating.

The Ideal Man

If one reads the popular literature on this topic, listens to talk shows or accepts the set of images of "ideal" men portrayed in contemporary film and television, one gets the impression there is a fairly universal conception of what constitutes an ideal man.

The Ideal Man

- Gray at the temples, maybe a few lines (sufficient evidence of character) and naked can be mistaken for a nineteen-year-old Olympian
- Not afraid to cry: demonstrated this once in desperate agony over losing someone close to him (This behavior must not be replicated more than once a decade!)
- Favorite television shows are any starring Kerry Washington
- Has the conversational mannerisms of a well-known talk show host. (No, it's not Oprah Winfrey or Maury Povich. Guess again.)
- Is a card-caring member of N.O.W.
- Is terribly rugged-looking while meticulously-dressed in his Armani and Brooks Brothers clothes
- Would never encourage a significant other to get an abortion but is unequivocally committed to Pro-choice
- Financially secure
- Never notices how attractive he is in the eyes of other women
- Well-read in the self-help literature
- Ryan Gosling is his favorite actor
- Is an outdoorsman type, handy around the house and always impeccably clean

- Believes in equality between the sexes despite his powerful "Gregory Peck-like" persona and ability to always be that "strong shoulder" to lean on

- Has a strong erotic drive that operates only when you're interested

- Loves you to socialize with your girlfriends and seeks out male companionship only when you want to be alone

- Loves to cook, wash dishes, clean house, do yard work, mind the children, and after a long day of work there is nothing he enjoys more than to prepare you a bath, brush your hair and rub your back and your feet

Not even on television has this composite appeared. If it cannot be found in fiction, what are the chances of finding it in reality? Would anyone really want this character?

Obviously, it is too much to ask of any one man that he be all these things. Mere mortals could never be so accomplished. On the other hand, is it too much to ask the ideal man at least *strive* to be all these things? Ideals are not about what people do or are but rather what people *should do* or *should become.*

In creating an image of an ideal man, there is no expectation the ideal will be realized in any one person. The closer a man is to the ideal, presumably, the more he will be appreciated and sought after by women. Any man who really cares about respect and appreciates women will do all he can to move from where he is now closer to the ideal as his talents and resources allow. Having said all this, a question remains: is the above portrayal of the ideal man an accurate depiction of women's folk wisdom about such matters?

The answer is a resounding "No." There are several reasons for this. First, capturing the essence of the ideal man is even trickier than capturing the essence of the social scientist's notion of an "average" person who is characterized by a set of statistics describing group propensities. It is unlikely any one person neatly displays a set of properties identical to *all* the statistical norms of his or her sex. Indeed, such a person would be quite extraordinary rather than ordinary. Each individual represents an unique constellation of attributes, some held in common with the majority and some not. Human individuality makes the instance of one truly average person well-nigh an impossibility. The concept of an average person alludes to *group* characteristics; it describes no *one*.

The essence of an *ideal* man in the context of adult single life is similarly inaccessible. The public ideal represents a distillation of women's predilections not the actual preference of any one woman. Since women are as individualistic as men, there is no reason to believe women share a common image of an ideal man, not even a modestly finite set of images! The truly ideal man for one woman will no doubt be different from that of all her sisters.

Would it not be useful for a man to know many women are changing their minds about what counts as an attribute or a defect in a man? For example, in the 1950s women looked with scorn upon a man who chose to stay at home and be a house-daddy while his wife went off to work. Today, the experts, talk-show hosts and audiences tell the world all that has changed. (Has it?) If a change in attribute is easily within a man's reach and if it will result in his becoming more desirable to large numbers of women, is this not the sort of thing that could cause a man to change his life? Surely it is. With the goal of improving one's general marketability, men are likely to continue the search for traits which most women value.

But no one man will ever possess the entire range of attributes descriptive of women's aggregate notion of an ideal man. If such a man exists, there is still no guarantee even one woman will find the personification of these qualities *ideal* for her! Nevertheless, it seems likely the more attributes of the ideal man any one man can possess, the more initial appeal he will have to an inordinately large number of women.

Before men begin running about trying to reconstruct their personalities and behavior patterns to bring them more into compliance with the ideal, it might be useful to step back and ask women just how *ideal* are the attributes publicly proclaimed as ideal. For example, on the abortion issue, clearly millions of women are in favor of the right to abortion as well as millions who oppose it. What is the "ideal" position most women really want a man to hold on this issue?

I queried forty women from eight cities and one rural community what they thought would be ideal in a man. The qualities the women mentioned are incorporated in the description of the ideal man above.

After an initial response, I asked, "Since there is no ideal man, and since what may be ideal for one woman may not be ideal for another, tell me what would be ideal for you. Imagine you are sitting with four or five of your dearest girlfriends from high school and it is two o'clock Saturday morning during a class reunion weekend. Pretend each of you is telling the others about her ideal man. What would you say?"

The responses the women gave to this question were different from their responses to the general question. Besides descriptions of physical appearance, the women said things many experts believe only their mothers would say. For example:

> A thirty-year-old mortgage banker said, "I want a man who is a real gentleman."
>
> A thirty-nine-year old Ph.D., biochemist and medical doctor said, "Well, for me, I'm kind of old-fashioned. I want a man with traditional values such as family, home and all that. Don't get me wrong. I don't think that's the way all men should be. I believe what I said before. But for me, I want a more traditional guy. Maybe it's just the way I was brought up."
>
> A twenty-nine-year old assistant to a bank president said, "I want a hero. I do! Some guy to sweep me off my feet."
>
> A forty-three-year old stockbroker said, "A guy with style. A gentleman who opens doors and treats a woman like a lady. I compete with men every day. In many ways, I live the feminist dream. But when it comes to a man in my personal life, I want a Prince Charming. I know that sounds silly and romantic, but you asked."
>
> A thirty-one-year old specialist in early child care confessed, "I want a man who is confident and will take care of me. I don't want him controlling me, but I do want someone to take care of me."
>
> A thirty-nine-year old lawyer said, "I want a lover and a companion. I want us to have two careers, separate responsibilities for work and shared responsibilities for home. If I were to get sick, I would like to feel confident that he would and could take care of me. I am a feminist in my public behavior and profession, but I think what goes on between two lovers is different. There is no equality in the bedroom, and I'd just as soon have him be the more dominant."

> And finally, a thirty-three-year old school teacher said, "I think he has to respect me for doing my thing. I don't want anyone trying to tie me down. However, if I get married again, I'd like the guy to be religious and have conservative political values. In my old age, I'm sounding more like my parents. I think that on many issues, such as crime and drug use, right is right and wrong is wrong. I want a guy with firm convictions."

These are only a few examples, but they clearly show a dissonance between the public image women endorse and the private image each holds of her own ideal man.

Divorced women, in particular, foster a private image of the ideal man that is very "fifties." This is in sharp contrast to what they originally proclaimed as the essence of their ideal man. For example, as one sophisticated real estate broker in her late thirties observed:

> I am very much a feminist. I encourage my son to regard women as feminists prescribe. Maybe the next generation will be different when their children grow up. For myself, however, I want someone like my father. I never thought I'd say that. After two divorces, your image of what's ideal changes. Because of the time and place I grew up, I need a man I feel I can depend on. And at this point in my life, I'm perfectly willing to be a wife—something like my mother—but with a job, not a career.

Several things account for the dissonance between the alleged public image and the private image of the ideal man. But it may be important to remember all the women surveyed on this issue were divorced and members of the baby boom generation. It may well be the dissonance referred to is characteristic of divorced women or perhaps baby boomers and not women generally. However, since this book is about post-divorce, it is the experience of divorcees largely from the baby boom generation that matters most in these pages.

Baby boomers brought about many changes in the social fabric of society. Collectively, their condemnations and prescriptions wrought much good on the social and political level and much bad on the personal level. The baby boomer's condemnation of war and advocacy of equal rights and opportunities for women and minorities did much to increase the social consciousness and moral splendor of Western Civilization. However, their tolerance and even advocacy of drug use and promiscuous sex produced much debris in the personal lives of many of today's middle-class adults. The millions of divorced baby boomers who learned so much about sexual activity failed to learn anything at all about intimacy, love and commitment. They profess to want love and intimacy but remain emotionally paralyzed when the opportunity for commitment presents itself.

Angry authors of self-help books blame, *en masse*, the members of one or the other sex. But such explanations are too simple. As lawyer Wendy Kaminer decries in her book *I'm Dysfunctional, You're Dysfunctional*, it's time to declare the emperor has no clothes. It's time to pick up oneself by the bootstraps and begin to make a go of it. There is no advantage to declaring oneself a perennial victim.

The social changes of the sixties and seventies were no more wrought by men than by women. Together the sexes created a world many now sense is if not hostile to at least unsupportive of authentic personal intimacy. Free love, which encourages consenting adults to regard the other as a product of one's own self-gratification, deprives each person of personal respect. It distracts people from the obligation to see each human as a person deserving equal and ultimate respect. Baby boomers are now looking beyond play and the chance to exploit sexual partners and want very much to experience intimacy. But so many remain ignorant of how to do so. As one forty-year-old woman, working for a management consulting firm, lamented:

> All I want is to find somebody I can love and share with the rest of my life. He can be rich or poor, sophisticated or not. Is that asking so much? I've thrown away my shopping list for the *ideal* man. I want a man who wants to share his soul with me.

There is reason to believe divorce is a more confounding experience now than ever before. If one divorced in the 1930s, one could see the abandoned relationship did not approximate that enjoyed by so many of one's married peers. People shared a roughly hewn sense of what was expected in marriage and what good marriages were supposed to look like. There was, as it were, a delimited set of standards against which to compare one's own marriage. That has all changed as sociologist Robert Bellah and his colleagues so ably illustrate in *The Good Society*.

Marriage now has many different forms, and there seems to be an inexhaustible set of lists for comparing the merit of each. Some lists of marital pathology are nearly identical to what thirty years ago many couples believed was satisfactory. For example, in a book titled *Co-dependency*, the author contrasts traits characteristic of a healthy relationship with those of a pathologic, co-dependent relationship. The so-called healthy relationship the author espouses reminds one of the rhetoric used to recommend open marriages two decades ago. The co-dependent list by contrast, looks like an update of the traditional Christian marriage vow. Without getting drawn into the debate on whether this is good or bad, suffice it to say varying public perceptions of what marriage should be like are expanding with the whims of fashion in pop psychology and the film media. Meanwhile, baby boomers remain adrift in a sea of self-help books and films portraying failed marriages, extra-marital romance and so on.

The social turmoil created by the self-helpers and media moguls is a major factor in the apparent dissonance existing between the divorced women's images of what's ideal in a man. Too many experts have taken to telling women what is "ideal." Instead, they need to be asking women, "What do you really want in a man?"

In the wake of so many failed fashions, baby boomers look with envy upon their idealized notions of the past when, with all of society's short-sightedness and prejudice, there was something sustaining and rewarding in personal relationships. Divorced baby boomers tend to be a tragic lot looking to the past for a future they fear is lost. The country singing group The Judds produced a song in the mid-1980s which revealed this forlorn theme dramatically . . . the title, "Grandpa, Tell Me About the Good Old Days."

What Men Think Women Want

Today's middle-class, middle-aged male grew up at a time when men were expected to be gallant, polite, chivalrous, and gentlemanly toward women. It was also a time when men were encouraged to deliberately ignore some of those qualities to demonstrate to women that each man was really meant to be the master of his house. Once again, one can see how the creation of public image distorted the individual's perception of appropriate personal ideals.

Women want *shared intimacy* with a man. Men were under the mistaken impression that *access* to intimacy was a male prerogative. Women rebelled against this chauvinism and against all the social practices associated with it. The rebellion prompted great confusion among men. Men were left wondering whether or not they should open doors and pull out chairs for women. Outraged feminists screamed these gestures were symbols of men's continued attempt to oppress them. More traditionally-oriented women were offended if men neglected these niceties. What were men to do?

The story of an old and feeble professor illustrates how intensely befuddling the problem is. The old professor, who had already survived three heart attacks and two open heart surgeries was about to get on an elevator. A woman in about her mid-twenties was also about to get on. The kindly professor reached his arm in the elevator, holding the door and stepped back so the woman could get in first. The woman became irate and loudly denounced him for attempting to subjugate women in this way. She berated him continuously as the elevator rose three floors. On the fourth floor, the professor stepped off and slowly, anxiously, made his way toward his office. Once there, he reached for his heart medicine and took a tablet to relieve the pain. All the gentleman had intended was to show respect for the young woman (as he had been taught in his childhood). The irate woman's response made him feel like a mean and wicked henchman of a male-dominated establishment. "What am I to do?" he pondered. Is it wrong to be a gentleman? How does an old man show he respects women if not in these ways?

The old professor's experience has been shared in one way or another by most middle-aged, middle-class men today. Still, as every single male knows, to fail to do these things for some women risks making one look crude and brutish. Men, or at least many men, understand the arrogant and domineering ways of the past need changing. They remain at a loss, however, in trying to understand which changes are necessary in the company of which women. In chorus men cry out, "What do women want of us?"

The Moral of the Story

The sources of dissonance and confusion regarding the "ideal man" are evident. First, the experts and the media have not taken the time to listen to what the majority of women think. Instead, the public demagogues have created models and set about imposing them on the minds of the populace. Second, it is not at all clear there is much to be gained by ferreting out statistical norms indicating constellations of attributes the majority of women would favor in a man. The intimacy of relationships demands individuals address each other as individuals and not as mere variants of a statistical norm. To find an ideal man, each woman must begin with the Socratic dictum "Know thyself." With self-knowledge comes an understanding of what type of man and what type of relationship she should be seeking.

For men, the message is very similar. The man's task should not be to fashion himself in a way he hopes will attract a bevy of women to his side. Rather, his task is to know enough about himself so he honestly projects his best qualities. Women deserve the chance to know a man for who he genuinely is and not some image he designed to catch their fancy temporarily. Similarly, each man deserves a woman who is attracted to him and not some role he is playing for her. In short, self-knowledge and honest expression of character is essential for finding and guaranteeing happy *lifelong* relationships.

Given the diversity of individuals within each of the sexes, there is a potential good match out there for each and every man and woman. As one old Missouri farmer so colorfully put it, "For every scrubby mule there is a scrubby bush to tie it to." No one should think of oneself as "scrubby," but if I understand the farmer, he is saying happiness can be found in a relationship by each and every person if we'll all just have the courage to be ourselves.

4

What do Men Want in a Woman?

It is tempting to begin and end this chapter by asking the reader to recall the refrain from a song in the musical, *My Fair Lady*: "Why can't a woman be more like a man?" Men, it is suggested, often find women a confusing and befuddling lot. Things would seemingly be so much easier if only women could be more like men!

While a gender-neutral species might be less complex, it is unlikely members of either *sex* would be happier if everyone were truly indistinct in major psychological and emotional respects. In the first major awakening of feminist awareness in the 1960s and the 1970s, a few proclaimed the coming of a gender-neutral utopia. These social pioneers encouraged people to think of the sexes as in every way identical (except, of course, in matters bearing upon procreation). Fortunately, most would agree, this goal attracted few adherents. Nearly everyone agreed women should be afforded equal opportunity in the workplace, before the courts, and in politics, but the ideal of a gender-neutral society had little appeal.

The Feminist View of the Matter

The 1980s saw significant changes in the feminist movement. Perhaps the most noteworthy were initiated by Stanford educator Nel Noddings, Harvard psychologist Carol Gilligan, and television personality, editor, and author Gloria Steinem who celebrated the differences between men and women.

They began insisting women be respected and rewarded for their unique talents *as women*. The demand for equal civil and employment opportunities remained, but no longer were women encouraged to trade away their gender distinctiveness to secure their rights. If women's manifest gender traits make them less ruthless and provide them greater longevity, who would be so foolish as to trade this away?

Women who have successfully adopted the corporate male lifestyle are increasingly vulnerable to the same longevity and illnesses as men. To the extent they acquire the "win at all costs" approach to life, they risk acquiring social and psychological traits *inhibiting* the emotional development of many corporate males. For example, as Carol Gilligan's research suggests, men in general are not very good at understanding or creating intimate relationships with others. Beyond the intimacy extended to their families, males seem virtually bankrupt. Sometimes this is an asset for men, but more often it is not. Research documents the fact men have little emotional difficulty in coping with a move from one city to another. Women often find such moves quite troubling. Under earlier male-dominated interpretations of this phenomenon, it was thought men's sense of independence sustained them through such times and women's dependence on others prohibited them from enjoying the adventure of a move. Recent feminist interpretation of this phenomenon suggest something quite different is afoot. Indeed, men are quite independent and it does not bother most to leave behind their old neighborhood and friends. The principal reason for this is men's bonding is a surface phenomenon. This allows them to abandon old friendships with a minimal sense of loss. Women form networks of relationships that are strongly INTERDEPENDENT.

Women bond with friends in deeper and more intimate ways than men. It is unfair to describe women's success in building and maintaining relationships as evidence of emotional weakness or dependency because the bonding occurring among women is strongly supportive. Women are there for each other in times of need. Men are not or, at least, not as much or in the same way. Women are prepared to help and receive help from their friends. Men work out deals. For men, the effort expended in behalf of another man is often evaluated in terms of the likelihood of a return in kind. This makes men sound heartless and ruthless, and some are, but certainly not all. Yet most have lived their separate social and professional lives in environments where such thinking was common.

Before condemning men too harshly, remember one reason men develop such hard driving, egocentric personalities is because society, a society composed of *men AND women,* is quick to applaud men for their manifest achievements and little more. For example, most public school teachers—male and female—have a tendency to reinforce competitiveness in men on the one hand, and complacency and cooperativeness among women on the other.

Men who reject the mad chase for status and power often live different lives from their esteemed peers. The country doctor, preacher or high school teacher are but examples of this truly exceptional lifestyle. But such modest characters are not elevated by the public to the heroic status of a Bill Gates, a Bill Clinton or a Ben Affleck.

Men are taught to be ambitious and successful in ways demonstrable through the accumulation of great wealth and power. There is tolerance for alternative lifestyles among men but little encouragement. When a man moves from one locale to another, he abandons one set of competitors for another. The woman leaves behind a network of friends in which each person depends on her as much as she depends on them. Before the reader concludes this paints too rosy a picture of women's friendships, it is important to note that female "cattiness" toward one another is also evident.

The folk wisdom has it that cattiness is a female trait and is certainly no virtue, yet cattiness rarely prevents women from coming to the aid of a friend in trouble. This inclination to help a friend, even one who is the object of envy and subtly displayed hostility, has always amazed men because they tend to see the world of friendships as having three categories: like, dislike and neutral in feeling. They cannot understand how a woman can ostensibly dislike a "friend," and yet rush to her assistance when she is in need. Women do for friends what men do only for family. For a woman to move, to disassociate herself physically from her friends, approximates, at least somewhat, the decision to leave a family behind. For men, this is not at all the case. Indeed, when one looks at male-dominated occupations today, it is evident many men are comfortable with leaving their families for long periods of time.

While the ability to leave behind friends in one's quest for career advancement is generally seen as a character strength by men, this independence (perhaps one should say "anti-dependence") makes them perilously vulnerable when their marginally few sources of intimacy are destroyed. For example, data based on insurance claims illustrates that in the year following a divorce or the death of a family member, men are two to three times more likely than women to suffer a morbid event, including death or serious illness requiring hospitalization. Numerous studies of a more specific sort show that during such periods men are much more susceptible than women to each of the following: heart attack, stroke, suicide, and cancer. In short, men may gain some entrepreneurial advantage by limiting their expression of intimacy, but the price they pay in terms of few and strong friendships and limited emotional support is exorbitantly high.

Feminist research freely admits there are important psychological differences between men and women and revel in the differences. They now encourage women to take pride in their femininity and ignore earlier rhetoric encouraging women to become man-like which implicitly hinted the male worldview was right and good and the feminine worldview inadequate. This is decidedly not in the best interests of anyone. Women have so much to offer the world *as women*. "New Wave feminists" rightly argue men might be better off and live happier lives if they learn from women the joy of friendship and ways for sustaining emotional as well as business networks. I agree.

The species does well when it utilizes as many talents and virtues from its reservoir of resources as possible. Men and women both have much to gain by taking New Wave feminism to heart. Women, by virtue of their gender, have many attributes meriting admiration, and so do men. We all gain when all recognize this fact.

The Male View of the Matter

What about it, guys? Would you really be happier if only a woman could be more like a man? One Texas oil man was unhesitating in his response: "You betcha. I don't know about other men, but I know I can't figure women out. Men, I understand. If women were more like men, I wouldn't walk around confused so much of the time."

Some women have become more man-like. Certainly, the woman entrepreneur, complete with ulcers and the "everybody uses everybody" attitude is no different from her male counterpart. Many more women have entered the male world of participatory sports than at any time previously. A few of these women are as single-minded in their quest for visible achievement as any man. But the majority of women have, in a sense, feminized sports by bringing with them a sense of fun. One inveterate runner with nearly thirty years of experience said:

> When I started, there were virtually no women runners. For that matter, there were few men runners. Runners were a smelly lot, and most of the time they looked disgraceful. They might carry around two pairs of sweat socks, shorts, shoes, and one or two t-shirts or a sweatshirt for weeks at a time before getting them washed. You ran by yourself in the wee hours of the morning or in the evening after work. One winter day in about 1972, I was running in the field house at a local university on a one-seventh mile track. Around and round I'd go all by myself. Suddenly, this beautiful, long-legged girl appeared. She was running pretty fast. I just knew, being a girl, she would drop out after a lap or two. Actually, since she was so pretty, I thought she might not make a single lap. Well, she surprised me. She had this graceful stride, and she virtually flew around the track. As she gained on me, I began getting worried. She might pass me! A moment later, she was right on my heels. I began sprinting. She was still gaining on me. I had three more miles to go in my workout, but there was no way I was going to let her pass me. I also knew that if I stayed on the track, there was not much I could do to stop her. So I decided to fake it. I sprinted my heart out for about forty yards and then stopped, panting and acting as though I had just finished my (intended) six-mile workout. The girl kept flying. When I came back out of the locker room, showered, changed and shaved, she was still running. I knew then things were about to change.
>
> Today, lots of women pass me when I run. I've gotten used to that, and I don't mind it a bit. But women have changed the running scene in other ways, too. For one thing, they have brought fashion to the track. A lot of women look downright exciting in their running outfits. If you want those women to notice you, and most of us do, you take care to wear nice CLEAN clothes. Women TALK when they run, listen to stereos and just seem to PLAY. Now many guys do that, but it seems that women were instrumental in changing the running scene from simple exercise and meditation to fun and play. I still enjoy the long solitary run. But since my divorce, that is almost always my second choice. Running with a lady friend is a great way to relax, exercise and enjoy her company. Unless she is a real serious runner, you find that it is easy for the

two of you to adopt a pace that makes it easy to socialize for three to ten miles.

Many women are more than my equal in running. But unlike my experience of some years ago, I don't think that takes anything away from my manliness or from their femininity. If anything, I think women runners are prettier, more graceful and more fun to be with than most other women. If they left the running scene that might be the one thing that would get me to give it up, too.

As the runner's experience shows, women can and are doing more previously male-dominated activities than ever before, proving by the millions they can do these things as well as or better than many men. Nevertheless, this has not resulted in any loss of femininity or attraction between the sexes. A woman can perform an activity as competently as a man, yet do it with a style that is different, a style characteristic of women and often absent in men. The self-conscious awareness of each person for his or her own sexual role as well as that of the other need do nothing to affect the performance of either nor inhibit the delight each takes in the other as an object of romantic attention.

Would men really be happier if women were more like men? I think not. As philosopher Roger Scruton argues, to the observer there is an intriguing aura that seems to envelop members of the opposite sex. A man can never know, experience and understand as a woman does those things nor can a woman know, experience and understand as a man. This does not mean communication between members of opposing sexes is impossible nor does it mean that the sexes must compete with one another. Just the opposite is true.

Viennese philosopher Ludwig Wittgenstein introduced the notion of "forms of life" to show why and how people sometimes succeed in communicating with one another and why they sometimes fail. Wittgenstein claims people succeed in communicating with one another only to the extent they share in a common form of life (or "walked a mile in the other's shoes," as the folk idiom has it). Imagine two women who have never before met. Each is outgoing. Each woman has a twelve-year-old daughter and has recently given birth to a child. The women chance to meet in their obstetrician's office and strike up a conversation about their recent deliveries. Is it likely that much shared communication could occur between the two? More than either could share with her own daughter? More than either could share with her husband, whom she loves dearly and with whom she participated in Lamaze? More than to either woman's married but childless sister?

Having shared deeply in nearly identical experiences, the two women can communicate very effectively with one another. The limited extent of communication in other cases is often a function of the absence of *shared experience.* Experiences held in common bring together aspects of people's forms of life, allowing them to communicate with great success. In contrast, no communication is likely to succeed if there isn't a base of relevant shared experience. For communication between people to be successful, there must be considerable overlap between their respective forms of life.

The form of life women participate in overlaps and has many points of contact with that of men, yet the two are not identical. Men and women advance in their understanding of the other sex vicariously through a loving and intimate relationship with a member of the other sex. No matter how deep and intimate the relationship, the two will never come to understand the world fully *as* a member of the other's sex, but this prospect should not in the least strike lovers as disheartening. The depth and length of any romantic relationship is directly proportional to how much one can learn of the other as an individual and of the other *as* a member of the opposite sex. The successful development of the relationship moves each person to a fuller understanding of the other. Neither becomes fully transparent to the other, hence romantic mystery is never exhausted. If the enchantment disappears, it will not be because either knows too much about the other.

The difference between men and women, as determined by their differing sexual roles, is one of the things that makes relationships worth pursuing. There would be little benefit to men or women if the species became gender-neutral in every respect (beyond those required for procreation). If men learned to respect genuinely, to appreciate and to revel in the differences between themselves and women, they would find the social world in which they live infinitely more interesting.

In the previous chapter, I showed there is no publicly-conceived ideal man for any woman and the attempt to assemble statistical generalizations about traits most women fancy is unlikely to help any man in his romantic life. A central theme in much that has been written throughout this book, and in particular in the last several chapters, is that middle-aged adults need to learn about, and rejoice in, their own individuality as well as respect the individuality of others. For example, too many men are quick to declare their ideal woman should be pretty, understanding, caring, fun-filled and so forth. These words really do not mean much. Aesthetic tastes vary greatly among men. What strikes one man as pretty may not strike another as such. What it takes to understand or be caring towards one woman may be unhelpful in caring for another. Quick and careless assessments of the ideal, even by and for the individual, are not very informative and tend even to be misleading.

The Ideal Woman

- Her face and body never age beyond twenty-five

- Is matched in maturity. You both remember the Beatles, you're both coming to grips with your mortality and her pension balance meets or, better yet, exceeds yours

- Is exceedingly healthy and devoted to caring for you in your old age

- Adores you and has no idea all other men see her as Helen of Troy

- Is an extraordinary athlete but never quite as good as you in the sports in which the two of you participate

- Any display of sexual interest on your part immediately dispels any headache, fatigue or stress that may have previously afflicted her

- Loves the outdoors and working with her hands always with her hair clean and fragrant, her face radiant and her skin forever delicate while sporting an eternal, wrinkle-free tan

- Reads the sports section, plays poker and can beat any man except you

- Hates to shop, go to expensive restaurants, volunteer in children's school activities and, most of all, she hates Gerorge Clooney

- Is well-read, cultured, a gourmet cook, and can be fascinated for hours on end by stories of your daily triumphs

- Loves to debate and entertain challenging If . . . then . . . hypotheticals.

There was a story about an old man (103 years old) sitting on a corner crying. A police officer happened by and said, "Hey ol'timer, what's the matter?" The old man replied, "I just got married a few days ago." He went on to describe his new bride as the ideal woman above. The police officer immediately recognized the ideal and in astonishment declared, "What have you got to cry about?" The old man sniffed and said, "I forgot where I live." Part of the humor in stories such as this is the idea anyone could ever find such "ideal mates" in the first place. For the person who confuses fact and fiction, life may be forever lonely.

Looking for the Ideal Within

The reader of this book has already acquired a fairly extensive repertoire of experience. The reader's life narrative and its product, a determinate and unique web of beliefs, are substantially developed by now. In short, the reader's individuality is irrevocably established. This does not mean there will be no further changes. People can, and do change, anything that is, except one's life-locating principles. The problem is all too often people want to change too much or change things that ought not to be changed. Worse yet, many of the changes they seek to initiate, they seek only so they can match up to someone else's ideal. For example, consider men who *developed* hard driving, egocentric and life-threatening approaches to life not because it was innate to them but rather because their parents, the media and their peers expected it of them.

If there is an "ideal" women should work towards in order to be more appealing to men, it must start with something as simple as respect for individuality. Women should not encourage men to seek material gain, power and status any more than men should expect women to be forever pretty, charming or unabashedly attentive to the men in their lives. The ideal in any woman, just as the ideal in any man, begins with self-respect for one's own individuality and respect and delight in the individuality of others.

Everyone knows he or she can always benefit from improvement. To love is to want to be one's best for one's lover. To paraphrase Aristotle, it is the sincere desire to exercise all one's excellences excellently that leads to self-fulfillment, something presumably everyone seeks.

To love is also a matter of wanting the best for one's beloved. This involves making recommendations from time to time and giving encouragement to one's lover as he or she attempts various improvements in his or her life. To love is radically different from the desire to become an architect of human character. Women, an increasing number of men claim, no longer understand this.

Men who believe they have been victimized by women's attempts to wholly re-design them are angry, disappointed, frustrated, and confused. All these men ever wanted was to be everything the woman felt they could be. In trying to become their lovers' ideals, the men accomplished little and often lost the relationship altogether. A thirty-eight-year old engineer working in middle management for a large oil concern tells the following story:

> Becky helped put me through my MBA. She never got to finish her undergraduate degree. We had two children in the first five years of marriage. I did not try to keep her barefoot and pregnant. I did not try to keep her at home taking care of the kids. I did not discourage her in any way from seeking work or going back to college.
>
> We have moved to a classy neighborhood. We drive BMWs and Volvos. No one in our family has a NEED for much of anything. I've been real lucky in my career.
>
> From out of nowhere, Becky started complaining that I've imprisoned her, that she has not had a chance to become her own person. I reminded her that she wanted both the kids and that I kept protesting that we might not be financially stable enough to support the second child. She insisted we should take the chance because she wanted to have two kids while she was still young. She wanted to stay home with the kids until they went to school. When she wanted to return to school, I cheered her on and was happy she was using a portion of our family income for that purpose. When she had class in the evenings or had to study, I baby-sat the kids and fixed dinner. When she wanted to spend time studying

with her girlfriends, I saw no reason to object. When she changed majors three times, I continued to encourage her to pursue a degree. During all this, she got nastier and nastier towards me. She claimed I was trying to control her life and smother her personal growth and development. I couldn't figure it out. I'm doing my job, my work around the house and nearly all the jobs she used to do around the house. I served as both mother and father to the kids and as her number one cheerleader in whatever she chose to do. Still, I was accused of being a beast who just wanted to suffocate her in my world. The friends she developed in college all started talking the same way about their husbands. I have no idea about their home situations, but I know I did everything I could to help her get what she wanted out of life.

Finally, two of her college friends got divorced, and she and the other two began going for drinks at night after class. I didn't like that, and I objected. After all, I was doing all I could to cover home and job so she could "find" herself, finish school and become happy again. Two weeks before graduation, she told me she was leaving the kids and me. She said it just didn't work anymore. She said she had grown, and I hadn't. She said there was nothing wrong with me, but she just couldn't live surrounded by me and all I represented. Two months later, she moved in with a psychology graduate student four years her junior.

I have no idea what I could have done differently to save the marriage. It seemed the more I did what she asked, the angrier she got. Now I look back at the whole thing with resentment. If she was going to throw the whole relationship away anyway, why did I waste so many years helping her do it?

Her psychology friend left her after a year or so, and every few months she calls me and wants to talk about the old times. I think she wants to get together again, but there is no way I will ever get caught up with a nut like that again. The kids and I are doing fine now. I date occasionally, but as soon as the woman I'm dating starts talking about her needs or how I could change, I leave. I got burned in that game once before, and I'm not falling for it again.

There is, no doubt, another untold side to the story above, and one anecdote does not make good a general claim. The story, however, is not atypical. The number of men who are sympathetic with the engineer's disenchantment seems to be growing each year. For the purposes of this discussion, it makes no difference whether or not the engineer's perspective is accurate. What matters is his perspective is shared by a growing number of men. This story does not indict women or men but reflects how difficult it is for people to respect and reciprocally nurture the individuality of another. For a long time, women claimed too little attention was given their individuality. Now, it seems that cry is growing louder from an increasing number of men and their literary champions who extol the virtues of finding fire in the belly or a warrior from deep within. One movement countering another won't work in the domain of romance.

Changing Selves

Men agree the one thing they want from a beloved is acceptance to be who they are. They claim if women understood men better, they would not condemn all the gender-related idiosyncrasies that tend to separate men from women. Men note they are not asking for anything more than what feminists have advocated for women. The men *claim* they have learned to grant this to women, and now it is time for women to reciprocate if there is to be mutual respect for interpersonal development on everyone's part. Many men accuse women of entering romantic relationships determined at the outset to change the man to the woman's idiosyncratic notion of the ideal. *The ideal woman,* or so these men charge, should not embark upon a relationship unless she is content with all major aspects of the man as he was when each committed to the other.

Divorced women often relate how much they tried to change to satisfy the idiosyncratic demands of an ex-husband. Like their male counterparts, these women chant in unison, "Nothing I did for him was ever really appreciated. Nothing I did ever seemed good enough." As one tawny-haired forty-one-year old university administrator declared, "I tried and tried to become everything he wanted, but all he did was complain. Finally, I couldn't take it anymore. If I had stayed with him, I think I would have gone crazy. So I just packed up and walked out."

Another woman, slightly over-weight and graying, but generally in good shape for her fifty-one years said:

> I managed the books for his medical practice for years. The accountants were always amazed at how orderly everything always

was. For his part, he complained that I was disorganized at work and at home. As the years went on, he kept harping that I was getting worse. Finally, he came home one night and told me I just wasn't right for him, and he was leaving. Well, the old fool left and a month after our divorce was finalized, he married a twenty-seven-year old nurse.

In the cases above, the women confessed that after the divorce, each felt like little more than a shell of her former self and their efforts were for months, and sometimes years, directed toward re-building a sense of self.

Rebuilding a sense of self can be a perilous adventure. The university administrator whose story was recounted above developed a sense of self that was, for a while, excessively egocentric and selfish. For example, she often took pleasure in announcing, "I have learned to put myself first. If you do not care for yourself first who else will? . . . Certainly not some man!" While this woman reconstructed a strong sense of independence, the cost was high. Her particular sense of independence precluded further social growth. As long as she maintains an angry emphasis on a "me-first" perspective she will remain angry at men and will not learn to respect men nor socialize with them as equals.

Reconstructing a sense of self is a process in which the person studies his or her own life narrative to learn what has been written and what should now constitute appropriate future entries. Future entries cannot be radically different from the plot as it has unfolded thus far. Without maintaining some sense of continuity in one's identity, it is all too easy to lose control.

A dramatic shift in plot leads people to fear there is little in their lives that makes sense. In the case of Tolstoy's *Anna Karenina*, the discontinuity of her life narrative forces Anna to commit suicide. In the case of the university administrator, she had been a sharing person but became a me-first negotiator. Her short-term gains in personal independence are the result of a pronounced discontinuity in her life narrative, and one worries the short-term strength afforded by her "me-first" perspective may not fit together with her forty-year history. There may come a day when she concludes the collective attitudes and experiences of her "two lives" do not fit well together. If this occurs, she will know full well the existentialist's angst, a condition wherein one feels alien to her own life and all that surrounds her, a condition each of us risks, thus repeating the fall of Anna Karenina.

The reconstruction of a sense of self should be just that: a re-awakening to, and development of, the best you are. It is not a matter of creating a new person. The maintenance of a sense of self flourishes only when the important people in your life respect the evolution consistent with your own internal life narrative. The one great work of art each person pens is his or her own life narrative. Since each person only gets one chance at this (with no opportunity for editing), one should take care the story always remains under his or her own control.

An Assault on Love and the Point of Courtship

Lovers write their beloved into their plots, but they should never turn over authorship to the other nor assume authorship of the other's story.

The attempt to change a lover is freighted with danger and hardship. Love, by its very nature, transforms people. But lovers do not effectively change loved ones through explicit recommendations. Indeed, the very act of making such recommendations suggests how little the lover values the (alleged) beloved, even if the lover and beloved agree the beloved can and should change in specified ways. No one can execute a set of directives pertaining to character development (the fabric of the life locating principles) without considerable allowance for interpretive error. What the two think they are agreeing to may produce changes the beloved never intended. To what extent can love exist between people whose desire to change each other radically is an admission that neither finds much ideal in the other in the first place?

No one is responsible for *loving* another. No one has to accept another as an extenuation of his or her ideal. Presumably, courtship is a procedure for avoiding just these difficulties. Courtship, that period beyond romance and infatuation, is a period when two people consider what it would be like to undertake a common life project. As Robert Louis Stevenson observed, "Marriage is a long conversation occasioned by numerous disputes." Courtship is a period in which each party learns just how ideal the other is likely to be for him or her. When the beloved is recognized as ideal, that recognition produces in the lover new ideals and new dreams of the ideal relationship. In other words, it is through viewing the beloved *as* an ideal that the lover becomes transformed. It is through loving another that a person learns what love is *for him* or *for her*.

Ideals of any sort are generally half-formed and poorly understood and so it is with ideal lovers and ideal relationships. When a person comes to see another as ideal and as worthy of one's love, this makes concrete the individual's notion of the ideal. With knowledge of what is ideal in a mate comes an evolving appreciation of what is ideal in a relationship. No explicit directive prior to the occasion of love can have so much appeal and meaning. With a changing view of what matters in life, one naturally changes, not through response to commands but through desire to act in concert with another and with compatibly held ideals.

Neither partner senses any loss in these transformations. In a loving relationship, the transformations are received joyfully and are valued as evidence of the couple's unity. The deeper the love, the deeper the transformations. On occasion, there may be radical transformations that would be destructive to one or the other person's life-locating principles. At that point, to borrow a line from the movie *The Accidental Tourist*, "It doesn't matter how much you love someone, what matters is who you are when you are with that person." When the depth of the transformations threatens the continuity of either lover's life narrative, the lovers must part ways for the mutual survival of each.

The intensity of hate an ex-lover experiences reflects an awareness he or she has lost his or her moorings and suggests one's life narrative, both chapter and verse, have been dramatically changed as a result of the previous union. Though courtship (or for the unfortunate ones, marriage) may reveal that things are not right between the lovers, dissolution of a relationship causes lovers to abandon what each previously perceived (perhaps mistakenly) as truly ideal in a mate or in a relationship. This is a profoundly unsettling and confusing experience, and it takes time to regain a sense of the continuing course of one's life narrative.

Men are much more likely to suffer a morbid event following divorce or death of a spouse than are women. For most middle-class women there is a network of friends, a support group that helps her maintain a sense of continuity as she makes the transition from married to single. For men, the matter is usually quite different. Without the strong network of friends at hand, a man's departure from married life is usually a much more radical departure from the plot of his life narrative. Unable to deal with this radical shift alone, he suffers a morbid tragedy. In contrast, a woman's friends help protect her somewhat while she risks fairly substantial changes in her life narrative.

Ex-lovers must re-acquaint themselves with new half-formed visions of ideals. This inevitably takes place in the context of transformed and poorly-conceived new world views. The adoption of new ideals is a clumsy and painful process. The transformative powers of love are truly its greatest blessing as well as its most fearful curse.

The changes that take place between lovers are not under the control of either party. They occur solely because each has become a part of the other's life. In contrast, the attempt to direct changes in a beloved leads not to transformation at all but rather to resentment and dispute. In fact, the deliberate attempt to re-make a beloved will keep aspiring lovers from developing deep and sustaining love.

Courtship is the period in which love is given full throttle. Courtship is not meant as a last opportunity to change the other. Rather, it is a period for showing a loved one how much he or she is valued. Courtship is also a period in which one person learns from another's example what is truly ideal in a lover and what is truly ideal in a relationship. If courtship is spent with each lover trying to re-form the other, their prospects for sharing in a life project are dim. If, instead, courtship is a period of learning "how to feel for the other," their love will deepen, ideals will crystalize conjointly and the prospects for lasting happiness are optimized.

Ideal lovers love one another *as is*. They may eagerly take part in helping the other learn about self. They may try to change and modify *minor* traits or qualities, but in general, lovers admire the fundamental aspects of each other's character. They see no point in trying to re-make the other. The moral of the story can be summed up in three principles.

First, **know yourself.** Only by knowing yourself will you learn what is ideal for you in a lover and a relationship. Second, be **patient** and **tolerant.** If the intuitions of a self-knowing person indicate this is a love to be pursued, *allow it* to happen. If the transformations of love which subsequently occur tend to make you uncomfortable with your evolving life narrative, accept that fact and end the relationship. Do not contrive to force the other into an inappropriate role. If you must end a courting relationship, do so not by condemning it or the other person, but treasure the love you shared and the transformations it produced. But then move on. Third, be mindful of **the point of courtship.** Do not hurry into marriage. Exploit the opportunities courtship provides to learn about the other, the evolving relationship and the effect its transformations have on you. A fully developed courtship will produce a sustainable marriage. A hurried courtship will only result in another hurried divorce.

Final Note on Attempting to Change the Other

As psychologist Leila Tov-Ruach notes, lovers are naturally inclined to seek good for the beloved. However, since lovers are seldom as adept as they may think in identifying what is in the best interest of the other, their efforts in this direction can be bothersome and even destructive. Before attempting to change the beloved in any directed way, lovers need to communicate so lover and beloved discuss the *wish of both* to change one in specific and prescribed ways. For example, if a man is quick to anger and his lover attempts to manipulate him so he will become more patient, she may be surprised to find her efforts only intensify his quickness toward anger. She may also find she is becoming the favorite target. On the other hand, if *each* agree he needs to develop greater self-control and patience, then the two can work together to form a plan for altering his behavior.

On occasion one lover may be traumatized by an outside event: loss of a job, death of a parent or friend, or some other catastrophe. These events can lead to sudden changes in an individual ranging from the onset of alcohol abuse and depression at the extreme to a general increase in irritability or introversion in less extreme cases. During these periods, the troubled partner is not in a position to engage in lengthy and considered discussion leading to cooperative action. If one's beloved is in real trouble, and the trouble is reflected in dramatically self-destructive attitudes, a spouse has little choice but to act alone. This paternalistic initiative is necessary lest the lover and relationship both erode beyond repair. The lover acting alone becomes the only chance either has for *restoring* the beloved to patterns more consistent with his or her life narrative.

The important concept here is *restore*. The lover should never attempt to initiate dramatic changes just because *the lover believes these will be for the better*. On the other hand, when the events of the world sharply deflect the beloved from continuing a consistent and satisfying life narrative, then the lover's actions should aim at giving back to the beloved full editorial authority over his or her own story. Knowing the difference between intrusions which compromise autonomy and those which restore it requires much thought and selflessness of intention. It is not enough merely to act out of love in behalf of another. The actions must *be in the best interest* of the beloved and no one else.

Summary

What do men want in a woman? They do not want women to be more like men. Each man, just like each woman, wants a set of qualities which uniquely complement his own unique set of propensities, foibles and talents. And he, like most any woman, wants something more. What he wants, however, as philosopher Robert Brown explains in his book *Analyzing Love,* is indefinable. He wants that special feeling provoking him to write the other into his life narrative, henceforth to tell a story of two together.

It may seem to the reader the last two chapters end with the same moral: men and women want to be respected both for their gender distinctions and for their individuality. Why then did I not include this all in one brief chapter? I didn't believe most readers would appreciate the symmetry between the sexes if the subject were treated in one homogeneous chapter.

Too many divorcees fail to appreciate how gender enriches their lives because gender also is seen as a distraction. When that happens, people fail to appreciate both their own individuality and that of others. The two chapters and the preceding discussion appear to be digressions into the course of love and not a discussion of gender-specific desires. The reader has already recognized that what at first appears to be a digression is in fact a *commentary on the tolerance men and women must have for the ebb and flow occuring between them.* The individuality of gender specific personalities is what makes tolerance of ebb and flow necessary. What men and women want from each other is respect and the unique opportunity to know the other as an individual and as an instance of his or her gender. This cannot evolve if one of the people is imprisoned in his or her own sense of gender or unwilling to let the other live through his or her gender.

Notes on the Ebb and Flow

1. Men do not want women to be men.
2. Women do not want men to be women.
3. Divorcees have already written many chapters of their life narratives. They cannot abruptly change the course of plot development without suffering severe and long-lasting distortion. Abrupt change of life narrative was the cause of Anna Karenina's torment.
4. Love transforms people.
5. The intimacy experienced by lovers causes each to see the world differently.
6. No lover ever brought about effective change in a beloved by issuing an order.
7. Respect people of the opposite sex for their gender.
8. Respect people for their individuality.
9. Know thyself.
10. Men want to know and be known by women.
11. Women want to know and be known by men.

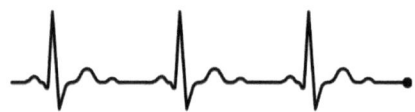

5

What is a Good Date?

Imagine two people, a man and a woman, each of whom is a good catch for the other. Each has the potential to be truly ideal for the other. Fortune smiles on the two, and they meet and agree to a date. What could be more perfect? Is it not inevitable in such cases the two are destined to fall in love and live happily ever after? Is it even possible that two good catches, each so ideally suited to the other, could find an outing together unsatisfactory—not to be repeated? Absolutely!

People can be right for each other, but the events of a first date can make further association unlikely. Every adult single is well aware of this. Consequently, at one time or another every single has taken great pains to ensure a date will go just right.

Executing a great date is no easy task. While an individual has control over himself or herself, there is virtually no control over the other person, and worldly events may intrude in destructive and unpredictable ways. For example, it is difficult to be romantic if food poisoning strikes, the seat of one's pants tears or if one spills spaghetti sauce on a date's thousand-dollar suit or dress. The couple could be on the verge of a romance made in heaven, but such disasters can vanquish any prospects for romance. Divorcees are acutely aware of these ever-threatening liabilities. They are also aware a great first date can lure people into a hasty romance that ends up in a hasty marriage and then divorce. Too, if the divorcee is not careful, he or she may become enamored with a person on the first date and then be devastated upon learning the feelings are not reciprocated. In short, first dates are not to be taken lightly since they can have profound consequences for individuals as well as future couples.

There is no couple, no sharing, no togetherness prior to the first date. Each participant looks upon the first date as an episode to be turned to one's advantage as quickly as possible. Though many would deny it, first dates typically are egocentric affairs. Each person hopes to seize control of the momentum in order to shorten the evening if it is not enjoyable and lengthen it if it is. (Things are perceived as going well on a first date if the other person is, in some way, attractive and, more important, is awe struck by your attractiveness.)

Ideally, cupid's deadliest arrows will find their mark in the heart of the other. The other becoming smitten is not only flattering to you but affords you the time you need to evaluate your feelings and your respect for the other. With the attention of the other focused upon you, you may comfortably control the extent and the pace of development of any relationship. Singles unhesitatingly regard this as an enviable position. And much of what determines if one is to hold such a position is established on that first date and, to a much lesser degree, the several dates which follow.

Because first dates are so important, it is tempting to over-plan events and strategies for making the date a success. By falling victim to over-planning, one will be disappointed by a date conspicuously contrived and awkward. On the other hand, if a person suspects a prospective date may be a good catch, it would be imprudent to treat the opportunity in an overly casual or slip-shod manner. The prospects for a romantic future between two people depend heavily on what transpires during the few hours of the first date.

There is an obvious rationality accompanying the ego-centricism of each person's approach to the first date. By ascending to a position of control early on in the relationship, one is able to protect himself or herself from harm and can pace the nurturing of a budding romance. The ego-centricism of a first date is about being vulnerable to psychological injury and the person's wanting to possess, in a sense, the heart of another. Consequently, anything you can do to cause the other to become smitten, while remaining protected from the indignities of unreciprocated affection, seems a good thing indeed.

I should comment on a possibility the reader may have considered, the possibility that during the first date each person becomes equally smitten with the other. Surely, this is an appealing outcome for both. Or so it may seem. Generally speaking, it is not. When each person becomes smitten by the other, and it happens early on in a relationship, the romance tends to proceed in a reckless and wayward manner. High school students are warned not to take these experiences too seriously because their suddenness and intensity earmark them as nothing more than puppy love. Among adults, participants are warned against being swept away in a fit of passion.

When two people are reciprocally smitten on the heels of a first or second date, the relationship typically takes on an intensity and urgency virtually impossible to sustain. As a result, it soon spends itself before anything approaching erotic love can evolve. Consequently, it seems a good thing that in most enduring relationships, one person is sufficiently in control, in the early stages, to nurture the pace of the romance in a way that fosters durability as opposed to eventual futility.

First dates with someone believed to be a good catch are very important. It is in both persons' best interests for at least one of the two to remain in sufficient control to nurture the development of the relationship at a pace comfortable for both. And it is typically in the individual's own best interest to be the one in control.

There is no way to ensure any date will work out as planned. Dating involves taking chances, chances with one's heart and chances with one's ego. At the very least, people hope a *good date* will produce fun and a really *great date*, romance, or at least the promise thereof. Through the next six examples I hope to show two things. First, people's conception of a good first date varies considerably, and what strikes a person as good or romantic is as ripe with biographical insight into the personality and character of the individual speaking as it is descriptive of a common feature of human experience. Second, there are at least two elements common to nearly everyone's conception of a truly great, that is, romantic, first date: pace and romance. There exists in the folk wisdom the etchings of what constitutes the heart of a picture-perfect date.

Fool's Fancy

First dates do not always go well. Sometimes the experience is intolerable. The person one is with may be a boorish lout, an antiquated bore, a pompous snob or things may fail because of unanticipated events that create embarrassment for one or both of the parties.

Everyone seems to have at least one story to share of an embarrassing first date:

> Diane, a slightly overweight woman with long tawny-colored hair and a successful career as a real estate agent, tells of a time when she was twenty-nine and going to church with a very proper and attractive thirty-one-year old man, Norm. The two had met at a neighborhood block party. When they learned they belonged to the same church, they decided to attend together and have brunch afterwards. Diane was dressed quite stylishly in a white shift dress and heels. As she and Norm ascended the stairs into the church vestibule, her girdle and nylons fell right to her ankles. She stepped out of the nylons and girdle and, with as much poise as she could muster, stuffed them into her purse. "What else could I do?" she said, smiling. What else could I do? Throughout church, I perspired as I have never done before. I could feel droplets of sweat running down my sides and my back. At brunch, I began hating my date. I felt he was probably laughing at me and by now, in my soiled dress, there seemed little hope he, or any man in his right mind, could find me attractive. When we got back to my house, I nearly slammed the door in Norm's face and ran to the bedroom and cried. I never saw him again.

Mark, a twenty-eight-year old stylishly attired man related an equally humiliating account:

> I took this girl to dinner. My story has been shown a dozen times in the movies, and it always makes the audience laugh. But when it happens to you, it's not very funny. While at the restaurant, I went to the men's room. You have probably already guessed what happened. Walking back, I had about twelve inches of toilet paper stuck to my shoe. People were looking at me and smiling. I smiled back. I fancied the idea that people were looking at me and smiling because of my appearance or the way I carried myself. I arrived at the table and my bimbo date was smiling from ear to ear. I got a big stupid grin on my face because of the way she was looking. I thought she was really glad to see me. The date had gone well up to that point. She motioned for me to draw near. I leaned forward. Giggling, she said, "You've got some toilet paper stuck to your shoe." I was furious. Here I was engaged in an act of public

humiliation, and she was laughing at me. We hardly spoke for the rest of the night. For the next twenty minutes she would blurt out a brief giggle and then say, "I'm sorry. I'm not laughing at you, but it is funny." After I took her home, my only thoughts were, "I wish this night had never happened. I hope she doesn't tell any of my friends. And I hope I never see her again."

Dates such as those above clearly do not end in romance. On the other hand, moments of embarrassment do not always destroy the possibility of romance on a first date. If the people involved have a sense of humor and do not take themselves too seriously, they may find an embarrassing episode can break the tension of a first date and allow both parties to feel more relaxed.

Lane, a thirty-year-old attorney who was trim but otherwise very ordinary in appearance tells the following story of a first date that led to a two-year romance:

> Periodically I would see this woman attorney in the courthouse. She had incredible poise and almost noble bearing. We met formally at a monthly bar association meeting. The next day I asked her to dinner. She accepted. I wanted everything to be just perfect. We went to a restaurant that was a little more expensive than I could afford. I had called ahead to find out what the chef recommended as his finest cuisine. When we got to the restaurant, I told her I was familiar with the menu and suggested, if she did not mind, that I order for the both of us. I told her I had in mind " . . . a delicately spiced entree of quail with . . . " and I went on with the spiel I had memorized. When at last the dinner was served, it was a relief to us both. I felt so awkward around her that I didn't know how to behave. Consequently, we had little of substance to say to one another. I later learned that she, too, was a little intimidated by me—not by my poise mind you, but she had been told I was very bright.
>
> Dinner gave us a chance to avoid conversation in part and concentrate on eating. What little conversation we engaged in pertained to dinner. As we ate, I kept glancing over toward her. My God, she was pretty and so proper and graceful in everything she did. Then it happened. A piece of quail she was cutting flipped off her plate and on to her lap. She seemed a bit embarrassed but handled it with the most quiet demeanor. Then, barely a moment later, as she was about to take a bite of quail from her fork, the

piece slid off and landed on the bodice of her dress. She looked up, and her eyes filled with mirth. We both laughed and began talking at ease about how difficult it is to eat quail. I confessed that I had only been to this restaurant once before and told her how I planned to appear so polished in ordering the dinner. We laughed and laughed. She told me how she feared appearing stupid in my eyes, and I told her how much I feared being identified as just an ordinary middle-class kind of guy.

I don't think I ever had so much fun on a first date. All the embarrassment did was erode the inhibiting tensions we both felt. Now, on first dates, I am almost tempted to plan an embarrassing incident just so we can get past the walls, feel relaxed and get to know one another.

A thirty-three-year old actuarial with clean-cut looks and a page boy haircut, Sally, tells of a first date about which she says, had she known of the immediate, physical outcome, she would have declined. As things turned out, Sally fell madly in love and, unfortunately, was heartbroken when three months later the romance came to an end:

> I met Steve at a fun run. He was one of those plain-looking guys you never notice unless they walk right up to you and announce their presence. He was in moderately good shape—by no means a hunk. He was thirty-six and an assistant principal at a junior high school.
>
> We wound up running next to each other in the race. We talked about nothing special. He asked for my phone number and with some hesitancy I gave it to him. I figured, if he called with a good idea and I had nothing else to do, then I would go out with him. He called and asked me to go on a picnic Sunday. That sounded like it could be a drag . . . a picnic. I hadn't been on a picnic in years. I thought maybe I should give it a try. This guy sure seemed safe enough. The worst that could happen, I supposed, was that I might die of boredom.
>
> He picked me up in a Ford Bronco and we drove off the road to the backside of a nearby recreational lake out in the country. Just as we were driving up a small knoll, there was a loud "bang!" He had a flat tire. I felt sorry for him. He was comfortable to be with, no red flags were up but no anticipation of romance either. I knew he wanted the date to go well, and the flat tire could really detract from the atmosphere he was hoping to create.

The flat was only the beginning. He had no jack with which to change the flat. He had just gotten a new spare tire and apparently the service station had forgotten to replace the jack. We were miles away from anything. I wasn't happy by it all, but most guys I know would have gone nuts at a time like this. You know, they get angry, cuss out the service station people, apologize profusely and then sweat and fume. Steve apologized but never got angry and never lost control. We walked to a farm house and called up a wrecker to come and help us. We waited back by the truck for nearly three hours before the wrecker got there. We had our picnic a few yards from the truck. At times, we were concerned the wrecker would not find us. But at other times, Steve had us both laughing so hard about the ridiculousness of it all, being found no longer seemed to matter.

We talked about so much. None of the talk was romantic, and there was never any sexual innuendos. He had a nice way of finding out about me. I felt in those few hours he learned things about me I try not to tell anyone until we have gone together for months. I also learned about him. His life had not been glamorous but it was interesting. By the time we started home, I felt as if he was a long lost childhood friend.

At my apartment, we laughed once again about the day. I wanted him to kiss me. He was beginning to look very handsome to me. He never did kiss me and never said he would call me. He walked away and for two terrible days, I anguished over whether or not I would ever see him again. I had never met a man before or since who in a single day seemed to be able to walk away with a part of me and leave behind a part of himself. If the date had gone perfectly, I don't know if that would have happened.

Embarrassment is not the unrelenting foe of romance some believe it to be. When events beyond one's control result in embarrassment to a person, the individual's immediate response to the situation determines how others will subsequently perceive the person. In the first two situations, the embarrassed parties were over-wrought with how the situation reflected on them personally. Both Diane and Mark dwelled on how others perceived her or him as a result of their respective embarrassments. They each confessed to feeling fear or anger at the very thought that others might be amused by what happened to them. In contrast to such narcissistic concerns, the reaction of Lane and Steve showed neither person was so preoccupied with herself or himself that either forgot when on a date you have a duty to make the occasion as pleasant as possible for the person you are with.

The narcissistic person is so self-centered that public embarrassment makes it impossible to think of anything or anyone else besides oneself. A less narcissistic, other-directed person, while genuinely embarrassed, remains committed to making the best of an awkward time for the sake of others. As Sally commented in describing her reaction to Steve, " . . . most other men would . . . get angry, cuss out the service station people, apologize profusely and then sweat and fume." Such men are not concerned with how this behavior affects the mood or happiness of their dates. They are concerned only with how *they* are seen by others. Unfortunately, for the egocentric-minded individual, those around him do see him for what he is, an ill-tempered Narcissus who on a moment's notice forgets about the happiness of others and instead retreats into intense self-interest and self-deprecation. Diane's case shows this to be equally true of the narcissistic woman.

There is no protocol or set of skills enabling a person to negotiate successfully each and every moment of unanticipated embarrassment. What allows an individual to turn an embarrassment to his or her advantage is strength of character, genuine confidence and an unselfish attitude toward others. When on a date, if one's goals are to learn about another, share something of him or herself and accept responsibility for sharing a cordial and pleasant engagement, then the perils attendant to embarrassment can be circumvented. What better way to demonstrate one's sense of humor, inner strength and charm to a prospective lover than to show one can turn potential disaster into an occasion for mirth and congeniality? What better way to show one is genuinely attentive to the well-being of others than to show restraint at a time of personal embarrassment? This surely contributes to a good date.

The Gold Digger's Delight

Popular novels, television shows and movies often equate the spawning of romance with exotic encounters, luxuriously appointed surroundings, the expenditure of large sums of money or a garish display of bravado. Sometimes, several of the above are intertwined to portray a spectacularly romantic encounter. As university studies have shown, society has begun to mirror media fantasies rather than the other way around. There is perhaps no better evidence of this than the ordinary movie-goer's dream of a romantic date, a gold digger's delight.

Trudi, a svelte model in her late thirties and still well-respected for her work in the industry, related the following account (beyond the ears of her current (and fourth) husband):

> I have gone on a number of spectacular first or second dates in my time. Because of my business, and, I suppose, my success in the business, I have occasion to come across a number of rich and powerful men. The kind of men movies are made about! Anyway, on more than one occasion, the first date a man might ask me on would be to go to New York or Aspen for a weekend. Sometimes, our first date might be dinner at which time the gentleman might suggest I accompany him to Miami on business the following week. If the man was at all interesting, I would accept without a moment's hesitation. You knew what would be expected of you, but women have long been putting out for men for far less. After all, for a long time, that is what a lot of people thought capped off a truly romantic evening, isn't it?
>
> Anyway, I've been to fabulous places, stayed in luxurious hotels, eaten at the finest restaurants, been chauffeured about in limousines and even travelled in a private Lear jet. Now you find me one woman who doesn't think that is romantic and who wouldn't do the same if she got the chance. By the way, I am no tramp. I was privy to opportunities other women only dream about, and I took advantage of them. I've lived romance. I've had some sensational dates. What more do you want to know?

"Are you happy in your current marriage?" I asked. "That's a hard one," Trudi replied. "My husband's real boring. He never wants to go anywhere or do anything. He has no friends that we socialize with. I think we might need to part ways, but what's this got to do with romantic first dates?" "Nothing," I replied. "Nothing at all."

Helen, an attractive middle-aged woman was invited to a country club dance by a debonair, wealthy, handsome, older man. Rudy was a man shortly to become a senior citizen. Helen could ably serve as his Jennifer. Helen confessed:

> I never really liked Rudy, but he was insistent. I gambled and said, 'Look I'd like to go with you, but I have nothing to wear.' And [she smiled] with a flutter of my eyelashes, I left the matter there. The next day, Rudy called and said he was having something sent over to me from an expensive clothier. A van pulled up and they brought into my house a rack of fabulously expensive ball gowns along with shoes, purses and all the accessories. The people from the store said Rudy had called and told them I could pick out a couple of dresses and everything that went with each. Needless to say, I went to the ball.
>
> The evening of the ball, Rudy picked me up in a rented limousine. Everything was so chic. That was one of my most romantic dates. He was a pathetic little man, but he sure knew how to treat a woman.

This couple eventually married and, hundreds of thousands of dollars later, divorced. I leave it to the reader to speculate why the marriage, and the divorce, took place.

Both of these accounts illustrate extremely glamorous dates. The question that remains, however, is whether or not glamour and romance are identical? If there is enough glitz and excessive spending will that produce a romantic encounter? (The reader should not mistake sexual encounters with romantic encounters here. The two are not always the same though the cinema smash of the '80s *Pretty Woman* certainly failed to make the distinction.) What is romance? Does romance serve a purpose? Before attempting to answer these questions, consider a few other scenarios, both those including some atypical role reversal as well as those of different types of romantic first dates.

An interesting role reversal of the gold digger's delight is provided by Lon, a slightly overweight, personable and very wholesome-looking thirty-nine-year old former salesman. Lon had divorced his wife just six months before he met Mary, the president of a local bank.

> We met once before we went out. In short order, Mary invited me to spend a week in Acapulco to celebrate my birthday. That night, we wound up in bed together. I never had any strong feelings toward her so I didn't understand the big rush. I am no Patrick Swayze. Why Mary would want to take me to Acapulco for my birthday astonishes me. I was, to put it mildly, flattered beyond belief.

Flattery aside, I couldn't understand why Mary would do this. We didn't know each other well enough to have any special feelings toward one another so what was the point? She asked me to go to Acapulco even before we went to bed. The bedroom encounter was easy enough to explain. We were both divorced only a short time and were a little horny. The invitation was a whole different story. I knew if I went, I would probably fall in love with the glamour the lady offered. This I might later mistake for love of the person, at least for a while. No woman had ever offered to entertain me that way. Other women I dated at the time gave me presents for my birthday, but these were more modest and somehow seemed in better taste. They were the sorts of gifts that could be accepted in a friendly way with no strings attached. I remember thinking, "Why not accept the trip? You only go through life once and I already lost fourteen years of my life in the previous marriage. I deserve some goodies. It's not like I'm taking anything from this lady. It's being offered!" I just couldn't get used to the idea. I felt, you know, if I accepted I would be a gigolo. It's an awkward feeling. You know you want to go on the trip. The woman was certainly attractive enough, pleasant and all that. But the feeling that I was being bought is something I don't think I could live with.

I also feared it might turn into a sort of addiction. You do it once, and there are other women with plenty of money that they don't know what to do with and they might be interested in purchasing your time and body, too. If you were just selling your time and body, it wouldn't be bad. In a sense, that's what you do at work. But this was different. This was a matter of selling a piece of your character. And once that is gone, no amount of exercise or going without sleep will let you buy back, or catch up on, what you have lost.

Later, I started feeling resentful toward Mary because I realized her action meant that she thought my heart, or at least my services, could be bought. I don't think it ever occurred to her that the price I would pay for being bought would be irredeemable in character. The more I thought about it, the more I realized how little romance was involved in the original date.

Are such dates romantic or are they something else? Is the former salesman a narrow-minded prude or is the model what she denied being, a tramp? Is there some truly romantic option in between?

Lon objected to the feeling of being bought because that feeling made it impossible to experience romance or even appreciate the original date. In contrast, Trudi found such ventures incredibly romantic. It is worth noting she felt compelled to assert, "And I'm no tramp," reflecting what she anticipated others might say. In presenting these three scenarios to a variety of men and women for comment, Trudi's self-proclamations found no endorsement among the women. One very jaded, divorced man quipped, "It sounds like business as usual." For the most part, the men agreed with the women that Trudi's approach to dating lacked character and probably prevented her from ever experiencing romance. Non-feminist women were often quick to denounce the moral character of Trudi and applaud the decision of Lon. As one former non-feminist model observed:

> I've seen my share of people like that, both men and women. There is no room in their world for ordinary feelings. They are out to get all they can. They are very materialistic, and they see other people and even their own bodies as products to be traded. I don't think they even know what romance is. They just know how to "act" at life as if the life they live amounts to no more than a role in some B-rated movie.

Feminists were particularly incensed by both Helen's intent on attending the charity ball and Trudi's sense of romance. A former leader in a university's women's studies program said:

> Women like that make it rough for all the rest of us. They puff up the outrageous egos of rich old male chauvinists and encourage them to see women as subservient to their wishes. Women shouldn't have to cater to men for travel or access to the finer things in life. Romance should not be seen as a function of what a man can buy for you. Real romance is something that occurs when equals address each other as equals.
>
> One of the reasons many women today insist on paying their own way on dates is to avoid being compromised by a man. No one should find herself beholden to anyone on a date. A woman should always address a man as a moral equal. The sugar daddy phenomenon should have been outlawed with other forms of slavery.
>
> Being enchanted by another is, or ought to be, a matter of being thrilled by the other's company and noticing that he is equally thrilled by yours. Every time a man gets to use a woman,

such as in the case of the model, he is more likely to see other women that way in the future.

Finally, in response to the three scenarios, two stylishly-dressed career women in their mid-fifties said they thought Lon sounded like a good guy. The world would be much better if there were more people like him. They also dismissed Trudi's claim that she was no tramp as a defensive mechanism borne out of her own self-conscious fear of guilt. There is no doubt that this woman is a user and that offends everyone's basic sense of morality. On the other hand, they admitted that it is possible to imagine Trudi's exploits in a romantic way:

> After all, when such character roles are a major part of a motion picture or opera is it not because the role evokes sentiments of romance, pity or sympathy? Sometimes, the role can evoke all three sentiments as in the case of Natasha from the movie *Dr. Zhivago*. The truth is, things can be romantic whether they are morally good or morally evil and whether they evoke pity or admiration on the part of an observer. Romance occurs whenever our hearts go pitter patter as a result of some sexual, or potentially sexual, liaison.

Finally, one feminist thought Trudi should be pitied because she exhibited no strength of character at all. She hypothesized this was probably a woman who was raised by a very domineering father and, like the character Glenn Close played in the movie *Dangerous Liaisons*, spent a life time seeking the approval of men as well as their downfall.

The impropriety of the women in the stories above was universally condemned by women with whom I spoke and nearly as much so by men. In contrast, Lon was generally approved of as a decent sort. Most people also thought the women did not understand romance and their dates could not have been romantic in the truest sense of the word. Yet there were holdouts, such as the two career women who seemed, in part, willing to echo the refrain from Tina Turner's song, "What's love got to do with it?" They admitted what they were willing to call romance existed largely as a function of the bragging rights Helen and Trudi acquired and not what most people think of as a deeply private and blissful commitment.

So the question of what counts as romance is central to evaluating a genuinely good date. Do breath-taking first dates, fueled by excessive expenditures of funds and dramatic surroundings produce romance? Do they constitute a good date in and of themselves? Do such accoutrements and the addition of two pleasant enough personalities secure a good date? A romantic date? Do such dates make the occasion of love more likely? Do such dates simply make one greedier for similar-type dates in the future regardless of the person? Are romance and awe the same thing? Are romance and desire the same thing? After reviewing five more sets of first dates, the reader may conclude the answers to these questions are self-evident.

Heroes' Homage

Most of today's divorced singles grew up at a time when somewhere along the way, they fantasized about the handsome prince sweeping the princess off her feet. The fantasy ends with the two of them riding into the sunset to enjoy a life in which both live happily ever after. At one time or another every *boy*, from fourteen to sixty-four has yearned for the opportunity to commit some act of heroism in the presence of the newest femme fatale in his life. *Girls* from fourteen to sixty-four have similarly fantasized the new man in their life has the potential to be a dashing prince or, as the refrain and title from a pop song of the early 1980s exclaims, "I want a hero!"

Sometimes one does get to act in heroic fashion in the presence of a date. As the ancient Greeks noted long ago, character traits exist which nearly everyone admires, called the virtues. The philosopher David Hume, as long ago as the eighteenth century, observed people are compelled to admire manifestations of virtue out of an innate sense of social sympathy. Indeed, as Hume explains, even in a fictional account of some heroic or uncommonly just deed, the reader or listener is naturally stirred to admiration of those initiating such actions. To stir one's date so can be a good thing. Stirring others to admiration for oneself ought to mean the other's emotions become alive and receptive to the actor's words and deeds. In such cases, romance might not be far behind. During such adventures, cupid should have free reign targeting one's date and thereby securing a splendid and enduring romance. Alas, such is not always the case. Heroic deeds can produce feelings of respect and admiration without leading to romance. This is true even in cases where the act of heroism is performed in protection of the date's well-being.

Twenty-nine-year old Ron is a rough and tumble former college football player. He stands five feet nine inches tall and has thick, dark, curly hair. His jaw is square and his facial features are angular. Most would agree he is a handsome Germanic-looking man. He is an extremely cordial person, and this fits in well with his job as a marketing representative for a major office equipment concern. Ron's high-pitched voice makes him appear almost comical in light of his looks and his career success. Still, his gentle and amiable ways quickly distract people's attention from the irritating shrillness of his voice.

Emily, Ron's date, is only two inches shorter than he. At twenty-nine, she works as a secretary for one of Ron's corporate customers. Emily had met Ron at her office on three previous occasions when he came to call on her employer.

Both Ron and Emily speak well of each other. They did so before their first date and two years later still have nothing but high praise for one another. Their first date was extraordinarily memorable. It was the kind of stuff one expects in an episode of a television adventure series. It produced a story Ron should be proud of and which Emily admits telling numerous times. What the date did not produce was romance.

Ron and Emily went to the tourist district in the downtown section of the Midwestern city in which they live. Three youths in their late teens or early twenties stopped the couple and demanded money. The youths showed no weapons other than their unabashed hostility toward the couple. Ron, with Emily's arm through his, attempted to step past the menacing trio. Suddenly, one youth jabbed his palm into Ron's chest to stop him from proceeding. Meanwhile, another grabbed Emily's purse. Ron threw himself at the attackers, punching and kicking. In a few moments, the three youths were on the run, and Emily had her purse!

What could be more stimulating to romance? Ron acted as heroic as any Lancelot before the adoring eyes of his own Guinevere. But after that night, Ron and Emily dated only one more time when, three months later, Ron asked Emily to accompany him to a business banquet. When asked why no romance evolved from the first evening, both parties independently produced a rather similar rationale. Ron said, simply, "I don't know. Why should there be?" In response to the suggestion that his heroic action had the potential for causing many girls to swoon, Ron retorted:

> What I did was nothing special. I mean, I would have done what I did regardless of who I was with—even another guy. The kids were bullies. They pushed me and tried to steal a friend's money. I don't think I did anything special. In fact, since I didn't know if they were armed, I suppose we were lucky that I didn't get us killed.

When asked if Emily seemed impressed, Ron reported:

> Sure, I was impressed, too, I was impressed that the guys ran off. I thought I was going to get my butt kicked. Emily was real gracious and all, but she wasn't awestruck. And why should she be? Like I said, what I did wasn't that big of a deal.

Emily admits to being very impressed with Ron's speed, aggression and courage that night. However, she did not feel stirred by feelings of passion or romance:

> Ron's a very special kind of guy, a real athlete and not a person to be bullied. Don't get me wrong, he's not a tough-guy type at all, but he's not going to be pushed around. When I think about that night, I wonder why I didn't feel a rush of passion for Ron. The story sounds so wonderful each time I tell people about it. I don't know. I think it was just that I knew Ron did what he did almost out of instinct and not out of any special concern for me. I know that still doesn't sound right. Most of my girlfriends are surprised that I didn't have at least a passing fancy for Ron after the fight on the basis of some sort of animal magnetism if nothing else. All I can say is, you had to be there. It was Ron doing his thing. Ron has protocols he follows in life, and that sequence of events triggered a particular protocol. Ron and I talked about our attackers for a while at dinner that night. But even by the time we drove home he had already lost interest in the adventure. We kissed goodnight, almost in a business-like way. That's the way I expected Ron would be at the door even when I accepted the date. The next couple of times I saw him at the office, we talked and joked, and that was all there was to it. He's a good person and a nice-looking man, but there are just no sparks.

Our second date didn't happen until about two or three months later. He needed a date at the last minute for a banquet he was invited to attend. He called me and asked if I would go—as a friend. I did and that date was just like the first except there was no fight. I'm always happy to see Ron. But he'll never be more to me than just a nice guy I happen to know.

Contrast the story of Ron and Emily with the following story of Tony and Robbie. Tony is thirty-eight-years old and works as a hospital administrator. He is jovial and slightly overweight. The color of his facial skin, the red nose and the evident broken blood vessels in his face suggest he has spent too many nights out hoisting too many drinks. Robbie is a petite and attractive medical doctor also thirty-eight-years old and readily admits to being eager to re-marry and begin a family. On the way home from their first date, the couple pulled up to a traffic light. Across the intersection from where they sat, a pickup truck full of teenage boys pulled up behind a car with a boy and girl inside. The boys from the truck jumped out, ran up to the car in front, pulled a boy from the car and started kicking and beating him with their fists and with boards. As the traffic lights changed, cars kept driving past giving a wide berth to the street fight. Tony and Robbie drove to the nearest pay phone and called the police. Then Robbie said to Tony, "Get us back to the fight right away!"

When they arrived at the scene, the attackers were just leaving. The police had not yet arrived and no sirens could be heard. As the truck drove off, Tony and Robbie pulled up behind the car. The boy lay unconscious in a pool of blood and his girlfriend was standing in the street crying and screaming for help. Robbie leapt out of the car and immediately started giving aid to the boy. She directed Tony to turn on both car's emergency lights. Then, Robbie had Tony get the girl off the street to a nearby gas station where she could sit down and be cared for by the attendant. She also directed Tony to bring back some water. When Tony returned with the water, Robbie gave his hand a squeeze, thanked him and asked him to direct traffic away from the scene. By the time the police and an ambulance arrived, the boy had returned to consciousness.

Tony gave this assessment of the evening:

I couldn't believe how daring this little woman was. Heck, I was afraid the kids in the truck might return. She didn't seem worried. She just went right to work. There was no question she was in charge. She was in charge of the kid's care, me, of the whole situation. Throughout, she made me feel like I was a special part of it all, like I was an essential part of her team. In the midst of this disaster, she made me feel like I mattered. I drove home that night in love. I was already thinking marriage. Just four hours earlier, if anyone had asked, I would have proclaimed myself a confirmed bachelor.

Three months after this event, Tony and Robbie were dating one another exclusively. Tony's remarks suggest Robbie's heroics triggered his romantic feelings toward her. Why did Robbie's heroics stimulate awe and romance in Tony when Ron's heroics had no similar effect on Emily? Is it just that Tony and Emily are different or is something more universal involved?

In these and the few other stories involving first date acts of heroism I encountered, one feature had universal appeal. If, during the act of heroism, the date is made to feel special, either by being the intended object of a heroic effort or by being made to feel an integral part of the act, the effect is intensely romantic.

However, when the heroism occurs in a de-personalized or automaton-like fashion, dates are seldom stirred by romantic impulse. Some admit to *transient feelings of passion* after watching a date's heroic endeavor, but even in these cases, dates were quick to draw a distinction between feelings of awe and respect on the one hand, and feelings of passion and romance on the other. If heroic achievements are to inflame the romantic sensibilities of another, the other must sense that through it all the "hero" remains especially mindful of the presence and importance of his or her date.

Would most people be willing to go on a date in which they knew ahead of time an act of successful heroism was sure to result? Probably. Would they do so even if they knew the act would be performed in a de-personalized way? Probably so. In the light of such knowledge, does this suggest people need not experience romance for them to count a date as a good date? Perhaps. But before concluding good dates need not involve romance, one must ask if people would prefer an unromantic date with a soon-to-be hero or a genuinely romantic date with someone who could become that "special (albeit unheroic) other." The answer to this is always to prefer the "special other."

Prince's Princess

The Prince's Princess is a carefully planned romantic event initiated by a female suitor. (The following section, the Romantic Rendezvous, is an account of events initiated and under the explicit control of male suitors.) In the previous sections, I gave examples to show the roles of each date-mate need not be indelibly associated with one gender. So why here, the socially conscientious reader should ask, is gender assignment specific and treated as a distinctive characteristic? The answer is men find it difficult to consider women as equals when it comes to initiating romance. Throughout this book, I have tried to portray folk wisdom as it exists and not how some might wish it exists. I hope the following will reveal some male prejudices in this matter as well as some ways of overcoming them.

When asked to consider whether dates planned and engineered by women are "romantic," most men say no. The idea women can "romance" men, rather than just ask them out, is alien to most men. Men know women can create an environment conducive to romance, but denials of chauvinism aside, they *see* romance as something *they do* for the special women in their lives. Women believe they can be as "romantic" as any male when it comes to engineering dates. Male reticence is a vestige of earlier, more chauvinistic times.

Men still carry the burden for initiating the request for most dates, in particular, first dates. Whether or not the man initiates the date, there are occasions on which a woman immediately takes control of the situation. She may strongly recommend or even dictate the evening's activities. When the evening begins, she drapes herself on the man's arm, and "oohs" and "ahs" at his every action or comment. Finally, she lulls him into blissful acquiescence of her mastery over his emotions. The man who is swept off his feet believes he is on a pedestal she has built especially for him.

To illustrate an instance when the designing woman appears too desperate, consider the following experiences of Gary, a forty-seven-year old land management consultant:

Ginny, an attractive woman I met at a party, called and asked if I would escort her to an affair the following weekend. Ginny said she was a little embarrassed to be doing this, but her boss insisted the employees go. Since she wasn't dating anyone at the moment, she needed an escort. She also suggested this would be an opportunity for me to make some useful business contacts.

At the reception, it became apparent this was not a matter of business. Neither Ginny's boss nor any other employees from her work were in attendance. She hung on to my arm all night. She treated me like royalty and introduced me to people in a manner that made them think we were an "item." I became very uncomfortable with what was happening. On the way home, she quizzed me about my desire to get married again and what I looked for in a woman. She volunteered her desire to marry again and gave a loose description of her ideal man: a description which seemed tailor-made to what little she knew about me. Once back at her apartment, she made overtures meant to arouse me to passion. I was tempted briefly by the prospect of a one night stand, but she was just too pushy. The more Ginny pushed, the more I wanted out.

A few days later Ginny sent me a note thanking me for serving as her escort and indicating she would like to see me again. I thought my reaction to this woman was peculiar. She was attractive, and I should have been flattered. Her demeanor was too much, however. She seemed desperate to get me into her life. The fact that she hardly even knew me was too disturbing for me. I felt that if I gave into her at all, she would latch on to me and never let go. This may sound excessive, but in some small way she reminded me of the character played by Glenn Close in the movie *Fatal Attraction*. She needed a man in her life; nearly anyone would do. And once there, he would never again be free.

Now consider the following account by Will, a man who believes his date Lorna was a gold digger. Dark-haired and somewhat slight of build, Will was the product of an excellent education at the best private schools and Eastern universities. At thirty-three-years old, Will worked as a fund raiser for a charity. His family had fallen on hard times a few years before and this, Will believed, had a deleterious effect on his own ill-fated first marriage. Will reports:

> Because of my job, I have contact with a number of fairly well-heeled people. My own situation is not so enviable. I have little in

savings, no inheritance to look forward to and I was born in the wrong era. By that I mean money doesn't mean much to me. If I had been an adult when President Kennedy founded the Peace Corps, I would have joined and been happy to live the next twenty years in some third-world country. If I were not an atheist, I think I would have become a missionary. As it is, I am using my talents in a way that is relatively helpful to those whose illness is depriving them of future happiness. I am paid little for what I do, but I am proud of my work.

I asked out Lorna the evening we met at a charity fashion show held at the store where she worked as a sales clerk. Lorna was dynamite-looking and could easily pass for one of the models. We went to the ballet on our first date. The tickets were on the mezzanine level, the best I could afford. The day before the ballet, Lorna called to tell me how excited she was about our date. She said she arranged to take the day off so she could look her best for the evening. She then suggested we have dinner beforehand. I didn't have the money to spend for dinner and ballet so I made an excuse about having to work late until just before curtain time.

Throughout our date, she kept asking about the wealthy people I knew. She seemed too impressed when I introduced her to a couple of the charity's bigger supporters (whom we happened to meet while at the ballet). After the ballet, she kept asking if I had been to this restaurant or that. Of course, she named all the most expensive and trendy restaurants. She announced that she was hungry with all this talk of food and asked if I was hungry. I said no, but we could stop for her to get a bite. Without any hesitation, she accepted. She told me she talked about all the restaurants she knew of and asked if any sounded good to me. I told her I knew just the spot. I took her to a nice but inexpensive little hideaway. She ordered three drinks, the most expensive entree and dessert. I had salad and a glass of wine.

After dinner, Lorna recommended we go dancing. She then named the three or four most expensive nightclubs in town. I declined, saying I was tired and needed to go home. Throughout the night, she clung to my arm, kissed my check and acted as if she were thoroughly enamored with me. For at least six weeks after our date she called me once a week to talk. She repeated how much she would like to go out with me again. My impression was that Lorna thought I had money and a date with me meant that she would be treated in the grandest styles. That, of course, isn't the case. I grew up living that way, and I don't like it. And now, I can't afford it. After the first few weeks, when she'd call I told her

I had too much work to do and too little money for dating. That didn't deter her initially, but finally she got the message.

I wish I could have felt comfortable Lorna liked me for me. When she wasn't talking about the trappings of money, she was pleasant to be with. Nevertheless, I knew that people were of secondary concern in her mind. I cannot be comfortable with that sort of person no matter how much they seem to like me. I've met those kind of women before. They are just out to pick your pocket and when the cash runs thin, they walk out. No one needs to chance a relationship with that type of person.

Both Ginny and Lorna seemed serious about capturing the hearts, or at least the imaginations, of their intendeds. When Gary and Will each noticed their date's interest was not for the person but in what he represented, both men were put off by their dates' aggressions.

There is a third set of circumstances in which a woman's attempt to romance the man of her choice is destined to fail. This is the situation wherein the woman's efforts seem far too polished. Bub, a very handsome and dignified-looking fifty-one-year old corporate real estate broker shared the following observation and cautions:

> Sometimes you go out with a woman who knows all the right moves. She is attractive, dresses elegantly, is abreast of world events and is cultured besides. The woman is confident, intelligent and yet vulnerable. She makes you feel as if nothing in this world matters more to her at this very moment than your approval. This is a thoroughly delightful experience for a man and one many find well worth paying for . . . and do. The best call girls practice just this sort of expertise at making the whole experience seem dreamily enchanting. She makes it easy for the man to believe that, negotiated price aside, she genuinely finds him to be the most fascinating man in the world.
>
> The best call girls lead fairly normal lives. They do not service different clients night after night. They hold other jobs. They date. And, most important, they work a client only when necessary for money, to retain an especially valued customer or develop a lucrative relationship with a new potentially long-range customer. The skill and energy used by these women is enormous. It is easy to understand why few could manage a nightly schedule of customers. In a single night, they create an evening for a man that is very nearly perfect—too perfect.

If you travel frequently in your business, you may run across such women both in their capacity as call-girls and as an ordinary date made while engaging in business at her daytime place of employment. In the case of the former, you know what you are in for; in the case of the latter, the experience can be somewhat disarming. What appeared to be a promising and interesting date, initially, begins turning into something spectacular and exciting. You find yourself believing your date has fallen in love with you at very nearly first sight. You find yourself becoming awed by the fact that your date is so evidently taken with you. And then, you begin to become awed by the woman herself. If you have been down this road before, warning signals begin going off in your head. You realize everything really is all too perfect. At that point, you begin backing off and erecting protective barriers around your emotions. You decide to enjoy the evening but avoid naively falling victim to the woman's obvious talents.

I do not mean to suggest that every woman who comes off like one of the sirens of ancient Greek mythology is a call girl. That would surely be a crass and irresponsible generalization. My point is that when a woman is able deftly to sweep you away in a whirlwind of adoration, she didn't acquire this skill overnight or because you are such an inspiration. As the old saying goes, 'She's probably been around the block a few times,' and she knows how to manipulate GUYS LIKE YOU. It is usually foolish to proceed with this type of relationship because you will end up by getting hurt. When you start feeling you are a piece of clay being sculpted by this sorceress, you find yourself incredulous at the fact you are loving it. This is surely time to move on. The ugly truth of the matter is that your feelings are correct. You are being sculpted according to the will of another. You are an object in the hands of a master craftsperson and not a person enchanted by an equal, a genuine compatriot in the quest for love.

There may be much to object to in Bub's comments, but one impression he shared is supported by a number of men. When everything about an evening turns out too perfect, a man becomes suspicious that the woman is practicing a craft and not at all caught up in cupid's delirium. All three anecdotes reflect men's concern they be valued as individuals and not as a representative or means to something else. Of course, there are men who are content with being used if what they get in return is of comparable value. But when judging the *romantic* merit of a date, men are just as concerned as women they be valued for themselves and not as a means to some further goal.

When a "true" princess enchants her prince it is not because her *designs* leave him helpless. Rather, a prince falls under a princess' spell because she shows he is *uniquely precious* in her eyes. *Sincerity is the most potent aphrodisiac.*

The sincere expression of romantic intention inhibits a person's attempt to engineer an event. The romantic's plans get disrupted in multifarious ways. But all is not lost as long as the woman's date recognizes she holds him in genuinely, special respect, as the experience of an exotic-looking thirty-one-year old Eurasian airline stewardess and former model named Han rightly reveals:

> I put together a date that seemed to deteriorate throughout the evening. Much to my surprise, the man I was with became more charmed after each faux pas. I had never asked a man out before so I was understandably quite nervous when I asked Hank for a date. Hank is a salesman. One flight when he was returning home I sat down next to him, as I often had before on other flights. We chatted a few minutes. Hank never seemed to notice that I was flirting with him. I decided that if he didn't ask me out, I was going to ask him. Well, he didn't. So I did. Hank accepted.
>
> For our date, I suggested we go to a very chic restaurant. He had heard of it before and was clearly impressed. Hank volunteered to drive. When he came by to pick me up, I was wearing a shift with a very tight-fitting bodice. As I got into his car, one of the buttons on my dress popped off. It was too late to change dresses so I just pinned it. Now, instead of looking sexy, I felt I looked like a domestic trying to keep her old uniform together by any means possible. Hank seemed to take it all in stride. No leers and no despairing looks.
>
> When we got to the restaurant, it was closed. We drove around for an hour; first with me trying to decide where to go and then driving twenty-five minutes to get there. I settled on a little-farm house restaurant just outside of town. It was known for its good food, and it was quiet and potentially romantic. Upon our arrival, we learned the restaurant was going out of business in a couple of weeks. There were few customers and the waitresses didn't seem to care that the food they served was lukewarm and lacked luster in appearance. I was mortified. I kept reaching over for Hank's hand and telling him, "I'm really not very good at this I'm afraid, but I

want you to have a good time." The rest of the evening went okay but there was no moment that should have produced romance.

Months later, Hank said he could not get over the fact that I never seemed to lose interest in him or whether or not he was having a good time. He said he thought he was falling in love with me that first night as he watched me struggle to make something happen right. By the way, we did not have sex until after three or four weeks of almost constant dating. Heaven only knows why Hank thought he fell in love with me that first night but, I am glad he did.

Han's date with Hank taught her you do not have to treat a man like a prince to create desire or romance. You only need to show him it is him you value. The true princess makes a man feel noted precisely by the intentions she shows and not by the measured efforts of a skilled performance.

The woman who appears too desperate or too much like a gold digger or too experienced, presumably wants her date to find romance in their relationship. Why does such a woman fail and Han succeed? There seem to be two ingredients in Han's example: sincerity and pace. Sincerity has already been discussed at length in this section. If the princess's prince does not believe it is he who the princess fancies but rather something he represents, then he will remain invulnerable to cupid's arrows. If, on the other hand, a man believes his date truly sees him as something of a prince, he opens up and may begin seeing her as a romantic interest.

Pace is the other key ingredient in making men and women see each other as dashing princes and enchanting princesses. The woman who appears too desperate rushes things. Her intensity forces the man to become wary of her before he has much chance to learn about her in any depth. In dating, as in an election campaign, things seem to go best when they start out slowly, gain momentum, and then achieve a zenith of enthusiasm in a way that feels natural to each party. To the sincere woman, willing to be patient, the necessary information will become available. The princess-to-be will know she has such information at hand when the man's smile reaches *all the way* to his eyes. Once the intended prince shows he's willing, the female suitor can step up the campaign with actions that say, "You could be my prince."

Romantic Rendezvous

Romeo and Juliet were young lovers whose lives are believed by many to epitomize romance. Ballet performances as well as Shakespeare's play leap toward the audience with grand displays of youthful exuberance and passion. But passion, romance and exuberance are not the exclusive domain of youth. Divorcees re-entering the single world after years of marriage may still yearn for romance. Surely romance is the right of the middle-aged as much as it is of youth.

Middle-aged divorcees may yearn for romance, but often their previous love-trauma leaves them too jaded to appreciate the many opportunities for romance. On the other hand, some middle-aged divorced men believe they have romance down to a system. More often than not such over confidence reflects little more than their experience in trying to use women and being used by women in return. Romance needs a certain amount of innocence and a lot of sincerity. Such traits can never be the predictable product of a "system." The middle-aged man may need to look at the young male to recall the role of innovation in romance.

Throughout this book, I have encouraged the reader to value his or her age. Years are the pages upon which the hand of experience writes. An individual's life becomes richly-textured only if there are enough pages upon which to unfold an intriguing life narrative. But when it comes to romance, inexperience is sometimes an advantage. Youth provides insights which are sometimes opaque to older singles. The energy of youth keeps one's emotions ever close to the surface and free of the shackles of grave disappointment. Youth accesses corners of the imagination that older, more experienced men learn to ignore. For the middle-aged male suitor, it is worth the effort to risk exploring those corners of imagination and to again truly romance a woman.

Only a few years older than Shakespeare's Romeo, Matthew, a young man of twenty-two, successfully planned a date greatly exceeding the ambitions of worldly men twenty or more years his senior. Matthew is average in most respects. He plays no collegiate-level sports and holds no college-wide elective office. He is an average student majoring in American history and is a member of an unexceptional fraternity. Becky, the girl he romanced, is pretty, a member of the best sorority on campus and currently serves as a representative on the Sophomore

Class Council. She is not the most popular girl on campus nor even in the sophomore class. She does know everyone who is worth knowing and has dated some of the most popular boys on campus. Although Matthew and Becky met through a class they had together, they rarely spoke. Toward the end of the semester, Matthew asked her out for a Sunday afternoon. He chose Sunday afternoon, he said, because he thought she was less likely to turn him down than if he asked her for a Friday or Saturday evening. Becky explains how the date proceeded:

> I always thought Matthew was a nice, VERY average guy. He also struck me as extremely safe. So when he asked me out for a Sunday afternoon picnic I thought, "Why not, it might be fun."
>
> He picked me up in his car, and he drove about twelve miles out of town. He pulled over at a rest area just off the highway and parked the car. At first I thought he had no sense of pastoral scenery whereupon he got out and retrieved a two-seater bike he had locked to a tree. Out of his trunk he pulled helmets and goggles, and we were on our way. About three miles down a country road, we pedaled up to a picnic table at the edge of some farmer's pond. There, on the table, were four breakfast rolls in a pack, hot coffee in a styrofoam container and two small cartons of orange juice. This was really starting to be fun. I told him so, often. There was absolutely nothing sexual about it all at this point, just two people quickly becoming friends, actually playmates might be a better word for it. I felt like we were just kids having fun.
>
> After a while, we took off. Instead of heading back to the car, we pedaled off toward the state park. When we arrived at the picnic area, there were two of his fraternity brothers. They had laid out a white table cloth with a picnic basket on top, an ice bucket with some cheap champagne and two plastic tulip-shaped glasses. They told us to enjoy and they would return in an hour or so. We ate potato salad, cole slaw and Kentucky Fried Chicken while we sipped our champagne. No post-formal meal had ever tasted so good. When his friends returned to clean up, we left and rode over to the concession stand and rented a canoe for an hour. We just talked as we lazily floated along only yards from the shore. I kept looking at him disbelieving that I was seeing him as a handsome and appealing man.
>
> When we returned to the concession stand, our bike was gone and there, in its stead, was his car. He drove me home and kissed me once. I must confess, between the champagne and the glorious day, I was ready for much more. I went to sleep that night thinking

> I had met the man of my dreams. What more can I say? The last five months have been just wonderful. We talk a lot about the future . . .

When asked to read Becky's account of this day, women of all ages readily agreed the date sounded romantic. A few women who were a bit older or not in particularly good shape, quipped, "That sure seems like a lot of bike-riding" and "Did she have to help paddle the canoe, too?" But alembic humor aside, each woman interviewed said it was easy to see how Matthew swept Becky off her feet. Why did Matthew and Becky's date have such appeal? Rhonda, a thirty-five-year old manager of a theater company said:

> Because he made her feel special for herself. Everything was so planned out to be gentle, and attractive to her. There was no attempt to take advantage of the situation, to whisk her off to bed. The whole thing: Sunday afternoon, picnic, bicycle built for two, other people involved, it all says I think you are special and I want to get to know you. Apparently, there were not sexual overtones. All that can make a girl feel **REAL** special. And it's much different from the way most of us ever get treated by men.

An ardent feminist in her early thirties observed:

> I suppose you expect me to object to the way Matthew treated Becky. He certainly did put her on a pedestal, but he did so because he thought she was a special person. Most men you go out with in your thirties try to impress you with their boasting or throwing money around. If it works, they expect you to return the favor through sexual attention to them. Matthew worked hard to get to know Becky. And even when she became interested in him sexually he seemed intent on preserving their good feelings for one another for the long run. He did not risk losing the relationship by trying to exploit her amorous feelings of the moment. If more men understood how an approach like Matthew's can affect women, there would be more successful first dates and probably more successful romances.

Men's reaction to Matthew's date is much more varied. Many wrote the episode off as "cute" but nothing more than an expression of childish innocence. As Wilson, a forty-six-year old insurance agent said:

> That sort of thing can work for a kid, but adult women want you to spend money on them. At the very least, the glasses should have been crystal, the meal catered and the champagne, Don Perignon. Also, what kind of woman, besides a college kid, is going to want to pedal all over the countryside on a Sunday afternoon? Women today have to go to work the next day. That stuff may work when you're in college but not with today's liberated career woman.

A forty-four-year old commercial real estate salesman, Jack, expressed similar amusement at Matthew's efforts:

> Yeah, I can remember doing that sort of thing in high school, but who has time for all that today? That kid must have spent three days planning that date. If a guy my age tried to set up something like that today, most women would laugh at you for being a sap. I shouldn't say most women. Those who enjoy going to church socials and square dancing probably think it's fine, but those aren't the kind of women I go out with.

A doctor in his early fifties reflected:

> It does sound nice, and I'll bet any woman young enough and energetic enough would enjoy it. I bike ride sometimes with a date—but I don't think I would ever go to all the trouble the kid did. Not that I don't think it's beautiful, but I just think that is the sort of thing that is inspired by and belongs to youth.

Finally, a construction foreman in his late thirties said:

> I think it's a great idea. If I could get up enough nerve, I would try it myself. That's the kind of thing that could really misfire. If the woman doesn't have the same sense of romance you do, the whole thing could look hokey . . . fast. You could find yourself in the midst of one long, miserable day. Dinner, movies, spectator sports, and dancing are much safer fare.

All in all there were few men who felt comfortable with the idea they should plan a date as meticulously as Matthew. One or two announced that he had a fairly elaborate scheme for wooing a girl to bed on the first date but their schemes revealed little novelty and seemed best suited to the people described in "Gold Digger's Delight." These schemes also revealed sexual objectives whereas Matthew's objective focused only on attracting the fancy of Becky.

No one should fault men for fearing that the bravado shown by Matthew risks exposing one to charges of excessiveness and immaturity. After all, this was only a first date, not an anniversary or a proposal. Perhaps, when one is as young as Matthew, only an arm's length from childhood, the risk of appearing ridiculous and childish seems less grave. Perhaps as Matthew ages (particularly if he is unfortunate enough to experience divorce), he too will become more reserved when it comes to showing his affection for a woman he barely knows. Nevertheless, since the women interviewed seemed so unabashed in their approval of Matthew's efforts, men might again find such risks worth taking.

For example, a thirty-nine-year old writer named Tony, created a date something like Matthew's wholly by accident. Tony had been divorced for about six months and only recently started dating. He had no idea where one should go on dates or even what was available to singles in his city. One night, he met a woman named Catherine at a reception for an art exhibit.

Catherine was confident and quite worldly. Tony was unsure of himself and felt conspicuously out of place in a situation where the single's life was so clearly in evidence. He introduced himself to Catherine whereupon she promptly gave him her card and hurried off elsewhere. The meeting happened so fast he wasn't even sure what she looked like. Nevertheless, he liked her voice and evident self-assurance. A week later, Tony called Catherine and asked her to go out the following Sunday. He suggested something casual in the early afternoon. Catherine accepted.

On Sunday morning Tony opened the newspaper and looked for an idea. He noticed a classical music concert was being offered that afternoon in a little town. He assumed the town must be a suburb since the city paper covered it. He called Catherine and told her of his idea. She liked it. As it turned out, the concert was in a country town more than a hundred miles away. Consequently, their date involved a long drive in the country, a concert, and when they returned to the city, dinner and a late night stroll. Catherine became enamored with Tony by the end of the evening. She saw both he and their date as spectacularly romantic. He had pulled it all off quite by accident. Tony describes the date:

When I picked her up, she looked pale, sickly and older than I remembered her. I thought, "Oh well, if she's nice, I'll make a new friend and I'll get a chance to check out this concert facility." The drive lasted forever and Catherine told me much, too much, about herself. She seemed the victim of a pretty rough life. I tried to be as consoling as I could and friendly. What else was I to do when we were destined to be together for the next four to six hours or more?

Upon our return to the city, I never intended to have dinner and go for a walk—that was all her idea. Anyway, to make a long story short, a few days later I asked her out one more time. I did this at the last minute since something unexpected came up and I wanted a date.

A day or so after that second date she asked me out to a series of three musical events. I'm glad she did because as things developed, we fell deeply in love with one another. We even came to discuss the inevitability of marriage one day.

The interesting thing is I swept her off her feet by accident. I hadn't planned on such a lengthy date involving a drive down country roads and a concert at a charming little German farm town. Nor had I expected her to see in my friendly demeanor an interest in getting to know her as a person. I thought I was just being cordial. The reason I expressed no sexual interest in her is that I had none. I was resolved to just getting to know her. I have often thought when I look back at our first date that I never planned things any better.

As in the case with Matthew, the key to Tony's success in producing romance on his first date with Catherine was he made her feel she was special, special enough for planning a lengthy date. Circumstances also led her to believe his interest was with her as a person and not as a potential sexual object. What Matthew deliberately and successfully planned was, in a sense, replicated by Tony, unwittingly. What is curiously displayed in the above is that despite all one's efforts to look great and impress a person of the opposite sex, nothing is more impressive in the long run than to show the person you believe he or she is a very special human being, a person of character and substance whose friendship is prized in a singularly unique way.

Romance involves sharing insights with each other about one's life and one's sense of the world. Dates which reflect a preoccupation with immediate sexual satisfaction make clear one has little interest in the other *as a person*. Furthermore, sexual overtures mask any secondary concern one might have in sharing such views with another even at some later time.

In short, the message to men is identical to one they wish more women would heed, namely, treat and respect the other as a person, not as an object to be mastered, collected or in any way used. With this in mind, one may discover romance can be more natural than sex and more common than rejection.

Sadie Hawkins Day

Recall an event from high school designated "Sadie Hawkins Day." To go to a Sadie Hawkins Dance, a boy had to be invited by a girl. This created a spirit in which role reversals were not only accepted but demanded. The spirit of the Sadie Hawkins Dance extended well into the entire evening. The girls often drove and determined who, if anyone, the couple might "double" with. The girl generally planned the entire evening. The openness of Sadie Hawkins Day created an atmosphere wherein a girl's attempt to create romance was tolerated as was a boy's willingness to respond.

The twenty-first century has extended the Sadie Hawkins concept beyond a simple designated day. Women are asking men out from time to time. Among baby boomer men and their seniors, the acceptance of these practices is still received with much awkwardness. Asking a girl for a date was once seen as a symbol of growing up. It meant one was ascending to the role of adult manhood. This is one reason why boys are so eager to date at an increasingly younger age. Few men today will admit to chauvinistic ideologies or practices. But on the matter of dating, men continue to think romance results from their efforts and not from those of women. (It is amazing how few men realize their first skills in creating romance were probably instilled by some cleverer and very subtle coquette!) Consequently, when asked for a date by a woman, a substantial number of men admit to being flattered, but inconvenienced by the sense that romance is now a female prerogative.

It is difficult for the individual woman to overcome this male prejudice. On the other hand, if a group of women put together a Sadie Hawkins Day event of some kind, the community atmosphere frees each participant of male-female dichotomy that might otherwise *infect* their dates. Of course, Sadie Hawkins events no longer need occur on Sadie Hawkins Day alone.

The rise of women's business and professional groups increased women's groups sponsoring picnics, dances, dinners and so on. These events are ripe with possibilities. In each case, the woman is in control of the date's activities and the man expects her to be. If romance is on her mind, she has the opportunity to initiate an advance—much to the glee of a willing male.

Katy is a vice-president of an oil-drilling supply company. She is in her late thirties, attractive, personable and aggressive. Kim is a university administrator. He is plump, in his late forties, quiet but easy to get along with. On their "first date" nearly four years ago, Katy asked Kim to accompany her to a dance at her yacht club. The dance was not a Sadie Hawkins affair. The couple went through the motions, but there was no chemistry. The evening ended with each person politely bidding the other farewell and with no lingering interest to learn more about the other. When asked about the evening several years later, Katy observed:

> I wanted to go to the dance and needed an escort. I thought Kim might be interesting. He was polite and amiable throughout the evening, but I could never really draw him out. After a while I just gave up. I didn't have that much interest in him in the first place.

Kim's recollection of the evening was a similar story:

> I was flattered Katy asked me to the dance. I didn't know anyone at the dance, but that doesn't usually bother me. On the other hand, I do remember feeling like Katy's tag along. Not because of anything she did—quite the contrary. The club was clearly dominated by a good ol' boy set. Katy was accepted by them—as much as any independent woman was going to be—but I felt out of place. This was a dance where men brought their wives and dates, then there was Katy, the lonely divorcee (but she's very pretty mind you!), bringing along some guy she found. Katy didn't belong with the wives and girlfriends, and I didn't belong with the men. After an initial exchange of pleasantries, we sat alone. Katy tried to be friendly, but I'm afraid I just wanted out. Of course, I didn't say anything because I didn't want to offend her. On the other hand, it didn't seem to me that she would have found things different with any other guy. The social dynamics just didn't favor the presence

of a woman like Katy. I got bored, and I think Katy got a little embarrassed. She even said at one point, "I don't really care for these things I just came because I have a couple of customers here I always try to schmooze. My ex was the real sailor in the family."

Three years later with almost no other communication between the two, Katy again asked Kim for a date. This time it was to be a women's club Halloween party. This "first date" turned out to be a success. Katy and Kim have now been dating steadily for several months. What was the difference? No doubt, a shift in the implicit social conventions surrounding the event had something to do with it. As Katy explains:

> It's a group of interesting and accomplished women. It's a fun group to be with. I feel more relaxed with these people than with the good ol' boys of the yacht club and the wives' constant chatter about kids and gardens. Also, Kim was different. I don't know what it was, but he was much more talkative to me and everyone else. In fact, through a friendship Kim struck up with another fellow I think I may get the other fellow's company's account. Anyway, Kim and I got along great that night and so far it seems we make a great pair.

Katy felt comfortable with the group and felt, as a group, they secured an enjoyable evening for all. Katy also thought she sensed a difference in Kim. Kim's observation confirms Katy's assessment of the evening:

> When Kim asked me out three years later, I was surprised. I figured she was hard up, in-between boyfriends or whatever. We had only talked two or three times since the first time we dated. Katy is very pretty. I figured even if the night turned out to be a bomb, she wouldn't be hard to look at.
> It turned out to be fun. "We guys" were the dates and the women planned quite an affair. I met several guys who were in much the same boat I was: asked out by an attractive woman each of us barely knew. Even the husbands seemed responsive to the newcomers. I know Katy thought that I had changed significantly since our first date, but that wasn't true. The first time we were an odd couple out, so to speak. This time all the couples were just like us. It gave me more of a chance to get to meet people and enjoy myself.

It may be Kim's remarks describing the differences between the two first dates reflect little more than personal insecurity. Even if this is the case, Kim's reactions to the two situations are not uncommon. Kim, like many men, felt awkward in adapting to the role reversal. In addition, the first group was apparently a closed social set and did not understand the potential awkwardness they presented to Katy and Kim. In contrast, the second date took place among people who understood the social roles of the moment and were tolerant and supportive of them. The roles may have been radically different from what one normally expects, but their uniformity afforded an atmosphere of acceptance and congeniality.

Sadie Hawkins events will not, in and of themselves, create romance. They do break down some of the remaining encumbrances of the male ego, making it more natural for women to create a "prince's princess" if they choose. They establish the conditions under which a particular type of date, the prince's princess, is most likely to occur in circumstances optimally favorable for romance.

The Essence of a Good First Date

The safest thing one might say about good first dates is they are occasions for people to enjoy themselves. A criteria of success should be the eagerness of the parties to date again. That which looks so obvious at first blush is often misleading. So it is with this criteria of success.

It is not uncommon for two people to enjoy a sensational evening and yet never want to see each other again. Sometimes that first and wondrous encounter with another person cannot, and ought not to, lead to anything else. Their evening of passion or romance, if that is what it is, amounts to no more than "two ships passing in the night." Under such circumstances would either assent to *stepping back in time* and reliving that solitary encounter? Answering yes suggests the date was enjoyable. Nevertheless, subsequent encounters may be out of the question. For example, one or both of the parties may feel they rushed into something they now regret. The moment of the evening prior was beautiful, but the PACE was such that future encounters are, at best, unappealing. This happens both in cases of hurried physical intimacy as well as in cases where intimacy of mind and soul seem rushed as well.

People sometimes reveal the contents of the deepest recesses of their mind early on in a conversation only to regret it later. They are embarrassed they were so careless about expressing intimacy to a near stranger. The date partner may be guilty of no intrusion nor deserving of any rebuke, but one or both parties may conclude it is best to avoid further contact and thus avoid further embarrassment. Enjoying shared physical or emotional intimacy does not assure pursuit. Sharing enjoyable and memorable moments on a first date does not guarantee a desire on the part of either participant to continue a relationship.

Recall the example of the battling and heroic salesman Ron, discussed in Heroes' Homage. Ron defended his date from the attack of three young toughs. Emily, the woman he defended, admits to being awed by his valor and physical abilities, yet neither Ron nor Emily saw any spark of romance in the evening's affairs.

When asked if she would look forward to stepping back in time and reliving the events of that first date, Emily was unhesitating in her affirmation (just as she was unhesitating in her judgment there was no future for this pair). But is a good time all it takes to have a good date?

Imagine one's life could be segmented off into a series of time-slices and those time-slices which currently constitute your life are interchangeable with a set of alternatives. You only get one chance to remove a given, say, five-hour time slice and replace it with another. Once a substitution has been made, all that occurs afterward will be duly modified by the substitution. So imagine that in place of Emily's first date with Ron, a modern day knight, she could substitute a different sort of evening, a rather modest affair involving neither heroics or glitz nor anything else beyond the realization that she may be on the verge of an extraordinary ROMANCE. Which do you suppose Emily would choose? As one, very unpoetic, apartment manager explained, "Being witness to acts of heroism gives you something to talk about from time to time. ROMANCE changes your life forever. It's the better bet." Romance is the central goal of dating.

Some dates are more like business appointments or promotional appearances. In contrast, a genuine date is an *opportunity for ROMANCE.* "If that were not the case," a stoic-looking thirty-year-old nurse declared "sperm banks and prostitutes would be all that is needed to serve society's desire for future generations and pleasant distractions, respectively."

Truly great dates are not merely events which leave people with wonderful memories. Romance, or the potential for it, is necessary and something more is required, PACE, which is integral to long-range success.

PACE is the rate at which events happen and the cumulative effect they have on people's emotions. A good date is something of an emotional and intellectual feast. With each course, one needs time to savor the offerings of the moment. One cannot rush from one course to the next in gluttonous fashion or one will fail to savor the offerings of the moment. Rushing forward to consuming large bits and chunks of the next course may make one overlook many savory morsels. After each course, time is needed to reflect upon the treasures of the past moment and to anticipate those of the next. The "two ships passing in the night" phenomenon can be explained in the context of this analogy as a rushed meal. Much eaten was good but much more was neglected and left behind. The haste of the situation turns what should be a deliberate and enjoyable delight into a blur of ineffective, sensual responses.

Just as the glutton is embarrassed by his own lack of discrimination, so too date-mates can be embarrassed by rushing through a potentially beautiful affair, turning all into a series of half-digested, half-understood and quickly discarded sensations. While a feast moves dramatically toward a crescendo, which it achieves with the main course, it ends with something light, allowing the pace of the event to relax. This is a common feature of truly great dates, leading to satisfaction and a desire to continue learning about the other on subsequent dates. Failure to pace a date leads one or both parties to distraction and confusion.

To ensure an appropriate pace, monitor your date's reactions. Is he or she enjoying himself or herself? Is it time to move on to another activity or another topic of conversation? Do the two of you need a chance to reflect about what has transpired? Do you or your date need to reflect about what is likely to happen shortly? As the episodes of Fool's Fancy demonstrate, well-paced attentiveness to the other—even in the most unexpected and disastrous circumstances—can turn a mere date into a great date: an occasion for ROMANCE.

ROMANCE is an enchantment of mind which leads to a peculiar desire to learn more about another. This desire does not focus on one single aspect of the other person. It is not the other's role as a stockbroker, a professor or a doctor that accounts for the attraction, nor is it the other's biceps, mile run records, luxurious hair, or shapely legs. The desire of romance is more general. It is a desire to learn all there is about the other and is never satiated as long as the romance survives. Unlike a desire such as thirst, the intensity of which diminishes to the extent one drinks (unsalted fluids), the desire to learn more of a romantic interest is continually inflamed as one learns. Romantic longings lead to further questions and a passion for more answers about the other.

Romance is also an enchantment of the heart. This is the chemistry people say they are looking for in a relationship. Enchantment of the heart causes people to seek out each other's company. In its most intense form, this includes sexual intercourse, but it is also captured in the urge sweethearts have just to be with each other, hear the other's voice, and, most important, see the other's continued responsiveness to your expressions of attention. Enchantment of the heart also diminishes one's propensity for calculating strategies to manipulate the other. Obviously, much time and energy is spent manipulating intended date-mates during periods of infatuation, but as infatuation gives way to romance, people inevitably become more careless and fear less Machiavellism in their beloved's responses.

People who cannot let go of the urge to manipulate never really understand or experience romance. They do not understand the feelings of being *destined* to seek out the company of the other rather than the control of the other. Romantics want to possess the other but not at the cost of corrupting the other's freedom. Lust for the other's company may approach, but it need not be obsessive, nor pursued in Quixotic fashion. The individual recognizes the *feel* of romance by the effect it has on one's ability to regulate fully ordinary behavior. It also noticeably affects the skills one ordinarily relies upon to control the behavior of an attractive consort.

Romance is not a single discrete experience contrasted with the absence of romance. That is to say, it is not at all like being pregnant. Romance is *felt* as a matter of degree. At some moments, one may feel more romantic about a beloved than at others, and some people are more predisposed to experiencing romance. Nevertheless, some capacity for romance seems to be a part of the emotional repertoire of nearly every adult single.

Romance makes people susceptible to delights and ambitions they might otherwise miss, exposing them to anxieties and tragedies they might well want to avoid. For example, romance bestows upon lovers opportunities for intimacy, enhanced self-esteem, elation, and the possibility of one day achieving erotic love. In contrast, unrequited passion makes one susceptible to fits of jealousy, depression and anxiety. For better or worse, romance can substantially alter a person's life narrative. Few other events can so affect the human psyche (save morbid events such as severe illnesses, death of a loved one or spiritual revelation). No other experience is so widely sought after.

Romance opens people to new experiences. As Plato observed, the object of our romantic intention awakens in us thoughts of beauty and truth. Indeed, it is *because* we feel romantic towards another that he or she appears increasingly more beautiful as our romantic awakening evolves. Furthermore, romance leads us to reflect on the "truth" of our feelings. And, finally, romance causes us to contemplate merging our life narrative with that of another.

Pace paves the way for romance. Romance makes possible new adventures, new feelings and even new (presumably), enhanced lifestyles.

Fun, interest, novelty and such, all contribute to romance, but none are central to it or even to the notion of a good date. No instance of the Gold Digger's Delight will ever count as a genuinely good date because these qualities are the most either person can hope to achieve. They are central to the encounter, not romance. Since the gold digger and the gold digger's date are exploiting each other while risking self-exploitation, neither regards the other as much of a person and neither sees him or herself as honorable or anything special. Only the surrounding events are special. The people are just incidental. As one world famous European salon operator noted in reading through an earlier draft of this chapter, "I like what you do with the Gold Digger's Delight. You got it right. It's all dicks and boobs, bucks and diamonds." No one's life is altered by a Gold Digger's Delight (unless it's the first time one actually "sold out"). At best, all one walks away with is bragging rights to sex and luxury.

In contrast, romance is profound and private. No one "brags" about genuine romance. It is too personal, too frail and too treasured to be bandied about in casual conversation. One may share with friends the events leading to a current romance, but such sharing is done in hushed and respectful tones. Bragging about one's romance objectifies it. It blasphemes the special intimacy evolving between lovers by treating it as a sort of trophy or an award for outstanding personal performance. In romance, the personal gets lost in the sharing.

Summary

Given the length of this chapter the reader may anticipate a similarly lengthy list of do's and don'ts. Actually, the moral of the chapter is that such a list is not necessary because there are really very few things one needs to remember to secure a good first date.

1. Forget the razzle dazzle. Do not try to buy another human being and do not allow anyone to buy you.

2. If you like the other person, show it. This is a matter of being attentive to their interests and not to their sex, power or position.

3. Pace yourself. The "Two ships passing in the night" phenomenon is at best a very small footnote in the life of any person. Don't risk a potentially rewarding relationship on the prospect of a quick score.

4. Enjoy the other's company. Do not try to manipulate. Things go much better, much more natural, much more as they *should* if you just remember to "Think Friendly."

5. Do not be afraid of romance. Let the cards fall where they may. If you stay in the game, the cards will come your way.

6. Forget ideologies. Address the other person as a person.

7. Remember any event can be turned into an opportunity for romance. Do not fall apart because things did not go as planned.

8. Remember, too, no event can guarantee romance. Planning an evening of entertainment can be a good idea, but do not associate specific romantic ambitions with any given event.

9. Relax! A date is supposed to be a good time for you both. Your date will find it easier to relax and enjoy the occasion if you are able to do so.

10. Above all, remember: No one ever said every date was meant to be a *good* date. As one avid baseball fan observed, "Some you win, some you lose and some get rained out. The ones you win make all the others worth the price."

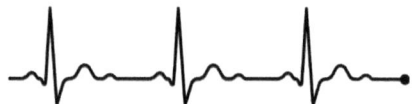

6

Is Marriage a Good Idea?

This question evokes a quick and cynical response from many divorcees: "It must be since so many people do it. . . again and again and again." Cynical divorcees may bolster their disdain by noting government statistics which, they say, show approximately half of all marriages ending in divorce. What these people don't know is that pollsters extraordinaire, Louis Harris and George Gallup, have both pointed out that government data do not distinguish the skewed impact of a relatively small minority (constituting what some have dubbed the "Drew Barrymore Syndrome"). This syndrome occurs when a person marries and divorces with the casualness of a ninth-grader "going with" and "breaking up with" a boyfriend or a girlfriend. Gallup and Harris estimate the number of permanent first-time marriages at somewhere between 60% and 72%, respectively. Statistically speaking, *very, very few people* get married more than twice.

The people with numerous marriages to their credit are like the gunslinger of the old west. They exist and are the object of much public comment, but they are few in number and represent very much the exception rather than the rule.

As every reader of this book knows, divorce is a brutalizing experience, so much so that few people are emotionally, intellectually or morally prepared to deal with it more than once. Obviously, those who move in and out of marriage with abandon need the attention of counselors and merit study by skilled researchers. For most people, marriage is taken seriously. Most people whose marriages do dissolve become more resolute never to repeat this tragic experience a second time.

Those who divorce once differ statistically from those who never divorce. But those who divorce once, represent a group substantially larger and quite different from those who divorce a multiplicity of times. For the most part, I have directed my attention to the larger group of divorcees though I hope much is said that every adult will find helpful, whether the victim of multiple divorces, a single but soured marriage, or even those contemplating either divorce or marriage for the first time. The intent of this chapter is to identify the virtues of marriage and thereby dispel any self-defeating notions you may be harboring that cripple your opportunity to marry again successfully.

The Collective Suspicion

I began asking divorcees what I took to be a rather innocuous question: "Besides progeny, what, if anything, *justifies* the institution of marriage from the perspective of a woman (man)?" I expected the two sexes to produce similar answers roughly in the same proportion. This did not happen.

The women interviewed were white, middle- or upper-class and professional. Their occupations included corporate executives, engineers, financial officers, teachers, doctors, lawyers, and nurses. Out of 103 women queried, 89 thought the institution of marriage was justifiable from the perspective of a woman: "It gives two people the chance to share their lives"; "It provides an opportunity for intimacy"; "It gives you someone to share your life with"; and finally, "Who wants to lie on her deathbed with no one especially caring about the passage of her life?"

The first 112 men interviewed came from the following occupational classifications: doctors, lawyers, university professors, Ph.Ds. in private practice or corporate work, accountants, school teachers, and business management. Not one offered a justification supporting marriage.

Like the 103 women interviewed, all the men had divorced at least once. And like the women, the men ranged in age from twenty-six to fifty-five. The men said things like, "As soon as you say 'I do,' the woman says, 'not tonight'"; "It's a man's world as long as you're single"; "The law of supply and demand puts everything in your favor"; "As soon as you commit to a woman the backrub, sex and concern all stop. So who needs it?"; "As long as you're single and healthy you can have all the companionship you'd ever want from women. As soon as you marry, you lose your options and get nothing in return but a lot of responsibility." And, finally, one lamented, "It's a one-way street. When a man marries he must contribute to, if not be solely responsible for, the financial well-being of the family. Women bounce in and out of the world of work without prejudice. If a man is out of work for a few months, both his friends and her friends immediately look upon him as a parasite. I'd just as soon be responsible for myself and myself alone."

The response of these men will shock many readers. I must caution that while my survey was not done with the scientific rigor of a Gallop or Harris Poll, it did include individuals from every region of the country. In addition, since it was done in a casual and informal manner participants' responses were likely to be more candid than in response to a standardized questionnaire. Despite the limits of this investigation, it is alarming to consider that out of over one hundred divorced professional men there was nary a one who could identify, or would, a justifying factor for the institution of marriage—from the man's perspective.

Stirred on by this outrage, I pursued the matter further, ultimately interviewing over three hundred men with roughly the same academic/occupational and socio/economic background as the original group. In this group, half the respondents were married. These results were better, but they were hardly encouraging. Out of just over three hundred men surveyed, only forty-seven offered justifications for the institution of marriage. Thirteen of these men were married, meaning over eighty married men surveyed did not offer a justification for marriage other than providing for offspring. To make matters worse, in my desperation to find reasons justifying the institution, the married men I interviewed were deliberately selected because they appeared to be happy with life. They were active as Little League coaches, in YMCA father/daughter functions, pursued diverse outside interests with their wives such as golf, bowling, bridge, antiquing, and dancing. They were, in short, middle-aged men who seemed comfortable in their marriages.

The married men who did offer justifications for marriage sometimes cited reasons that would offend their wives. For example, a dozen men cited as one justification a version of the "You wouldn't want to get sick or be left all alone on your deathbed would you?" While this may lead some men and women to seek marriage, it is not at all clear their regard is for the person or even the institution rather than for themselves. If marriage is a cooperative venture, then it should be sustained by concern for the other, and appreciative attention for you by your spouse. Exploiting the institution as merely a hedge against getting sick or dying alone is parasitic. A healthy marriage requires more than desperate dependency to sustain it or to justify its existence.

Marriage requires an active investment of time and energy by both spouses to make it work. It is exasperating to find so many people who are unwilling to pay the full price of admission. This observation must be discouraging to a divorcee considering the prospect of a future marriage. The fault may be with the loss of virtue cited by award-winning historian James Lincoln Collier in his book The Rise of Selfishness in America. The problem may be with the technique in the study itself or it may just be the advent of the twenty-first century brings with it a transient pessimism. Social scientists no doubt need to make a systematic study of the causes of this cynicism. The fault may lie with the limited socio/economic class captured in the study. But for the reader's purposes, the most useful insights are those of the men and women who, after thinking about it, still found marriage valuable. Divorcees will learn more from people who make marriages work than from those who fail and fail again, or from sterile statistics that ring an incessantly foreboding alarm, or even from married friends and colleagues who are cynically bearing up under the weight of what they regard as an oppressive bond. Divorcees know all too well the pitfalls of marriage. They know too little about its success stories.

Insights of the Few

Roy, a bright, athletic and divorced professor of philosophy, has an East coast upbringing and a sound educational preparation from several of the finer universities in the Northeast. Roy mused:

> I can think of one thing that justifies marriage: the irrationality of love. Love is not the servant of reason. It's an irrational and often impulsive emotion. Consequently, love needs an institution both tolerant and protective of irrationality to sustain love. This is not to say that love cannot be sustained outside the bonds of marriage. It's only to recognize that marriage represents a way of insulating the couple from outside pressures and temptations and in doing so

allows the couple to relax somewhat in their knowledge that minor trials and tribulations are not likely to tear the relationship asunder as might otherwise be the case if they were operating on a mere boyfriend/girlfriend basis.

Deirdre, a divorced and remarried professor of education, widely known for her many books and articles flatly states:

> Marriage instills responsibilities on both parties that love alone does not. It takes enormous love to realize this about marriage and go ahead with the intention to commit oneself in marriage. This is what makes marriage so special.
>
> Our lives have ups and downs every day. They also have ups and downs that may last days, weeks or even months at a time. Lovers can tire of one another. If a "down period" seems uncommonly long, it is easy to think to oneself, "Look, I didn't sign on for this crap; if she (or he) doesn't snap out of it soon, I'm cutting out. I don't need to waste my time on this." On the other hand, if the couple is married, there is a sense in which everyone realizes that a duty does exist to see the other through bad times as well as good. Furthermore, when one's sense of duty finally begins to waver, if that should happen, the realization that the option, divorce, is a long and painful process may be enough to rejuvenate one's efforts to pull one's life partner out of the doldrums. Love alone has no such sustaining power. However, the sustaining power of marriage may allow people to realize new and ever deepening experiences of love as one's partner ultimately moves from a valley to a new emotional peak.
>
> You know, those who try to find love outside the bond of marriage usually find the same superficial love or passion with a multiplicity of partners. Deepening a loving relationship requires time and the willingness to travel through lots of peaks and valleys with another. As far as I can see, marriage is the only vehicle with enough staying power to help a couple make the trip.

For the most part, people who approve of marriage applaud its intimacy and the opportunity for sharing one's life with a spouse. To the cynical ear of the "post-modern" man or woman, these approbations may seem like nothing more than naive wishes for a tradition whose time has come and passed. If lovers *love*, the cynics say, then intimacy and all the rest abounds. When lovers cease loving (and they usually do, after a time) then all the rest vanishes as well, and no law or no political institution can make things any different. At first blush, there seems much to recommend this highly intellectualized conclusion. Still, the urge common to most people is to ignore the cynics' dismissive remarks and to seek the wedded bliss some couples enjoy year after year.

The words of Roy, the philosopher and of Dierdre, the professor of education, reveal something at which the others only hinted. Roy may not be right that love is irrational, but as everyone knows, the experience of love—of any kind of love—does detract from a strictly rational approach to life. This is good.

As nearly every episode of the television and movie series *Star Trek* illustrates, there is something amazingly resilient and valuable about the human emotional repertoire. Unlike the logic-being, Mr. Spock, who alternates between disgust with humans for their enslavement to passions and his own wish for a complete human repertoire of emotions, ordinary people take their full complement of emotions for granted. We revel in the joys of life through our emotions. More often than not, we use our intellect to exploit further opportunities for emotional satisfaction.

The courts, science, industry, and commerce strive for optimal rationality. Marriage, another equally artificial human enterprise, was never meant to be a harbinger of strictly rational pursuits. Marriage is a sanctuary and Garden of Eden for our emotional defeats and our elations. As Roy said, marriage is unique as an institution for it and it alone is designed to protect a person's emotional freedom and to nurture a couple's cooperative growth. Marriage provides a safe harbor away from the demands of the most IMMEDIATELY reasonable, the most IMMEDIATELY pleasurable, or the most IMMEDIATELY painful influences. It is a refuge from an automaton-like existence that often serves us well in our business affairs and in the distractions of an excessively hedonistic-like society beckoning to us during our leisure hours.

Dierdre's remarks are similarly insightful. Human life, being what it is, consists of many achievements and failures. For two people to make it through the thrills and mishaps of life, they need the resources of an institution both flexible and strong.

The question then is how to secure that cooperation so the union is of sufficient flexibility and sufficiently strong. In a contract between two parties, there is an exchange of promises and consideration (i.e., some goods, promises to perform or services exchange hands). Contracts, even the most open-ended, tend to be somewhat brittle. For example, if one party to an agreed upon exchange defaults, the other contracting party is released from further compliance. So contracts can be quite strong, but where is the flexibility?

Despite the fact the courts administer carefully defined aspects of marriage and its dissolution, marriage itself is something more than a mere legal artifact. It represents the commitment of two people to stay *together as one* through good times and bad. Should an unforeseen mishap affect the life of one of the members, whether sickness, personal, social or business misfortune, it is expected the other person will see the partner through to new good times again. There is no ledger to be kept. No point at which one person says to the other, "Your account is overdrawn. I'm closing the books on this affair." In a healthy marriage, the two accept the idea they have come to address the world as one. Consequently, a mishap to the one is equally a mishap to the other. Together, they have promised to work things through despite a myriad of changing circumstances.

Together does not mean equally! Fate may inflict one spouse with multiple sclerosis and bestow upon the other an extraordinary business opportunity. In each case, the *couple's* ability to respond to the world is disrupted. Disproportionate shifts in the fortunes of each partner may be viewed in the eye of an economist as representing debits or credits in each individual's account. Yet it is not only the individual who suffers or benefits from such events, it is *the couple* which is disadvantaged in the case of serious illness and it is *the couple* which is benefitted by the enhanced business or professional opportunity.

To see matters in this way requires the parties involved possess certain virtues. For example, the individual in the weaker position must have the confidence, courage and trust in the other to accept help from the spouse without feeling resentment or diminished self-esteem. The person in the stronger position must be trustworthy, compassionate and manifest a sense of duty towards the other disadvantaged partner. Indeed, the person in the stronger position must value his or her advantages as a shared resource of the couple. Couples who successfully respond to the challenges of married life are those who see marriage as a single life-long project, a project the two have freely undertaken in a cooperative and INTERDEPENDENT way. When two people see the world from the viewpoint of a single cooperative enterprise (It's you and me against the world, Honey!), then fortune and misfortune are not seen as boons and afflictions to one, but to both. Marriages that achieve this sort of interdependence are successful by anyone's standards, but this success does not come easily.

Marital interdependence is difficult to achieve because the media and other social forces tend to promote the happiness of the individual at the expense of nearly every other consideration. The alleged war between the sexes further diminishes the likelihood of marital interdependence to the extent this war seems to be raging around and within a given married couple. As a result of such turmoil, spouses may find it difficult to address the world as one team rather than each as adversarial competitors.

Finally, life-long commitments are made difficult by talk show experts and self-help book authors who speak of commitment as itself a form of co-dependency, an ideological vestige from the 1950s, from television shows like *Lassie, Leave It to Beaver, Father Knows Best, The Donna Reed Show,* and so on. These commentators promote a view of marriage in which the contracting parties are urged to move on whenever the couple's cost-benefit product is in the red. But successful marriages, according to common folk wisdom, are those which serve as a refuge from any alleged wars between the sexes. The successful marriages of folk wisdom encourage rather than discourage dependency between partners.

Marriages cannot survive if the participants do not get beyond their respective sexual identities. Similarly, marriages cannot survive if each party remains objectively distant from the other's interests, goals and ambitions. Everyone must depend on another at some time in life. What more comforting thought than one's avowed life partner will unhesitatingly shoulder a disproportionate burden when things become too overwhelming for one person alone? The dependency one sees in successful marriages is not a pathologic social condition. It is not the much maligned co-dependency of current pop psychology. It is an *interdependency* in which each spouse readily assumes the role of leadership and responsibility when the situation demands.

The interdependency of a successful marriage is a vehicle for *extending and enhancing the range and quality of one's life experiences.* It is not a set of shackles. It does involve, as many of the men surveyed above decry, an increase in the responsibilities and obligations one owes another person, but such duties are not oppressive when FULLY ASSUMED BY EACH. The sense of love characterizing marriage in its various stages is sufficient to overcome most obstacles. From the blinding delight of romance, common in the early stages of marriage, to the more mature erotic love that evolves through mutual commitment, acceptance of one's marital duties should not seem a heavy or unwelcome burden.

The erotic love of mature marriage evolves from a relationship in which one's best friend is also one's most treasured and intimate lover. Erotic love, once attained, need never again be lost—except in the context of jealousy. Circumstances may change, particularly changes in one's physical health. These changes may make sexual intercourse less frequent or even impossible. Nevertheless, erotic love, once achieved, may be sustained without the continued reinforcement of passion and sexuality. Erotic love is the optimal bond occurring between lovers. Erotic love is not what brings people together in romance. It is an emergent property of an already existing union. Erotic love is such a profound bonding between people that if lost, it affects one's very sense of self and future self as well. The experience of erotic love situates one's sense of union at the border of one's own life-locating principles.

The language of erotic love and marriage does not fit in well with the sterile scientific-sounding language common in today's self-help and pop psychology market. So much the worse for such literature. Roy was on to a wonderful bit of folk wisdom when he declared marriage to be a peculiar institution designed for the protection of love, that most irrational of emotions. (Please note, irrational does not mean mindless or stupid.) People in successful marriages see the institution as *extending and enhancing* each spouse's sense of self. Through the experiences of the beloved, each lover experiences more of the world than is possible alone. In addition to increasing the range of each partner's experiences, marital intimacy leads to a greater appreciation for the sublime. Seen in this way, it is mindless to condemn marriage, or more directly, one's spouse, as a delimiting factor in one's own attempt to grow and develop. Sound marriages do just the opposite. They help people grow and develop. However, no one can achieve intimacy and union with another merely as a result of "figuring out" it leads to his or her advantage.

Passions arise not out of reason but out of something else, something not entirely rational. One hopes that before marriage, rational faculties have led the individual to avert obvious disaster despite the immediacy of arousal. Even so, the early years of what promises to be a good marriage are fraught with danger.

No marriage begins on the impenetrable foundation of erotic love. Mature, erotic love takes time to develop: the passion and romance of premarital bliss will wax and wane. Do not fret. Be patient. Given time, passion and romance always return to lovers in some form. When the romance of marriage is at low ebb, you or your spouse may be vulnerable to romantic exploitation by others. A transient indiscretion under such conditions can lead to the destruction of a potentially strong marriage. The formality of marriage with its rituals, protective laws, the wearing of rings and so on, all coalesce to protect the marriage during periods in which it is most vulnerable. Protected from outside intrusions, a couple will find romance nearly always returns and sets the stage for a deeper and even richer experience of togetherness in the future.

Deirdre aptly notes a successful marriage is both a sanctuary and a Garden of Eden. Besides the comfort marriage extends to one expressing an emotion, the *shared* expression of emotions achieves other ends as well. For example, the free expression of one's joys, sorrows, anger, pride, and various other emotional responses to the world invite one's spouse to share in those experiences and to learn more about what makes the other who he or she is. Sharing experiences both creates and reaffirms a bond of reciprocal trust which is the cornerstone of every good marriage.

Finally, Deirdre indicated that marriage, unlike other mere contractual relationships, provides the flexibility needed for love to grow ... to grow beyond passion. In a strictly contractual relation (no matter how generously worded), if the exchange of goods becomes inequitable, that is to say, when the debits on one side well exceed the credits, there are sufficient grounds for ending the relationship.

Traditionally, this is not the way the folk wisdom has conceived of marriage. The entries appropriate to any ledger of marriage are too intangible. There is no way to keep an accurate balance sheet. Look about you. Have you noticed that couples who constantly talk about the present accounting of their relationship are but a step away from divorce?

No one can foresee the forces which will affect the individuals in a marriage. The agreement to unite against all odds is not a risk one undertakes as might an expert in decision theory or classical economics. There are no mathematical formulas or logical deductions which reveal the extent of one's risk when marrying. The decision to marry cannot be calculated on the basis of anticipated advantages and disadvantages. The decision must be based solely on the prospect of cooperative growth and mutual resolve to keep the covenant.

The material advantages and disadvantages affecting a marriage should not weigh as a factor in its maintenance. Whatever they amount to, they were not, or should not have been, a part of the decision to live as one in the first place.

The decision to live as one should reflect mutual compatibility between persons and not an alliance between self-seeking entrepreneurs. The decision to marry is as rational as it should be when it reflects the agreement of two people wherein each regards the other as a source of inspiration during the best of times and a source of strength during the worst of times. In short, when contemplating marriage, the primary question one should ask is not "Is the anticipated balance between advantages and disadvantages in my favor (as one asks when negotiating a contract)?" but rather "Is this person sufficiently compatible with me so that together the good times will be better and the bad times more bearable?" This is clearly not the stuff of an ordinary contract but rather of an especially unique covenant. It is not a bargain but two unilateral promises, each guaranteeing the commitment of one person to both the welfare and happiness of the other. The nature of this commitment is most vividly evident in the lives of those who are about to complete a long and resilient marriage.

The Experience of Veterans

Rookies may look forward to marriage as the source of eternal, poetic bliss. Many divorcees look back on marriage as a source of diminished self-concept, wasted effort, tragedy, responsibility, guilt, and exploitation. Both of these sets of impressions are skewed. In the rookies' case, the impressions are skewed by a lack of experience. In the divorcees' case, they are skewed by the wrong sort of experience.

What is the right sort of experience for marriage? Is it reserved for only a select few? If only a select few, who might these few be, and how do you identify them?

It is hard to imagine anyone so discerning he or she could identify a set of ideal marriages. Consequently, one's ambition must be more modest. Perhaps by identifying couples who were able to make a go of it for thirty or more years, one might uncover the minimal requirements for sustaining a marriage.

To this end, I proceeded to meet with some forty or so senior citizen couples. The conversation with the first couple set the tone for the rest of the interviews. The husband, Kenneth, was nearly eighty. He had snow white hair and a burly build. Kenneth had been retired from his accounting practice for over ten years. While Kenneth and his wife, Sylvia, lived all their lives in the northeast, they had traveled frequently throughout the country and had been to Europe once. Sylvia was seventy-one and carried herself with the elegance and charm of a woman once thought to be quite handsome and sophisticated. Sylvia had worked as a secretary, then as a homemaker and finally as a banker. They had three children and several grandchildren. I asked, "If divorce were as prevalent and accepted in your day as it seems to be now, would the two of you have divorced?" After a few moments' silence, Sylvia turned to Kenneth, smiled, and then they both laughed. Turning toward me she said, "Sure!" but she then went on to explain:

> When we were in our thirties and forties we argued and fought frequently. Sometimes it seemed we quarreled day in and day out with no relief. We argued about the children, about money, about where to vacation . . . we argued about arguing. If there was one thing we did a lot, it was arguing. People didn't get divorced in those days. If we thought that was an option, I am sure we would have exercised it. But it wasn't an option. You just had to set your mind on the idea that you were going to make the best of it. Suddenly, one day you wake up and you know you've made it. You made it! There is no longer any question of whether or not you will be able to endure it—you did. At that point, you just know you will be together until the very end and the thought becomes very pleasant and terribly reassuring.

Kenneth chimed in with the following illustration to which Sylvia nodded in hearty agreement:

> During our thirties and forties it was like going through a tunnel with no end in sight. Our married life, and for us that pretty much meant our world, was dark and bleak. Then one day, you see the light at the end of the tunnel. It's just the way Sylvia describes it. All of a sudden, you know you made it through all the trials. From that point on, you know you will be together until the end, and that is a happy thought. It's also very romantic. You feel a desire for the other person's company almost the way you did when you first married except perhaps now the feeling is deeper and much less precarious.

When talking to each of the other couples, I related the story told me by Sylvia and Kenneth. Everyone indicated their own experience had been somewhat similar. The thirties and forties seem to be periods of rough going for everyone. Then, sometime in one's fifties, there is an almost spontaneous cessation of conflict and renewed commitment or, at least, resolution on the part of each that the two are destined to share fully in each other's joys and sorrows until the very end.

There was only one woman, Sarah, who confessed she could not empathize with this experience. Sarah had been married for thirty-one years, but *this was her second marriage!* Perhaps this was why she did not identify with the experience of her peers or even her husband who, by the way, was surprised to learn they did not have the same sense of their current relationship. Sarah was not unhappy with her current marriage. She just could not identify with the feeling that suddenly, now, they know the marriage is forever. She felt she and her husband argue now as much as ever, but since neither of them is very argumentative in the first place, this is not a problem.

There is no reason to believe the people interviewed shared the kind of eternal love and romance extolled by poets. These are ordinary people, people who spent most of their lifetimes together and who are still together as the end of life draws near. These people endured difficult times together. They admitted to blaming their spouse for difficulties experienced during various times of distress. They paid their dues. The admission fee may have been higher for some than for others, but now all seem agreed the cost was well worth it.

There is no shortcut for getting to know another person intimately or for revealing yourself to the other. Through each decade of twenty, thirty, forty or more years of marriage, one learns of the details making one's spouse who he or she is now. Since many of the experiences have been shared fully and equally by each, the two learn to see one world in ways ever more compatible.

The phenomenology of lasting marriage is aptly illustrated in a touching movie produced in the early 1980s, *On Golden Pond*, with Henry Fonda and Katherine Hepburn in the lead roles. The movie shows a wonderful romance of two elderly people who loved, respected, understood, and appreciated the way each confronted the world. They were not of one mind in their thoughts about the world, but they were of one heart in wanting to share with the other all their remaining experiences had to offer. Their marriage had become a common life project drawing indiscriminately on the resources of each. This is what the covenant of marriage is designed to achieve. And if the covenant is blessed with erotic love, so much the better.

Why Marriage is Not for Everyone

Not everyone regards marriage as a desirable state within which to spend one's adult years. For example, some people choose a life of celibacy for religious reasons. Other people choose a life of promiscuity because it seems like more fun than any alternative. There are others who avoid marriage because they fear it or because they have not had the opportunity to embrace it. Still others, often divorcees or the adult children of divorce, think marriage is anachronistic in the modern world of disposable goods and disposable relationships. Finally, there are those, again typically divorcees and adult children of divorce, who despise the institution. They genuinely believe marriage inevitably leads to exploitative relationships. The existentialist writer Jean Paul Sartre thought this was true of love. There are no doubt other reasons people have for avoiding marriage, but these are the reasons most often cited.

A person espousing any one of these reasons may one day fall in love. The beloved may be keen on the idea of marriage. Disagreement between lovers regarding the value of marriage can become a source of constant agitation. One of the persons will be forced to relent in his or her position and adopt that of the other. Or one may hold tenaciously to one's position as a point of debate but in practice accede to the wishes of the other, ultimately adopting a form of togetherness he or she believes is potentially harmful or despicable. In any case, one day the lovers will realize, despite their love for one another, they are confronting a clash of life-locating principles. And such conflicts underscore the fact these people are wrong for each other. Fortunately, since ideologies regarding marriage are rarely life-locating principles, it is generally possible for two people to resolve their differences.

Individuals deeply antagonistic toward marriage are unlikely to change their beliefs even when these beliefs are not life-locating. There are several reasons for their continued obstinacy. First, who is going to spend the time it would take to convince these antagonistic people they should change their minds? People who are antagonistic toward an idea, any idea, have generally dug in their heels and are not open to contrary opinion. This may change after much time has passed, but few marriage-oriented people risk such an investment on someone whose mind may never change. Second, the old saying "Birds of a feather flock together" is true in this case. People antagonistic towards marriage try to select friends and date-mates who think as they do. As a consequence, they are seldom confronted with opposing belief systems. Third, the media tends to reinforce antagonisms toward traditionally-conceived bonds of marriage. The media does this by deprecating marriage as a decaying vestige of an earlier and less complicated era, a time when church-going and extended families were common. Even the image of the nuclear family is quickly giving way in the media to an image of adults pairing only " . . . as long as our love shall last." This tentative portrayal of marriage, and ultimately family, intensifies the feelings of those already fearful. The nuclear family may become even less a bulwark of stability in the future. Finally, statistics decrying the slow death of marriage and an inexhaustible supply of self-help books touting open relationships, how to survive divorce, exposing the alleged faults of the other sex, and prescriptions for ensuring the well-being of "old number one," make the very idea of a lifetime of happiness with one other person appear outrageously naive. It is easy to see why another divorcee would not be predisposed towards marriage. With all this in mind, it may well be the most challenging task is to remain mindful of the alleged benefits marriage bestows on couples!

Is Marriage Dying?

Government statistics throughout the eighties and nineties show *there was a sharp increase in the marriage rate and a decrease in the divorce rate*, and pollsters Gallup and Harris cite data showing many more marriages last a lifetime than was originally believed. The earlier misconceptions about massive increases in divorce during the 60s, 70s and 80s were the result of earlier examinations of the number of divorces each year in comparison to the number of marriages. This crude comparison failed to take into account the fact individuals who divorce often get counted often. In contrast, those who marry for life get counted only once.

Once one's view of marriage becomes jaundiced, it doesn't change just because one falls in love. When a person falls in love, however, he or she may marry to keep a beloved. When this happens, the original contempt for marriage may eventually be transferred to contempt for the spouse. It is too tempting for an estranged spouse to blame the entirety of his or her troubles on the institution or the person who cajoled her or him into marriage in the first place. Once these temptations are lived, the demise of the marriage is all but assured. In short, it is folly to pursue a marriage with someone who sees no good in the institution regardless of how he or she feels about you.

There are many challenges to surmount in a marriage even by two people resolute in their commitment both to the institution and to one another. A person who is unconvinced of marriage's good will not fight for its survival, much less its development. The uncommitted spouse has no sense or appreciation for the idea that marriage can be a *self-extending* experience. And yet it is!

Marriage is self-extending when two people pool their experience in making sense of the world. To understand marriage as a self-extending experience requires an individual to be confident and unselfish, to have high self-esteem, and to be prepared to risk a certain amount of dependency on the fortunes of another. To those who have difficulty understanding this idea, marriage is seen as *self-limiting*. For example, the selfish person is preoccupied with efforts directed toward self-gratification. Marriage, by contrast, requires a reciprocity of giving and consideration. To the selfish person, marriage is a shackle. Marriage *should be* viewed as a quest for cooperative gratification—not as an impediment to self-gratification. It is easy to see why it is in your own best interest to marry only if your intended is like-minded in viewing marriage as a self-extending institution. If you marry someone who is not prepared to assume his or her role in a marriage, you will do nothing more than subject two people to increasing anxiety (with divorce the only apparent relief). If the marriage is to result in a family, a husband or wife who cannot share with a mate will be no more able to share with a child. Children we bring into this world deserve better.

Marriage is the foundation of family, not the other way around. Many a divorcee is quick to bemoan this point. As Sally, a thirty-one-year old mother of two said:

> I thought if we had children, Bert would develop a greater sense of responsibility toward me and our family as a whole. As it turned out, responsibility just seemed to drive him further and further away. He saw us as depriving him of his place on the fast track. Bert seemed to have no remorse about how he continually failed me or our family.

Marriage is not for people who need to learn caring, responsibility, commitment, togetherness, interdependency and so on. It is only for those who already are sufficiently mature to possess those traits.

Those who see marriage as self-limiting are the takers and users of society because they misunderstand marriage. For them, a fortuitous marriage is a source of material reward and social status. These people are destined for unhappiness and failed marriages. No spouse can provide material goods, status, psychological reward or spiritual strength sufficient for satisfying the insatiable appetite of a selfish person. At the same time, selfish persons have almost nothing to give. They look to get from others, not to give.

After the first failed marriage or two, some selfish persons lose interest in marriage. They realize their entrepreneurial exploits are handicapped by marriage. Others continue looking for a "better deal" in a more rewarding relationship, a more lucrative association and so on. For this group, marriage is a field of opportunity where once the immediately available rewards are harvested, they look forward to greener pastures. They never give a moment's thought to what they can put back into the land, as it were, what joys are to be reaped in an attitude of unconditional giving.

The first attitude is reflected in the following boast of Bill, an aging financier, recently divorced from his fourth wife:

> (Laughing) When they start getting close to forty, I trade them in for a new model. Just kidding. Actually, I'm through with marriage. I just see no advantage to it for me.

The latter attitude is captured nicely in the confession of a woman model divorced several times:

> I want a man who can afford to take care of me the way I think I deserve. That sounds crass, I know. But I think a lot of myself. I think I deserve the best. Is that so wrong?
>
> Money isn't the only thing. He's got to be interesting and to want to have fun. My second husband was extremely wealthy, but he never wanted to do anything. He just wanted to hide me away at home. Needless to say, I found that most boring . . . intolerably so. I do expect to get married again, but I'm going to be more selective next time.

Children

Children complicate further the decision to re-marry. The divorcee who has custody of children must remember his or her first duty is to the children. When dating, and, more importantly, when considering marriage, you must ascertain the effect a new marriage will have on your children. The person marrying a divorcee with children is entering a marriage and acquiring a "family-on-loan." That is a tall order for someone inexperienced in family life or someone with little sense of what special duties one may owe others.

Children need so much and have themselves so little to give. In the ordinary case, marriage precedes the formation of a family. In like manner, one's duty to spouse precedes one's duty to children. Finally, a couple may choose to create a family. The challenge confronting many divorcees is the family already exists and the "outsider" must find a way to fit in. Any proposed marriage must adapt to pre-existing moral commitments and family obligations. This places an additional (and sometimes overwhelming) strain on a couple setting out to build one common life-long project. The challenge can be successfully engaged but not by people who are morally naive or insensitive to the nature of children. Love alone will not conquer all.

Summary

Many marriages fail. Divorcees have experienced only failed marriages. If your experience of marriage had been successful, you would still be married. Consequently, the questions you must ask yourself before remarrying are as follows:

1. What do I understand about marriage as an institution?

2. Do I view marriage as self-limiting? Or do I see it as self-extending? If the former, then you should not remarry at this time. If the latter, then you may be ready for marriage.

3. Do I understand marriage as the undertaking of a common life project? Or do I see marriage as just another form of going together? If the former, then you understand marriage demands you seek fulfillment of your mate's needs as well as your own. If the latter, then you should not covenant marriage. You may want to contract—for pleasure or romance, but this is not the stuff that "til death do us part" is made of!

4. Do I understand the ritual, the wearing of rings and the legal commitment, are all intended to deter others from intruding into the intimacy of the relationship? Or do I see such conventions as anachronisms from a more primitive past? If the former, then marriage for you is a sociopolitical institution to be valued and protected. If the latter, then for you it is little more than a rite of passage . . . so why bother?

5. Am I prepared to share my emotional ups and downs with my partner and reciprocate his or her attempts to share these with me? Or do I fear such revelations will destroy the romance? If the former, then marriage will provide you and your spouse with a comfort and emotional freedom seldom enjoyed by single people. If the latter, then make the most of the romance

you have but do not risk destroying it by twisting it into something it is not meant to be.

6. Do I feel I can risk becoming dependent on this person? Or do I fear I will be emotionally crippled if things do not work out? If the former, you trust your beloved. If the latter, you do not trust your beloved, in which case you are not yet prepared to risk your future with that person.

7. Do I feel my beloved can trust and depend on me fully? Or do I fear I may not handle such responsibility very well? If the former, you are ready to provide the marriage the strength and dependability it will require from time to time. If the latter, you may reconsider the disservice you risk doing to another should you marry.

8. Do I understand the feeling of romance will come and go? Will the waxing and waning of passion discourage me? If the former, then you know marriage requires intensity of *commitment* and not the constancy of passion. If the latter, then again, avoid marriage. As the lives of Don Juan, numerous movie stars and others of similar ilk show, one romantic relationship can always be superseded by another. This is not true of successful marriage. People just do not live long enough to experience such deep relationships, three, four or more times.

9. What does your proposed spouse understand about marriage?

10. Have you talked to your spouse about what matters in marriage? Are the two of you in agreement? If so, your prospects for success are good. If not, then why do you think the two of you share the "right stuff?"

11. In answering questions 1-7 above does your beloved show he or she has fully come to grips with the demands of marriage?

12. Are you seeking marriage now and with this partner because *this person* and *this union* are what you want FOR BETTER OR WORSE? Or, have you decided, in full acknowledgement of what marriage involves, that your partner is tolerable and

possibly the best buy on the current market, so why not? If the former, your chances of "making it through the tunnel" are optimal. If the latter, then you are not seeking marriage; you are settling for a facsimile.

13. Remember: there are attractive lifestyles outside of marriage. Do not marry solely because you lack sufficient creativity and courage to explore an alternative.

14. The decision to marry IS the decision to begin a common life project. It is the first decision two people make conjointly with the full knowledge it will forever affect the life of each. Thus, both tradition and the law construe marriage as the beginning of a set of promises freely and reciprocally entered into. Divorce, by contrast, requires but one person for its initiation, and this is as it should be. Divorce is an action pursued for the benefit of an individual and not, as in the case of marriage, for the benefit of a *cooperative* life-long union.

15. Remember there are no bargain marriages. You get what you pay for. The more you put into marriage, the more likely it is you will one day experience erotic love. If you go for a bargain, try to get more than you put into marriage, you will end up being disappointed by your role in a cheap and inferior product.

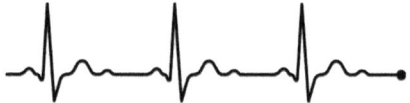

7

What Choices do I Have?

The previous chapters of this book ranged from what counts as a good catch to what counts as a good date, from what men and women want in a member of the opposite sex, to where to find available men and women. Finally, the risks and benefits of casting one's lot with the institution of marriage have been explored. What has not been discussed but only assumed up to this point is the idea there is for each reader the potential for passion, romance and erotic love. This may not always be the case. Perhaps the influences of society are such that there no longer are men attractive to women and women attractive to men. Just what kind of singles can the divorcee expect to meet?

Establishing a category of types has long been a favorite pastime for people gathered in their living rooms, the study, the local tavern, and the laboratory. Ordinary people often discuss with their peers: "What kind of men and women are out there?" Social scientists and theorists have flooded magazines, journals, book stands, and the Internet with their own contrived taxonomies.

Rather than subject the reader to one more idiosyncratic view of adult single life, I will let the respective populations of single men and women (between the ages of twenty-six and fifty-five) speak for themselves. I asked women who had been single for at least a year, "What kind of men are out there?" After accumulating several hundred accounts, I constructed a classification reflecting these accounts in the simplest manner possible. Then, taxonomy in hand, I asked an additional one hundred women to comment on the taxonomy. Specifically, my question was not is the taxonomy "true" but rather is it implausible or in any way seriously misleading. Finally, I polled thirty men. I explained to them the process I had followed thus far and asked each of them if they found the proposed taxonomy seriously misleading. Both women and men agreed the proposed taxonomy reflected *no obvious errors*. I followed precisely this process when constructing a taxonomy of available women.

What Kind Of Men Are Available?

Jerks, egomaniacs, priests, gays, the elusive prince . . . are but a few of the descriptions I heard when first posing this question. In addition, each woman's attempt to elaborate on her own sense of the matter is likely to differ significantly from that of her sisters. The search is no small task.

The search for common threads tying together individual impressions is complicated by the fact there is little consensual folk wisdom on this matter. Nevertheless, any taxonomy must be of manageable size so it can have practical value to the divorcee. Thus, the categories which follow are by no means exhaustive, detailed or in any other way exacting. They constitute, rather, a colorful portrayal of the kind of men divorced women are likely to meet.

The Corporate Climber

This is a man whose whole sense of identity is tied up with his achievements at work, the civic arena or with some other publicly visible exploit. Success in life is measured in terms of the applause it garners from an appropriate audience. A wife is an arm-piece, an accoutrement, meant to create, or at least enhance, the man's appearance. Like his European sedan, his passion for the "right" sport, his meticulously appointed attire and his appearance at select social events, the corporate climber's wife should be an asset to complement the image he presents to the world. As long as she is cooperative in presenting the image he wants, he has no other demands *nor interest* in her activities. He is likely to shy away from emotional or physical intimacy. Intimacy represents an invitation to proceed beyond public image. For the corporate climber, there may be so little beyond the image that the very thought of anyone discovering the "real him" is intensely threatening. In the most extreme cases, there may be no identity apart from the public image. This lack of private identity may explain why some men, disgraced while in public office, fired from a job, charged with a crime or subject to bankruptcy, commit suicide. When their public image becomes tarnished, all that makes life worth living for them is lost. As one spectacularly bejeweled and exquisitely dressed woman in her mid-forties attests:

> I wanted for no material good while I was married—jewels, furs, clothes, cars. Nothing I wanted was ever denied me. I didn't even have to ask. If there was something I wanted, I just ordered it. He also gave me a generous monthly allowance. What he didn't give me was attention. Except when we were entertaining or attending a social function, he paid no attention to me whatever. He didn't even want to have sex. I think I'm fairly attractive even now, or so I am told, but he never wanted to have anything to do with me. This wasn't the way things were the six months we dated before marrying!
>
> It wasn't a matter of him disliking me or losing interest in me. I am sure there were never other women in his life the whole time we were married. I don't think women count for much in his life. We never even had chatty little talks at night or on weekend mornings like other couples do. I wasn't disliked, and I wasn't a prisoner. I was more of a generously paid employee. When we would go out, he wanted me to look good, and he would act as if he were madly in love with me. I kept thinking that meant that things were about to turn around for us. They never did. The public show never made it to the bedroom. Finally, I realized that was all he was concerned with—the public show.
>
> I tried to make him jealous. I never cheated on him, but I started to go on more trips alone. That was another thing. He didn't mind traveling with me for business, but he loathed the idea of a vacation. If I wanted to travel by myself, he never had an objection. If he knew I had a lover in every port, I don't believe he would have said a thing as long as it did not become a scandal and as long as I was in top form the next time we had to entertain.
>
> I think the thing that amazed me the most was that after seven years when I asked him for a divorce, he was amazed. He protested, "Haven't I given you everything? What more do you want?" When I told him things like intimacy, love and sex, he thought I was just making excuses. The few times he told me he loved me he said it with the conviction of a person saying "Hello" to a neighbor.
>
> I think it hurt him when I left. I think it hurt his ego. And, in his own way, I do think he cared about me. Mostly, however, I think he worried about how it would look and how he would explain the divorce to his friends.

Comedians joke about the ubiquitous headache of married women. Wives of Corporate Climbers have quite a different story to tell. Hollywood and Madison Avenue lead the public to believe glamour ensures happiness. "Maybe money isn't everything, but it sure beats what's supposed to be in second place" or so the joke goes. But women who have been there are far from universal in their appreciation of glamour and far from universal in finding humor in such naive witticisms. As one divorced bank president declared:

> He didn't want a wife, he wanted a business associate. Now I have my own money, but unlike my ex, I know there are more important things in life than money. At this point in my life, when I go out with a man, I listen very carefully. If all he talks about is career and money, then I make it an evening, a very early evening. If I am going to have a man in my life again, then he must be able to *see* me as a person and want me to see him as a person. I don't need another business partner in my life.

Embittered Male

This is the new guy on the block. On the surface, he looks like the perfect mate. He's a Boy Scout but with a sense of humor. He is brave, clean, thrifty, polite, respectful of others, cooperative, looks to make the best of every situation and is willing to undertake any task or share any labor without concern for stereotypical sex roles. He genuinely believes marriage is for life. Family and commitment are his most treasured values though he has also proven himself a success at work and play. He is willing to share his feelings, and he is attentive to the introspections of others. When asked, he usually has sound advice to give. When the advice requested is beyond his realm of experience, he is smart enough to recognize this fact and is honest and confident enough to admit it. He is attractive, and women are quick to notice his presence. He is the kind of man a woman is proud to introduce to both her family and her friends.

This man looks like Mr. Right. His faults surely cannot be more extensive than leaving the cap off the toothpaste or showing a green thumb . . . while cooking. Unfortunately, there is something underneath—something almost sinister that makes him emotionally dangerous. He does not *like* women. He is not bisexual or anything like that, nothing so exotic or psychologically complex. He simply does not like women. When in a particularly open and vengeful mood, he may even confess to thinking women are just "nuts these days." He sounds like . . . he hates women!

This man is divorced. He was married for a long time and espoused feminist commitments both in word and deed. He did all the typical "male" chores around the house and cooked, made beds and helped with the dishes. He was a Brownie "Dad of the Year" and a Little League coach. While married he was always faithful—he probably never even flirted. He never struck his wife or children and seldom raised his voice. He has his irrational moments but is quick to apologize. He is slow to complain and quick to praise. If he drinks at all, he is temperate. While married, he seldom spent time with "the boys," preferring instead to be with his family or put in a few more hours at work. He avoids both prescription and non-prescription drugs (except for one daily aspirin and vitamins). He is health conscious, exercising and dieting as necessary. *He was abandoned by his wife.*

His wife never gave him any substantial reason for her departure. She assured him he was a wonderful father and a decent man. "We just grew apart," she complained. If she sought custody of the children at all, she returned them to his care within two years. He expressed a willingness to go to any length to preserve the marriage and the family. She refused, declaring there was no point. She told him this was not a matter of right or wrong just a matter of her need to follow her own path. Karma. What they had was wonderful, she reassured him, but the time for parting was undeniable. She dumped him, and there is a resounding thud still reverberating in his heart and mind.

Divorce scars. The embittered male is debilitated by his scars. He did everything right and would have done more. Not even his ex-wife denies that! "We were just too young when we married. We are two totally different people now, and we don't belong together," she may explain in conclusion. Unfortunately for him, he had no input in this decision.

Abandoned by his wife (see Avery Cornman's *50* for an amusing portrayal of this personality-type), his experience of single life is teaching him many women still find him attractive and desirable. This is both pleasing and confusing. Eventually, it fuels his residual anger for the woman who left him. Remember, anger is a result of moral indignation. He feels wronged and vengeful. He sees himself as betrayed and abandoned by the one person who was supposed to be his best friend. Fear of another abandonment and vindictive rage motivate his apprehension around other women. Beneath an obvious pleasing and stable veneer, his deepest emotions continue to seethe. He's glad women like him. But he is resolved never to let another woman hurt him. He will not risk becoming intimate ever again. When emotions approximating intimacy arise, he abruptly ends the relationship. To the women he meets he is a most unexpected anomaly. He seems so decent, yet he savagely disappears with the suddenness of the most insensitive male chauvinist.

Wanda, a twenty-eight-year old director of nursing at a psychiatric hospital relates the following experience:

> Jason was the most wonderful man. He was good looking, thirty-nine, held a good job, attended church and loved kids. I felt, "My Lord, this IS Robert Young's character from *Father Knows Best.*" Jason was bright and well-read. He did little things around my apartment just to help out. He took care of my car and never pressured me for sex. In fact, if I hadn't been more aggressive, I don't know if we would have even gone to bed. By the way, he was a great lover.
>
> As time went on, we saw more and more of each other. Things were going fine until I started using words like "love" and "living together." I didn't even get to the M-word (marriage). It wasn't like I was pushing for anything. We had dated for five months and been sleeping together for three. Two weeks after I first told him I loved him, he disappeared. Actually, the straw that broke the camel's back might have been my asking him, "Have you ever thought you might want to live with someone again?" (He was divorced a year earlier.) I suspect he was aware of what I was hinting at, but I know enough about men not to do a hard sell. I never heard from him again after that night. He screened his calls on his answering machine, never returned my calls and never responded to two letters I sent him. He left a shirt, pants, underwear, socks and three record albums at my apartment. He never came by, called or made any effort to retrieve them. He just disappeared!
>
> I know nothing happened to him. Four nights after our last date, I saw him going to a movie by himself. Jason really hurt me. I was also embarrassed by the fact that I had already began telling my friends we were an item and probably had a future together.

> I still haven't figured out why he left. My friends tell me I should just write it off to cold feet. But I don't think so. It has got to be more than that... what do you think?

"Cold feet," the fear of commitment, of reciprocal obligation, is typically viewed as a male affliction. (Recently though, some feminists claim as women become more independent they, too, become more resistant to giving up their independence.) Cold feet has been associated with the male of the species for so long most women have become adept at dealing with it or, at least, adept at avoiding men who suffer from it. Wanda is an extremely attractive, personable career woman. She is by no means an innocent in the ways of adult single life. The "cold feet" syndrome is not unknown to her. The situation she describes caught her off guard. Something different characterized Jason's adversity to intimacy, something she had not seen before, something she was not prepared for. That something is the central feature in the mutated personality of the embittered male: an aversion towards intimacy.

Historically, folk wisdom suggests men suffering from cold feet are unable to deal with the prospects of additional responsibility. It is true that commitment does extend responsibility but this is hardly a tragedy. In general, as people's social interests expand so, too, do their responsibilities. For example, a physician's responsibilities to a patient vary in proportion to the condition of the patient's health and the physician's previous specialized training. Similarly, a politician's responsibility to any given individual in his constituency varies in proportion to the size of the constituency, the extent of the individual's need and the ability of the politician to secure adequate relief. The roles one assumes in life determine the extent of one's responsibilities. For the person adverse to responsibility, there must be a proportionately delimiting interest in further social interaction.

The embittered male stands out as a most peculiar figure. By definition, he is someone quick to accept responsibility when there is no intimacy involved. In the context of his previous marriage, he showed himself prepared to give *all he has* in the pursuit of a common life project with another. The destruction of his marriage did not destroy his sense of responsibility, but it did shatter his ability to risk intimacy with another.

Whereas intimacy usually leads naturally and comfortably to increased responsibility, the embittered male is an exception to this general rule. Since he exudes a sense of responsibility in all his other affairs, women feel confident he'll do the same as intimacy evolves. To their surprise, he fades from view as the relationship develops. This paradoxical character is not something women have been taught to expect from men. Consequently, they are easily hurt when they encounter embittered males. Ominously, his numbers are increasing in epidemic proportions.

A twenty-seven-year old lawyer and athlete, Linda, denounces her last encounter with a forty-four-year old business professor, Randall, as follows:

> We knew each other for three or four months before going out the first time. Randall had a reputation for being a bit of a rogue, but sometimes that just goes with the territory. He was handsome, athletic and much in demand. You would expect him to be somewhat cavalier when it comes to dating. On the other hand, as you got to know Randall, he seemed very sensitive, very strong and very responsible in his work as well as in looking after his children. The more I got to know him, the more impressed I became. As you men like to say, he seemed like a real "stand-up" kind of guy.
>
> When Randall invited me to dinner the first time I was delighted. We went out frequently for several weeks without even the hint of any sexual overtures. I liked that he seemed more interested in me than in making another conquest—which I had no intention of becoming. Eventually, we became physically intimate. As we did so, the emotional intimacy I thought we shared began dissipating. Shortly thereafter, he dropped me and was out and about with another woman. I was astonished. I thought, "I've just been had!" As careful and worldly as I think I am, I can still be taken. I fell for his line. He got what he wanted and then split, damn it. The funny thing about vanity is that I still do not believe that he was just out to take me for a ride. There seemed to be too much respect and intimacy between us for a while. But once we got physical, he quickly tired of me and that was it. Being objective about it all, I suppose I should stop kidding myself and just admit that his whole approach to life is just one big act. He's just better than most others, and I was taken in.

Sometime after my talk with Linda, I was able to speak at length with Randall. I, too, was impressed by his apparent commitment to traditional family values and the time-honored virtues of trust, integrity, honesty, benevolence, and respect. Then when I asked about his relationship with Linda, a change seemed to come over him. Randall said, "Oh, Linda's a great gal, a little into herself, but why not? She has got a lot going for her. She is bright, pretty . . . she's just real neat." When asked why he left her if she was so appealing, Randall laughed:

> Hey, if you want a wife, Linda is probably as fine as they come. But who wants a wife? You think I am kidding? Women will do anything for you as long as you are just dating but as soon as they get you to say "I do" or commit in some other informal way, they are quick to say, "Only if you do this and this and this first." As long as you are free to walk, there are women available for sports, companionship, sex, whatever you would do with a wife or girlfriend. But just watch what happens as soon as they get you. Those reassuring talks, back-rubs, gourmet meals, even simple things like concern and attention disappear. Once they think they have you, all they can think about is what you can do for them. It's a one-way street, and I don't need to be a part of it.
>
> I'm honest with women. I don't lead them on. If they want to go out, be friends, have a good time then that's fine. But I make it clear all along I have no interest in developing a relationship with anyone. As long as they understand that, I will go out with them. If they want something more, they need to find it with someone else.

As the reader can hear, the tone of Randall's demeanor shifted significantly the longer he talked about relationships with women. He went from jovial and respectful to flip and hostile in a few short moments. Randall is angry with women. His personal history is most relevant to the point at hand. Randall had previously been married. He thought he was married for life. He thought there was no question but that she and he would raise a family, retire and hold each other's hand in that final hour. Such was not to be. Randall's wife decided her relationship to him was smothering her growth, so she divorced him. A year after the divorce, she freely gave him custody of their two children. To this day, nearly eight years later, Randall is unable to talk about her or the divorce without seething with anger. Though a scholar and a social scientist, he routinely overgeneralizes from the tragic and fateful experience of his first marriage to women generally. Randall now does not trust women. To protect himself, he has built a wall of sex-based prejudices. On the surface, he genuinely believes he is as committed as ever to traditional values. Randall does not see himself as violating any bond of trust to the women he dates. This is because, as he said, he makes no promises.

Randall departs only if and when it becomes clear the women he is romancing are beginning to think that something less casual may develop between them. He genuinely believes by strictly adhering to this policy he damages no one and is not responsible if anyone feels hurt because of his abrupt and unilateral decision to end an affair. Randall does not see himself as failing in any responsibility. Rather, he believes he is doing nothing more than protecting himself from abuses he subconsciously feels women are destined to reap on men. Whether or not Randall approves of the new "men's movement," he is quick to note he thoroughly understands it.

Embittered males are deceptively dangerous to women's emotional well-being. The danger is deceptive because they are good people and this shows through most of their daily actions. On the other hand, they are men who have been deeply hurt and who irrationally blame women for the excesses of their ex-wives. In practice, they are heartbreakers, love-them-and-leave-them cads. They are successful rakes because they do not appear to be scoundrels, nor at heart are they. Men like Randall do not fancy themselves as playboys. They are, however, obsessed with the fear they might once again be taken in by an abusive female.

Women readers of this section may find themselves wanting to exclaim, "What's wrong with these guys?" For centuries, women have been plagued by men who took advantage of them and then went their way. Women have learned to deal with such scoundrels, so why can't men? Just because one woman mistreats a man these men need to realize that not all women are like that. Nevertheless, smart as they seem, embittered males are unable to go beyond their new prejudices.

Twenty-five years ago, if a couple divorced, it was a pretty safe bet the cause was the man's drinking, philandering or desire to run off with another woman. Indeed, as government statistics show, until the late 1970s in this country, most divorces among the middle- and upper-classes were initiated by men. Things have changed. Now, in that same socio-economic group, most divorces are initiated by women. This change has left many men with their heads spinning. Some of these men were good husbands just like many women, married to philandering husbands, were good wives. None of them *deserved* to be rejected. Yet it happened. And as it did, the ranks of the embittered male population swelled. Perhaps because men are less prepared to deal with such uneven treatment, they do not handle it as well as their female counterparts. Instead, embittered males devise strategies to isolate themselves from further *risk of intimacy*. After reading this account of the embittered male, one woman commented:

> The scariest thing about this is that there do seem to be more of them. One of the first things I now try to find out about a divorced man is how he feels about his ex-wife. If he sees red at the mere thought of her I see the door and let myself out!

The Male Chauvinist Pig

This guy has been around for a long time and is easy to identify. He objectifies women and makes no pretense about it. He tends to be boastful and thinks the way to a woman's heart is gained by recounting his personal achievements. He views feminist criticism of his mannerisms as the irrational raving of a lunatic fringe of ugly, frustrated females. The narcissist usually sees himself as very manly, meaning he sees himself as a sportsman, accomplished in his career and having lots of male "buddies." He believes women expect to be taken care of regardless of anything they might say to the contrary. The male chauvinist over thirty has typically been married before and surprisingly, given his limited respect for women, he seems eager to marry again, and again, and again. He talks as if the most precious talents possessed by women are their sexual appetites and their wealth.

Women are quick to identify a male chauvinist and quick to sum up his character. Angie, a forty-year-old personnel manager for a sizeable corporation sneered:

> He wears his name on his belt, a gold chain around his neck and he's convinced the car, van or pick-up truck he drives is a turn-on to women. If he has enough money, the car may be a Jaguar and the belt and chain are set aside for a thousand- dollar suit and hundred-dollar tie, both of which have labels he is sure will impress you. He is extraordinarily insecure, despite his best efforts to the contrary. He needs a woman to tell him he's great. At the same time, he's trying to make any woman he's with feel that she is humbled by being part of the weaker sex.

Dale, a nurse working as director for a research project at a major medical school observed:

> These guys run around trying to make everyone believe that they are God's gift to women. They are always quick to talk about the women who are chasing them and about the hearts that they have broken. You can't help but doubt that any of it is true. If you go out with one of these guys more than two or three times, and particularly if you have sex with the guy, he'll start talking about marriage right away. Maybe it's all just talk, I don't know. I never stay around long enough to find out. Who wants to be with a guy who wears his heart on a coat sleeve? He probably has a tough time with women. That may be the reason he is so quick to make up stories about his alleged successes.

There is little reason to go on with an account of the male chauvinist. His motives are transparent and his prejudices are obvious. He is a user and a taker. He is out for what he can get from women and gives little thought to what he may have to give them. Women are quick to spot him. He constitutes little threat to most women.

As one twenty-five-year old school teacher, Brenda, declared, "When one woman tells another that her date was a jerk, the first thing that comes to mind is all you would associate with the words 'male chauvinist pig.'"

The Patient

Sophocles' Oedipus fell in love with his mother. Freudians claim every boy harbors a special longing for his mother as nurturer. Some grow into manhood harboring a now pathologic desire to be cared for by a woman as a mother might care for her son. Whether or not an individual man's desire to be mothered is a vestige of unsuccessful psychological development is a matter best left to psychiatric researchers. Many women, however, encounter men who seem driven to be under their care. Often these men suffer from a chronic disease such as diabetes, high blood pressure, angina, cirrhosis, chronic depression, schizophrenia or some maladaptive psychological disorder. Sometimes these men may simply be insecure and want someone to come home to for counsel and direction.

While some women enjoy the caregiver role, most become suspicious about men who require constant care, believing them to be emotionally crippled and unable to reciprocate when the woman needs her share of care, attention and nurturing. Evelyn, a vibrant and stately forty-six-year old woman manager of an expensive restaurant, explained:

> I've met a lot of these guys over the years. It seems the older I get, the more of them I meet. The chronic patient, the guy who needs—or thinks he needs . . . or might need—twenty-four hour medical care. It is not always easy to know that a guy you are going out with is a "patient." Some of these guys are quite successful in their careers. As you get to know them, you start realizing that they are obsessed with dying. The most important thing in the world to them is having someone there to mourn while they die. Well, I'm sorry, I gave at the office.
>
> I would like to get married again and share what's left of my time on earth with a man. But sharing isn't the same thing as becoming a nursemaid. I have no objection to going to any length to help the love of my life through any crisis of any duration. I hope I could count on him for the same. That doesn't mean I want to enter into a relationship where my role is nothing more than nursemaid, and for some guys that's all they want.
>
> By the way, I don't want to give the impression that it is just old guys who think they need a nursemaid. I'm fairly youthful looking for my age. I've gone out with several guys five to eight years younger than me. That generally is not a good idea. Some of the younger men you go out with think that because of your age you are an easy mark and desperate for some physical companionship. That may be true for some women, but I think if you keep yourself in shape and mentally alive then you aren't desperate for anything. Some of the other young guys a woman my age is likely to come across are guys who are trying to achieve social position through their association with me or they see me as a mother figure.
>
> I am no more of a mother than I am a nurse. I have one grown son already. I don't need to take on the responsibility of another because he wants to play act as my boyfriend. Young or old, some guys just can't face life on their own. They want a woman there to make it better just like Mamma used to do.
>
> I probably sound awful saying all this. I suppose I sound selfish myself. Well, I'm not. I just think there is a big difference between sharing life with another and becoming a surrogate mother to an adult male!

Heather, a soft-spoken twenty-eight-year old nurse who looked the picture of a Florence Nightingale complained:

> You know some men want to go out with you because you are a nurse. They think that because you've chosen to help the sick for a career that you want to spend every waking hour helping someone. I like to help people. I'd surely be glad to help the man in my life if he ever needed it. But I don't want a man so I can do more helping throughout the day. I don't want a man who wants me only because he thinks I will be a constant, private nurse to him.

Like the male chauvinist, the patient is seen by women as a user. He is not prepared to give of himself to a relationship but only to take from it. In contrast, the corporate executive is willing to contribute material goods to the relationship and something of his reputation as well. These things may be a distant second to emotional and physical intimacy but they are better than nothing. Even the embittered male is not trying to get something for nothing. He offers limited companionship and sexual enjoyment. He expects nothing more in return. The patient is a poor bet for women seeking a relationship in which a man and a woman genuinely share. The patient is a parasite. Most women want something more. Every person deserves more.

Something Else

Most women want an alternative to the men who fall into the categories above. Women from throughout the country concur on their authenticity. The question now is: Are the categories above exhaustive? I hope they are not. If they are the future of the species, it is in jeopardy since few available men would be sufficiently appealing to women. Things are not as bleak as the above suggests. There are single women who are happily involved with special men. Many of these couples are planning marriages and the majority of these marriages will last a lifetime. There are many alternatives to the type of men described in the first four categories. However, it is not feasible to lump them together in a manageable number of categories. The diversity is too great. The categories above evolved as women described general types of men to avoid. Stick with the guys from "something else" and you may find an appropriate romance.

Men should find it informative to read through the categories above so they might avoid falling into one of the undesirable categories. Of the men who read through earlier drafts of the above taxonomy, all affirmed they knew men who fit each category. They each saw themselves, however, as "something else" though a few admitted to being "embittered males." It might be worth it for each man to consider again how close he is to the disagreeable "bad bets" represented by the categories: corporate-climber, embittered male, patient and male chauvinist.

What Kind of Women Are Out there for Me?

Whereas women tend to build taxonomies of single men around specific personality constellations, men tend to begin with chronological indexes and associate both personality and physical attributes with age. These tendencies are not universally approved by members of either sex. For example, a few women divided men between those over forty, those thirty and above and those younger. The first group was said to be established, patient and mature. The second group was said to be energetic, challenging and a bit schizophrenic. The third group was said to be young . . . very young. Similarly, some men contrived categories of women based upon their career orientation, their hunger for money or status or their family orientation. In general, however, taxonomies of men based on personality were most appealing to divorced single women and taxonomies of women based on age were most appealing to divorced single men.

Whether in science or in the hunt for a compatible partner, taxonomies are made for the convenience of the user. A whale, for example, is a mammal and not a fish—not for any reason of nature's contrivance but rather because it lends itself to the simplicity and economy of the biologist's view of the world. Perhaps men should not be so quick to think about women in terms of age. Perhaps women should not be so quick to think of men in terms of stereotypical personality traits. However, members of each sex have found such homemade taxonomies useful in sizing up opportunities for interesting dates.

Twenty to Twenty-Five Year Old Women

Readers should remember the men surveyed are divorced and range in age from twenty-five to fifty-five with a distinct majority in their thirties and forties. All that needs to be said about this group is captured in the following few lines by Kirk, a slightly graying and amiable thirty-nine-year old journalist:

> The woman between the ages of twenty and twenty-five is amazing. She never has to lift a finger in exercise. All her muscles are smooth and resilient. Facial creams and make-up are a conspicuously unnecessary luxury. Their greatest beauty concern is still the unsightly pimple. Youth has its own beauty so every woman this age has some beauty to begin with. Pretty eyes, hair, all the rest just add to what's already there.
>
> Beautiful though they may be, these women are still children. They may be bright and earnest, but twenty-five years is rarely enough time for anyone to accumulate enough experience to find a place in the world. This is as true of men as it is of women. So while women this age are great to look at, it takes no time at all for someone my age to discover we have nothing in common. After the exchange of a few pleasantries, a comment or two on the state of the economy or the drudgery of work, there is nothing more to say. You don't want to talk to a girl this age about "your history" because it becomes all too obvious to you both that yours is too long and her's has barely begun.

Twenty-Five to Thirty

Carl, a fifty-year-old lawyer, well-established in his field, cultured and well-traveled declared:

> I love women of that age. They have all the beauty of a twenty-two year old. They are full of romance, zeal, idealistic, and with a great sense of adventure. The only bad thing about a woman in her late twenties is that she will shortly go through her early thirties.

William, a fifty-nine-year old business consultant and amateur athlete extraordinaire stated flatly:

> Women under twenty-five are too young and those over thirty too cynical. I have no plans in ever marrying again or becoming a part of a long-term relationship. So I keep my dating life limited to women who are fun, active and youthful, that is, under thirty.

And finally, a thirty-two-year old insurance salesman explained:

> I figured if I married again it would be to someone in that age span. But one of the things I have found is that so many in that age group are so career-minded they don't have much time for a social life. Those that don't have career prospects either want to marry someone who is established, usually much older, or they want to just keep dating as if all of life is an extension of high school.
>
> The high-powered career-minded type behaves like any other junior executive. She buys cars and clothes to impress. She puts in long hours at work, brown-noses the boss and takes up all the 'right' sports.

At first glance these three seem to be observing three very different groups. Yet, strictly speaking, there is only one set of single women between the ages of twenty-five and thirty. What accounts for such disparity in the three men's assessments?

A simple lesson learned in quantum physics and since exploited by students of the philosophy of science is instructive. In the realm of high energy physics, there are no observations free of the intrusive influence of researchers. In looking into the world of particle physics, the observer's presence disturbs all she or he wishes to see. Consequently, there are no observations free of effects caused by the observer.

When it comes to making sense of the opposite sex, single men (and women) will find the observations of their counterparts are contaminated by the predispositions they as observers bring with them. In the first two cases above, successful older men described women in their late twenties as exciting and romantic. The younger man sensed greater variety in this age group and was particularly struck by the fact some women in this age group are extremely career-minded. This latter observation may in part reflect the fact that men his age are in direct competition with these women. The older men observe and interact with these women in a way very different from the young man who must compete with such women in work situations. In any case, all three men seemed to agree women in their late twenties are attractive, energetic and desirable.

Thirty to Thirty-Five

At this age women are an enigma to men. Recall Carl's description of women in their late twenties: "The only bad thing about a woman in her late twenties is that she will shortly go through her early thirties." Pete, the thirty-six-year old owner of a high-tech bicycle shop observed:

> Women in their early thirties are just trouble. I will date women who are younger, but I will never marry one. I don't even want to attempt to make it through the early thirties with another woman. I'll date women a couple of years older than I am before I'll date one in her early thirties.

Leon, a fifty-six-year old business consultant and computer expert said:

> Women in their late twenties are the most fun to date. But you can't afford to get serious about a woman until she gets past her early thirties. I have been married twice before. Each time, the woman divorced me. One was thirty-one, and we had been married six years. The other was thirty-three, and we had been married five years. Something happens to a woman when she gets to her early thirties. She wants her life to go a million directions at once and a spouse is just in the way.

Finally, a thirty-three-year old accountant said:

> Women my own age are a pain. Their biological clocks are clamoring away. They want to be a senior partner or an executive vice-president by forty. They want a relationship that is "real." They want money. They want love. They want excitement. They want a family like Mom had. They want so much it's impossible to get it all, and they have no idea where to cut or how to compromise. A lot of them have already been divorced once. You can tell from what they say that the ex-husband got dumped because he was in the way. They're just a tangle of nerves and contradictory goals at this age.

The number of comments of similar ilk by men was overwhelming. Most surprising was women in their late thirties and forties when confronted with the men's comments, AGREED! As Ginger, a forty-six-year old woman (divorced twice before) said, while fingering a twenty-thousand-dollar string of pearls:

> The men are right. The early thirties are a very difficult time for a woman. You become acutely aware that your looks will not last forever. You begin exercising to fight gravity and cosmetics become the staff of life. You start thinking this may be your last chance to get it right. So you divorce your husband and take off for that one last fling, culminating, you hope, in a marriage to the man you deserve, Prince Charming.
>
> The early thirties are the period of greatest difficulty for a woman. I can tell you from experience that it is far more difficult than going through menopause. By the time you begin menopause, you pretty much know what you hope for in life and what you have reason to expect. You also know that transient emotional disturbances can be attributed to a physical event. In your thirties you are confused, but you are not even sure about that. You are convinced you know and understand so much . . . you just can't figure out what to do. The world around you seems full of last chances, and that's scary. When you get older, you know that even when you miss some last chances in some areas of life there will always be new opportunities elsewhere. Chances at certain opportunities may end, but the chance for a satisfactory future never ends. In your forties, you know that is true. In your thirties, you can't even understand what the words mean.

Finally Rita, a recently divorced woman working in the banking industry retorted:

> I don't know if I agree with the others. Here I am at thirty-three and I make more money than either of my parents. I am a success in my career. My personal life has been going fine since I got divorced. Before I got divorced, I never felt I could do things for me. Now I do.
>
> There was nothing wrong with my husband; we just wanted different things in life and grew in different directions. We have joint custody of our daughter and she spends most week-nights at her father's house. (He lives just two blocks away.) Now he's free to do his thing, and I'm free to do mine.

I asked, "What is your 'thing'? Do you want to get married again? Do you want more children? Do you want a man in your life? How important is your career? What would be an ideal situation for you in ten years?"

Rita responded:

> Gee, those are tough questions. Actually, I have thought about each of them . . . a lot! I am in a relationship right now so I know I want a man in my life. I don't *need* a man to be happy but I'd like someone to share my life with. I don't know if this is the guy, but someday I'd like to get married again. I'm in no rush. I don't have to get married within the next year. But in ten years, I expect I'll be married again. I'll probably have one more child. That's not a "have to," but it's something I'd like. I'm kind of an old-fashioned person. I think family is supremely important. I'm not a big career type. I think family comes first. I think career is important—particularly right now, but if I meet the right guy I think my priorities will change. I also think that the right guy will want me to continue to do well in my career.

As her remarks reveal, Rita is suffering some discontinuity of purpose. Also, there is a tinge of urgency, witness her remarks about having one more child, her current fellow may not be the right one, but she'll be married within ten years, and she may be willing to give up career aspirations for the right guy—though, of course, such a guy would not (by definition?) want her to.

Women in their late thirties and forties readily admit to empathizing with Rita's anxiety. They point out that such disparity of objectives was often the cause of seeking a divorce in their own early thirties along with an inept husband or the realization that they married too young. These sum up the reasons the majority of middle-class women give for initiating a divorce in their early thirties.

There is considerable agreement among men that women in their early thirties are a difficult lot. Sometimes men associate women turning thirty with adopting a harsh feminist and anti-male ideology. Whatever the reason and whether or not the early thirties does indeed represent a particularly trying developmental stage for women is again a matter meriting serious and sustained study by social scientists. A substantial number of men and a growing number of women believe, or at least allow, this may be a period of extraordinary difficulty for women. It is the time women are most likely to suffer from the "middle-aged crazies."

Thirty-Five to Forty

Loretta, a forty-four-year old consultant to state prisons and other correctional institutions said:

> As women enter their late thirties, they discover there is no such thing as a superwoman just as there is, nor ever has been, a superman. John Kennedy may have been a great president, but his performance as a husband apparently left much to be desired. My father was a great Dad, and I think he was a pretty good husband. He worked as a mailman. He never became a postmaster or received any supervisory assignment. Nobody gets to have it all. It seems that in their late thirties, women begin learning this. They are no longer rushing about trying to get it all or figure out what compromises they are reluctantly willing to make. They begin to relax and enjoy some of the things that make them happiest.

In general, men agreed women in their late thirties have resolved many of the difficulties and uncertainties that plagued them earlier in life. They have made decisions to live with certain trade-offs and they adapt better to uncertainty. A number of men also note despite the loss of youth, many women in their late thirties remain attractive because of increased efforts at exercise, more skilled use of cosmetics, better taste in dress, and greater poise and sophistication.

Forty and Above

Several decades ago a major news magazine pictured on its cover an attractive woman sitting in a garbage can. The title of the story, "Is there life for women after age 28?" The point of the story was that although women begin losing their youthful, good looks at twenty-eight, that is not the end for love, romance or an exciting career. In the late 1980s, *Playboy* magazine applauded the achievements and attractiveness of Gloria Steinem on the occasion of her fortieth birthday. The point of the story was a woman's thirties can be thoroughly enjoyed and turning forty did not forebode the final chapter of a woman's life.

Feminists encourage women to think of their forties and fifties as like any other decade of life. Those decades are to be lived and enjoyed and never bemoaned as a waning of life and opportunity. Apparently, the feminist message has been well-heeded. From the perspective of their male counterparts, many divorced single women have learned to live life much more comfortably and fully in their forties than they ever did in their twenties and thirties. In their forties, women adopt a roughly hewn life plan and slow down, "smelling the roses along the way." They exploit their past experiences for the benefit of the present. They do not lament the past or fantasize about the future. In short, divorced single women over forty are typically perceived by men as interesting companions.

As one forty-three-year old geologist, Stuart, said:

> Women my age are much more comfortable for me to be with than the younger ones. There are no biological clocks ticking. They've resolved themselves to the very real possibility they may never marry again. As a result, they are less likely to pressure men for marriage. They have taken control of their careers rather than the reverse. If they have children, the children are generally old enough to be of little nuisance. They've experienced many of the same historical events I have. They are appreciative of the effects age has on even healthy bodies—an appreciation no younger man or women can ever have. They have become more discriminating in their tastes and more likely to know the simple joys of companionship.

A better sales pitch one can hardly imagine! Yet when asked what age women he generally dated, Stuart said women between the age of twenty-eight and thirty-five. When asked why he did not date women closer to his own age, Stuart confessed:

> I don't know. I believe everything I said about women over forty and I have a lot of women friends my own age. But when it comes to dating, I choose to date women who are about ten years younger than me. They generally aren't as good at companionship as women closer to my age, but so what? Someday one of them will be. You look for different things in a date than in a "pal."
>
> A special younger woman might be exceptionally mature. Also, she can learn what the older woman knows. Just by getting older, she'll probably learn it. But an older woman can't look like a thirty-year- old and looks are important. Besides it's just natural for guys to be older and gals younger in a relationship. The only time you

even hear about it being the other way around is on a television talk show. That alone proves how rare it is.

I guess I don't really have a good answer to your question. I suppose because I never thought of myself as doing anything unusual or different from any of my friends, I never gave much thought to the question. And I don't suppose I will now, either. I like my life as it is so I probably won't give any thought to changing it.

Stuart's observation of women in their forties and of his own dating habits are unexceptional. This is a position endorsed by the vast majority of divorced single men questioned. They do not try to defend the rationality of their practices but are content to continue in their ways just as they have in the past. They simply believe "it's natural" or "all my friends do the same thing, so without thinking about it I do, too." Indeed, some are delighted to refer to a rule *Esquire* magazine once attributed to French folk wisdom that a man should be with "women half his age plus seven years."

As one owner of a small construction company pointed out:

This isn't unnatural or a 'male thing' only. We couldn't concentrate on younger women if the younger women were not equally enamored with dating older men. Right or wrong that's just the way it is.

The predilection on the part of men to date women who are much younger despite the fact they are more likely to enjoy the company of older women represents a serious quagmire for divorced singles. It brings to mind a line from a country and western song originally made popular by the movie *Urban Cowboy*: "Looking for love in all the wrong places."

If men feel most comfortable with women close to their own age, then why not date those women? Despite the obvious appeal of this recommendation, many men persist in dating younger women they admit are less likely to be compatible companions. With few exceptions, men claim they want more from a relationship than, say, mere sex or an associate to travel or attend functions with. One would think in light of one or more previous failed marriages, divorced middle-aged men would be more apt to utilize their taxonomies in a more promising manner. It seems, for the moment at least, most divorced men are destined to date within a population of women wherein they least expect to find a good friend and a suitable companion.

Summary

In light of most middle-aged men's actual dating practices, it is hardly surprising they are increasingly pessimistic about finding a mate. In contrast, women remain hopeful "something else" is out there. But hope is waning as encounters with the patient, the corporate climber, the male chauvinist and, most devastating, the embittered male, add up. Women, too, are becoming discouraged. Still, marriage rates are increasing, but after talking to so many men and women, it is hard to imagine why. Maybe more and more people are willing to settle for less just to escape the singles' scene and all that goes with it. On the other hand, maybe men who are "something else" are becoming more adept at finding appropriate soul-mates. Maybe women, too, are getting better at finding the men who are "something else."

For divorcees who continue to entertain the idea of finding a soul-mate, the following morals derived from the taxonomies above may be useful.

Women

1. Don't become jaded. "Something else" exists. If you become jaded, you will become something less than a "good catch" yourself. If you find yourself getting involved with the same type of loser, time and again, examine yourself, your dating practices and your social habitat. For example, people who are pathologically co-dependent seek out others of similar disposition. To break out of the cycle, you need to recognize your own weakness. If your dating practices center around "the fast life," you may be encouraging men to see you as someone to "date" and leave. Change your PACE and seek out men with some different interests. If your social habitat centers around a particular activity or institution, such as running or bars, change sports or nightlife habits and try a new sport or a new type of gathering place. Maybe tennis and church groups

have a greater number of YOUR TYPE OF "SOMETHING ELSE."

2. Remember, despite appearances to the contrary, most men want to find a woman whose companionship they can genuinely enjoy. You might become a bit more aggressive in seeking out a man closer to your own age. This will benefit both you and him. If you are convinced you prefer older men, learn something about his "culture." There really is a generation gap, and he is not likely to think you can traverse it. If you are one of the handful of women who prefer younger men, you might ask yourself why? Is it the same kind of public allure that has dominated men's habits for so long?

3. Be particularly wary of the embittered male! He is easy to mistake for something else. He is easy to love. The best way to get a closer look at his stripes is to engage him in a conversation about his previous wife (wives). If episodes he cites or the tone of his voice reveal anger, hurt, jealousy, or hate, be careful! Such traits are hidden in the mantle of every embittered male. They shield him from intimacy. Note that these are four of the five furies. Guilt has been omitted because men who feel guilt are generally not adverse to future relationships (and some of them may have learned a thing or two as a result of laboring under such guilt!). Men harboring long-term guilt have special problems and needs. These needs may turn them into a "patient" but seldom into an embittered male. When all the vestiges of a former relationship are gone, if a man still harbors intensely guarded feelings of hate, anger, hurt, or jealousy, he is a likely candidate for embittered male status so . . . BEWARE.

4. Whatever your age, you don't have to make any choice now or in the near future. In fact, a woman who is confident and relaxed, knowing any choices will be obvious when the time comes, is a woman who is generally appealing to men.

Men

1. Take a careful inventory of yourself. If you are a male chauvinist, a corporate climber or a patient, few women are going to be interested in you. Similarly, if you are an embittered male, wise women will abandon you. More important, if you discover you are an embittered male, you have a moral duty to protect others from the pain you feel victimized by. Straighten out your life before attempting to involve others in it.

2. If long-term companionship is appealing to you, then date women whose age makes it easier to relate to one another.

3. Free yourself from peer pressure. Date women for what appeals to you. Don't date women to impress friends or society-at-large.

8

Sharing

Divorcees are products of failed relationships. If you knew how to make marriage work, you would still be married. It is tempting to blame your divorce on your spouse. This is not a good idea. Chances are you played a significant role in the dissolution of your own marriage. But even if you did not, even if all responsibility for past failure is attributable to your spouse or others, you are still responsible for selecting the associations you made in the first place. What have you learned? How can you make more prudent decisions in the future?

Throughout the next part of this book you are encouraged to be cautiously optimistic about what life has yet to offer. I have talked a lot about preparing for single life but how should one prepare for re-marriage when the time comes? Re-marriage is not at all like a first-time marriage for anyone. How can you increase the odds of success the next time around?

The Political/Economic Theory of Marriage

On one level of analysis, marriage is a socio-political institution like that of a city, a corporation or a nation. Each of these socio-political units requires a measure of commitment from everyone involved. Political theorists speculate commitment is sustained by recognition of an implicit social contract. Participation involves following rules in an effort to optimize (or at least *satisfy*) personal benefits. This economic/managerial approach to understanding human relationships was so generally accepted throughout the sixties, seventies and eighties that it provoked three sociologists, a theologian and a philosopher to collaborate on a book *Habits of Heart* (R. N. Bellah, et al.). The managerial/therapeutic ideology the authors describe is based upon incessant calculations of costs and benefits by every self-interested person. The self-help books of the seventies and early eighties made abundantly clear what the authors claim: people had come to see the bonds of marriage as regulated by the distribution of personal advantages.

Therapists and self-help authors led the way, encouraging people to think of themselves first and of everyone else only to the extent there was a foreseeable advantage to doing so. This, Bellah and his colleagues contend, has not worked. The more we exact a price for maintaining relationships, the more we price them out of the market. Through numerous interviews, Bellah and his colleagues noticed that upon reflection most people were uncomfortable with the idea relationships should be valued only if they rendered a calculable bounty.

Such relationships are void of altruism, tenderness, serenity and all the intangible virtues most people hope will distinguish their relationships from more common ones. As people bought into the "give and take" economy of human personal relations, they increasingly lost out on the benefits afforded by these virtues.

The therapeutic attitude is modified in society at large, the authors claim, by a managerial ideology that views all utilization of human resources as a matter of showing bottom line advantages. Of course, to effectively anticipate bottom line advantages, one must subject prospective romances, friendships or marriages to a rigorous cost-benefit analysis.

The best analyses are done in a cold-blooded objective manner. However, successful romances, the best friendships and the best marriages all require much more. Despite the influence of "experts," ordinary people intuitively understand marriage, at least, requires more. Bellah's interviews show people have a need to see themselves, their beloveds, their community, and their work efforts as reflecting an importance extending beyond their immediate relation to self.

Psychologists Barry Schwartz and Jonathan Baron pointed out even business has been forced to recognize people need to feel they are working for something more than mere personal advantage. Major corporations now carefully develop corporate loyalty in their employees. They seek a sense of commitment from employees that extends beyond the "me first" mentality of the therapeutic society. In a similar vein, economist and decision theorist Robert Frank, in his book *Passion*

Within Reason, notes love often prompts people to act in ways contrary to self-interest. Without this feature, people would never notice love as a special quality in the first place. Frank goes on to detail how none of the current, decision-based models or economic, rational-person visions account for the constellation of phenomena so routinely evident in successful marriages. Indeed, the social evolution of marriage itself reveals how truly different it is from other more mundane economic and contractual relations.

My own interviews and encounters with divorcees reflect similar insights. Marriage *is* far more than a mere contractual relation; it is a covenant. The cornerstone of that covenant is commitment—and commitment toward another does not exist when all one is prepared to do is act out of self-interest. This notion is already abundantly clear to most divorcees. The question now is how to incorporate it into one's repertoire for nurturing a sustainable relationship.

Commitment involves such matters as being resolute when acting on behalf of persons, institutions or ideas to which one is committed. Commitment to spouse means constantly seeking opportunities to share with one's mate. Sharing is not trading. *Sharing involves giving to another without calculated expectation of return. Sharing is knowing how to accept gifts from another without taking.* People fully committed to sharing with another do not divorce. The intended reader's past is one of divorce, not of successful sharing. Consequently, before embarking on another trip to the altar, consider what you and your partner know about sharing. Any deficiencies must be addressed before either of you risks suffering the trauma of another misguided marriage.

Commitment

Commitment involves sharing. So, too, talk of sharing and talk of intimacy both lead back to talk of commitment. "Commitment" might seem a very ordinary word, denoting a very ordinary experience, yet its depths are suspiciously opaque. Every self-help book dealing with relationships, personal development, drug or alcohol dependency, dysfunctional families, business success, and so on devotes at least one chapter to commitment. The authors discuss how to achieve commitment presumably because in all these cases there is a lack of it. With so much attention, one would think at least the idea of commitment, even if not well understood in the past, must surely be clear by now. Still, each new self-help book insists it has something new and cute to offer. New and cute will no longer cut it. The self-help books have failed miserably in deepening our understanding of commitment and the television talk shows have fared far worse. The time has arrived when this topic must be treated more substantially.

Lovers speak freely of the beauty of their commitment. In contrast, divorcees and other veterans of love-trauma pore over reasons and causes for failed commitments. Victims of love-trauma were all once lovers, people who believed they and their partners understood well the language of commitment. Now, in the wake of shattered vows, they lament how little the concept of commitment was understood by either of them.

If people truly understand commitment, they do not find it so difficult to sustain. They recall commitments are bonds they freely accepted. They recall, too, it is each promisor's responsibility to nurture all that was entailed by previous vows. Commitments fail because one or the other failed in his or her responsibility. The libertine might protest, "Are there no fault-free failures?" Alas, there are not.

Because commitments are freely entered into, the bonds of obligation eagerly proposed and accepted by each, there are no fault-free failures. There are, however, many instances in which people are alleged to have entered into a commitment of, say, reciprocal love without understanding everything involved. These relationships do often fail, but not because there was a fault-free failure of commitment; they fail because the commitment alleged was only an illusion.

To commit to a common life project with a spouse requires extraordinary ego strength and great moral sophistication. Ego strength constitutes the courage required to do right by one's spouse. Common sense makes abundantly clear to every mature adult commitment requires the continued exercise of moral courage. Moral sophistication, on the other hand, is a matter of demanding integrity of oneself in the face of temptations. We are dealing here not with lofty philosophical abstractions, but the stuff of folk wisdom, of mature common sense. The more excellently people engage common sense in these matters the more sustainable their marriages.

Saying, Showing, Doing

How is it that the subject of so much poetry and art on the one hand, and philosophy and social science on the other, can be written off as best pursued through the *excellent* exercise of *common sense?* This should be easy to understand. Sharing is the most democratic of all concepts. It does not require special genius or a Ph.D. Consider what is required in learning, say, to ride a bicycle.

Imagine you know nothing at all of bicycle-riding, but you have just heard a lecture by a highly acclaimed expert detailing the relevant aspects of human physiology and the relationship of these to the physics of bicycling. Do you suppose you could walk from the lecture hall, climb on the first bike you see and ride away? What if, subsequent to the lecture, you are handed a copy of the speaker's written text and commit it to memory. So successful are you in memorizing the text you are able to deliver the same lecture yourself. At this point, could you imagine yourself hopping on the next bike you see and riding about in expert fashion? Your answer in each case must be a resounding "No!"

To learn to ride a bicycle proficiently, there are certain things you must experience, certain *sensibilities* you must acquire. The ability merely to "talk a good game" is no substitute for learning to do the real thing!

The exercise of skills is different from the task of storing bits and pieces of factual information. People do not come to the world knowing how to ride a bicycle. They *acquire* this capacity but not as they might knowledge of some fact. They learn to ride bicycles not merely as a result of being taught "right principles."

The problem of how people learn things which *cannot be taught* is explored at length by the British philosopher Gilbert Ryle in an essay entitled, "Can Virtue Be Taught?" Ryle noticed virtue was the sort of thing adults acquire to a greater or lesser degree regardless of the amount of formal schooling they enjoyed. Upon reflection, Ryle, ever the quintessential British scholar, concluded a lot of things were of this ilk. Ryle never addressed the capacity to love and make commitments as examples of such talents, but they are similar.

Most people learn to ride a bicycle by engaging in three very different types of activities. First, they are *instructed* in the points of riding a bicycle and the tasks performed by various devices such as brakes, pedals, steering mechanism, gears, and so on. Second, they are usually *shown how* to ride a bicycle by experienced bike riders who simply hop on and ride about a bit. Third, they are invited to do, to actually ride a bike. Of course, mishaps occur. These mishaps diminish in proportion to the length of practice attempted. Eventually, every new rider proceeds in expert fashion without further mishap or further assistance. (The idea of developing expertise in stages involving instruction, demonstration and practice is further unpacked in a five-stage approach by artificial intelligence researchers Hubert and Stuart Dreyfus in their book, *Mind over Matter*.)

Too many divorcees approach the commitment of marriage as an uninstructed and inexperienced child might approach bike riding. The result in each case is the novices are destined to do no more than fumble about. Most divorcees did have some "pre-nuptial" instruction, but it is often irrelevant or too little. For example, while in school divorcees-to-be learned the mechanics of copulation. At home, parents traditionally responded to their question, "How do you know when you're in love?" by asserting simply, "When you're in love you'll know it." This vacuous information, divorcees may recall, was all very discouraging. Equally discouraging was a parent's disapproving caution that the immediate love of one's life is only a passing fancy, an instance of puppy love. Many a teen has complained, "If they can't *tell me* what love is, how can they tell me this is just puppy love I'm feeling!"

Finally, finding no solace from other quarters, the divorcee-to-be may begin experimenting first hand by "trying out relationships." What this amounts to is sex, going steady, living together and sometimes all three. As many a victim of a failed marriage can attest, the responsibilities and bonding attendant upon marriage cannot be experienced—even vicariously—through any of these routes. A person can be an outstanding sexual partner, an attentive companion and a tolerable roommate and still not pass muster as a soul-mate. The sort of sharing that makes for a successful marriage stops at nothing short of unmitigated acceptance by two people in one common life project.

In a book entitled *The Examined Life*, philosopher Robert Nozick describes marriage as a union between two persons wherein the protective boundaries between individuals is erased. Nozick does not mean the parties to a marriage no longer retain any individuality. Anyone familiar with Nozick's work over the years knows he advocates individualism to the point of excess. Still, Nozick argues marriage affects individuality the way no other institution does or should do. To paraphrase Nozick, one can say in successful marriages, part of each person's identity incorporates essential elements from the identity of the other. What this amounts to is a spouse's happiness produces immediate and uninterpreted happiness in the mate. Similarly, any sadness or disgrace experienced by one produces similar sadness or disgrace in the other. It is important for the veteran of previous failed marriages to dwell on these examples for a moment. Nozick is not claiming one person *sympathizes* with the plight of his or her spouse. Perhaps even empathy is too weak a word here. Sex partners, friends, roommates, indeed even neighbors and business associates, can be cheered a bit or saddened by the events affecting another's life. But in the kind of shared undertaking constituting successful marriage, the *important* emotive events affecting one, affect, *in like manner,* the other.

Even after reading this, the traveler of failed marriage will probably still find such notions difficult to comprehend. It is not for lack of interest or seriousness the reader may fail to assimilate Nozick's point. The truth of such things must be experienced to be appreciated.

The market for self-help books and talk shows which claim to reveal the secrets of successful relationships would be less lucrative if there were fewer seekers after such truths. There are many seekers but limited means for finding truth. No self-help book and no talk show can ever provide their audiences with what they seek. One cannot learn about Nozick's "we-ness" or what I have described throughout as a "common life project" by reading, even by reading swell books such as this one or by listening to eloquent speakers. One must experience such sharing to understand it. Before the reader casts aside this book without reading the few remaining pages, let me hasten to add useful advice can expedite one's quest for the appropriate experience. Let's now turn to that advice and then send you on your way. The final leg of this journey towards self-discovery must be made by you and you alone.

Recall what is involved in learning to ride a bicycle. Essentially, there are three elements. First, one *describes* the salient features of the bike and how each is used to achieve one's goal. Second, one *shows* the learner how it is done. As the novice watches, he or she begins to notice adjustments made such as maintaining the rider's balance, preparing for a stop, turning, and so on. Third, the learner gets on the bike and *tries* to make a go of it. In the earliest efforts, one tries to keep in mind all he or she was told and *imagines* acting in expert fashion. Mistakes are inevitable. These mistakes cause the learner to pause, collect his or her thoughts and think how best to proceed next time. In doing all this, the person is trying to get a *feel* for success.

In like manner, before you or a beloved can begin to act in a genuinely sharing manner you each must *see sharing as demonstrated by a master.* To observe acts of sharing, expertly executed, each of you must also know what to look for. This preliminary goal requires further instruction.

You have been told about the phenomena of intimacy, sharing, and commitment. You have been advised to look for their appearance. Yet you are apt to feel you don't quite know how to identify intimacy, sharing and commitment even when each is before your eyes. We will try to make these phenomena more transparent by considering a few illuminating anecdotes. The best anecdotes are found in the texts of classic fiction, the remaining sections of this chapter, and most importantly in the lives of your friends and neighbors. To begin your study of intimacy, sharing and love, peruse Leo Tolstoy's *Anna Karenina*. Pay particular attention to the character Levin, whose life is a testament to commitment. For a more contemporary example, consider reading the screen play for *On Golden Pond*. Whatever literature you select, be sure the stories focus on the sharing aspects of love and not the zest of passion.

Look about the world. You need not be a philosopher, a psychologist or a cleric to share with others. Mother Theresa, Albert Schweitzer, Tom Dooley, and former President Jimmy Carter may all be Olympians when it comes to sharing, but the volunteer who counsels the terminally ill at your local hospital may be a world-class expert as well. So are many others who you pass every day. Each of these people possesses an understanding of love which is most fulfilling when cast in the context of romantic love.

Learning to share in romantic love, to become a "we," requires wisdom, not scholarly excellence. Regardless of your socio-economic status, if you look, you will find happily married couples in your world. Studies suggest the very poor and the upper-middle class may have a more difficult time finding appropriate examples, albeit for very different reasons, but the examples are there as well as in the broad middle-class.

Rich or poor, some people learned enough from books or parents, took adequate notice of successful married-types and, finally, put it all together in a package they could share with another. By watching the lives of such people, you can *imagine* much about what the sharing of love should *feel* like.

In the domain of shared love, everyone earns his or her own degree from the School of Hard Knocks. There just is no substitute for experience. However, the experiences must be of the right type. Some people engage in numerous affairs and yet remain innocent of love. Others marry a childhood sweetheart, a "first love" as it were, and manage to craft a wonderful relationship. The difference between the two is not a function of innate talent or mere chance. It is a function of being discriminate and focused enough to assimilate appropriate experience, that is, in knowing not all novel experience in the romantic domain is of equal worth.

Individuals of the first sort may well know the thrill of driving in shiny new cars, receiving a spray of three dozen arranged roses or weekend trips to exotic places. Individuals in the second group know more the meaning of a single rose, a well-intended but unpassionate kiss on the forehead, the presence of an attentive lover happy to share the beloved's expressions of insecurity as much as the beloved's boasts and delights.

Of course, not all who learned of love did so with a childhood sweetheart. For most who enter into successful marriages, there were previously a number of romantic misadventures. Nearly everyone stumbles in their early efforts. These encounters with unrequited "love" and "break-ups" with an early "steady" are not failures. They are a natural part of the trial and error curriculum that is the backbone of the School of Hard Knocks. In these early stages, one is in the process of getting the *feel* of things. In the case of riding a bicycle, it was a matter of getting a sense of balance and a feel for one's forward momentum. In the case of early romance, it is a matter of feeling what it is like to share and to accept another's efforts to reciprocate.

After the flame of romance dwindles, just as after one falls off one's bike, there is an opportunity for reflection, to recall what went wrong and then what to do to avoid such mishaps in the future. If this feedback loop is executed successfully, the resulting maturity helps the person be a better catch, a better lover.

Nearly everyone who sets out to ride a bicycle does so. Similarly, at least half the population attempting marriage sustains it on the first try. Moreover, even those whose first marriage failed learn from the experience. Studies show they are more likely to create a lasting relationship the second time around as long as they wait at least two years before re-marrying. Contrived recipes for securing marital bliss are discarded. They learn if marriage is to be a common project, any recipe for its success must be constructed by willing participants as they go.

Those who tried to systematize their first marriage, much the way a corporate business is systematized, learn the ledger-approach to relationships must be cast aside. The intangibles of marriage cannot be reliably recorded in columns of mutually agreed upon credits and debits. If one is always looking to keep the books balanced, ever distinctly in his or her favor, there is no time or interest in dissolving the boundaries between individual entities. It is only when individuals become committed to one another and the enterprise of forging a common life project can they truly forget about "getting their share." When this happens, they begin acting to give more than they have ever given before and expect less than they have ever before expected. Only such unselfish commitment will lead to the *flourishing* of a common life project. Such marriages promise erotic love.

Failure to Listen; Failure to Watch; Failure to Imagine and Act Conscientiously

There are those whose names appear regularly in the *National Enquirer* and publications of similar ilk who carelessly and desperately careen in and out of marriage. This pathetic lot seems ever in search of an elusive ill-defined experience. Before they can learn the lesson life makes freely available to all, they launch themselves into yet another precariously based relationship. The result leads them to abandon three, four, even five or more marriages. Fortunately, for society, the number of these people is relatively small (or so pollsters Louis Harris, Daniel Yankelovich and George Gallup all report).

Those who go through the courthouse doors in cyclic fashion, first for marriage then to divorce, another marriage and yet another divorce, skew the statistics such that doomsayers now predict the downfall of marriage and society itself. Human societies are extraordinarily resilient. The predictions of the doomsayers are premature to say the least. Marriage is probably less imperiled than the politicians and evangelists claim. In fact, the actual effect of all the adverse press may be rather positive. Nearly everyone now concludes marriage is a real challenge, and if they enter into marriage they had better be prepared for it. Later, at least among successful married-types, the challenge idea dissipates and in its stead is a concept of a sophisticated union between two mature adults.

The psychological stamina of baby boomers and their predecessors is beginning to wear thin. Boomers are learning they are not sufficiently resilient to avoid the disabling pain of repeated love-trauma. With this idea in mind, I will sketch some of the salient features of lasting relationships. By doing so, I hope to assist the reader in avoiding re-visiting errors of the past.

The lesson of your own love trauma may be that you are best served by remaining alone, happily alone. No dissolved boundaries to worry about. No concerns about being dependent on, or responsive to, the needs of anyone else. On the other hand, if union with another is your goal, then through these final anecdotes you may begin to SENSE how you ought to proceed to build a relationship invulnerable to love-trauma.

Read the following with care. Then be patient. Move forward at a snail's pace. You need not worry about missing opportunities at such a pace. As you learn more about what you are looking for, you are less likely to rush past it and more likely to spot it even from afar.

Whatever your age, however many years you have left, you do not need another confrontation with love trauma. You have been there, and now it's time to get on with life. You may have been charmed by the adventure of single life, but now you face the very intimidating prospect of again joining your life with that of another.

Lasting Relationships

Sharing is at the heart of long lasting relationships. Where there is sharing, love grows and marriage endures. Where there is no sharing, love diminishes proportionately and the foundation of marriage dissolves. But what is sharing and how do you make it happen?

As Robert Fulghum notes in his best-selling book, *All I Really Needed to Know I Learned in Kindergarten*, sharing is a matter of displaying an unselfish attitude toward others. When at no great cost to yourself you can improve the lives of others by sharing, you should do so. This pretty much says it all. What provides grist for volumes of philosophical musing is specifying what counts as an "unselfish attitude" and what is a matter of "at no great cost to yourself." Without venturing into such ticklish philosophical problems, I will simply trust that Fulghum is right and if the reader remembers the lessons of kindergarten, he or she has a respectable start.

Promoting the well-being of others, particularly when done at no great inconvenience to self, is a wonderful way for improving good will, the fortunes of others and society at large. Surely, partners to a marriage benefit whenever there is reciprocal improvement of goodwill and material well-being. But the sharing of marriage is special in other ways as well. While the sharing we learned in kindergarten is important, it is not enough to sustain a marriage.

In marriage, reciprocity is often out of the question. For example, in one of the most beautiful marriages I have ever observed, the wife, Wendy, recently learned she has cancer. Wendy's situation is terminal, and chemotherapy and radiation treatments have done nothing more than mercifully bring her closer to her final moments. Throughout it all, her husband, Ken, has given everything he has in energy and money. Through heart, mind and soul, Ken's one goal is to make his wife happy. Ken calculates no self-benefit. He cannot even imagine the shoe may one day be on the other foot and she will do the same for him. Ken does not ruminate about how such actions might be role-modeled by others and thus lead to a better world for all one day. Such ruminations *are the stuff of kindergarten*. But this is not the stuff of Ken's sharing of himself. Ken does not see himself as a hero. He wouldn't do this for just anyone nor would he do it to set an example for others. Ken is quick to remind his friends he is no Mother Theresa. He is doing what he is doing for Wendy and Wendy alone. No other reason matters. Ken is a good man and kindly disposed to all. But only his wife merits such complete and selfless effort.

For all Ken's efforts, there is only more suffering. Why, an economist might ask, would anyone suffer so, knowing there are no benefits nor any way to recoup one's losses? The answer is the sharing of marriage is very different from what motivates commerce or, for that matter, the kind of sharing moralists extol when they ask us to consider making a better world for all.

The sharing of marriage occurs between people holding few boundaries between them. Their life-narratives have been rewritten enabling them to share their destinies with another. It is not at all surprising then Ken seems to be dying a bit each day along with his wife. With her death, their union will be dissolved. There will never again be their "we." At that point, part of Ken will die. His life-narrative will be dramatically altered as never before and without his editor, Wendy, for support.

In long-term marriages, spouses often follow their mates into death. The power and beauty of a genuine loving union is extraordinary. Its dissolution can truly be overwhelming. There is an intimacy in the sharing occurring between lovers that cannot be duplicated in the sharing which occurs between friends, neighbors or fellow citizens. Thus, to understand the special sharing of life long lovers you must understand intimacy. In Ken's case, he persists for no other reason than he senses a oneness with his wife. This oneness embodies the virtue of intimacy.

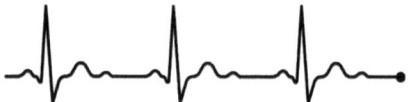

9

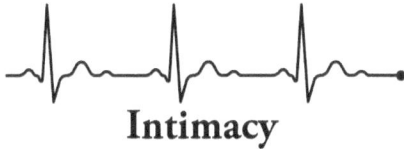
Intimacy

Intimacy, like commitment, is another term not well understood today. If you ask most people what intimacy is they are likely to respond it is a matter of sharing, perhaps even deep sharing or some such thing. Those still reveling in the wake of the 60s, free love movements, open marriages, and all may think of intimacy in purely sexual terms. That is, as a polite name for sex acts. None of this is *wrong*, at least not in any important sense. It just does not seem to say enough. Intimacy is far richer, far more revealing of character than anything implied in mere sexual complicity.

Victims of love trauma lament the absence of intimacy. Even the most superficial questioning of the victims reveals that in these thoughtful and introspective moments, their lament is not simply about a lack of sex, a sharing of worldly goods or even friendship. It is all of these and a bit more as well.

I have used the term erotic love by which I meant roughly a situation in which your most wondrous lover is also your best friend. I said there was more to it: the more is intimacy, intimacy that is whole and complete.

To get a complete picture of erotic love, consider the idea *there are three intimacies, the union of which changes simple sharing into the foundation of erotic love.* The three intimacies I have in mind are sexual, intellectual and emotional.

Sexual Intimacy

Sexual intimacy occurs when two people engage in sexual activity with one another. Note I have not used some more sterile term such as copulation. Copulation is involved in rape and names equally each act of procreation by every hermaphroditic animal species. But surely only the most careless speakers would describe all such acts as intimate. Sexual intimacy between people extends beyond biological efforts to reproduce. Sex may be pursued even when procreation is unlikely or unwanted.

Mere biological drives do not give the full story on sexual intimacy. Similarly, love and sharing do not tell the full story of sex, either. It is all too common for people to engage in sex with those they do not love and even, on occasion, fail or be unable to "have sex" with those they do love. So what is going on in sex seems to elude the sciences of biology and psychology as much as it does moral convention and theology.

Sex allows people to know the most sublime secrets of one another. This is not really as bold and lofty an idea as it may first appear. The simple truth is there are things we can say about ourselves and things we can only show.

Through sex you show things about yourself you could never put into words. This is not unique to sex. For example, a person can tell another the details of his or her training schedule. Yet only during the race does it become evident how well the athlete has trained. Similarly, actors and actresses can weep and laugh on command, but none is so talented he or she can blush on command. On the occasion of a blush, it is as if, as Roger Scruton explains, *the soul betrays the body*. The occasion of the blush informs everyone present the blushing individual is embarrassed by something that just occurred. In all such cases, the body shows more than the mouth can explain. This is why the touches and caresses of a lover often entice the beloved's body to reveal secrets of the soul he or she could never fully articulate—even if willing. In successful love-making, a meek person may display a voracious appetite for sex, an aggressive person may become meek and dependent, an extrovert may become quiet, while an introvert becomes demonstrative.

Not every sexual encounter is an act of love-making. Intercourse alone does not always cause partners to reveal vulnerabilities or share hidden aspects of themselves. For example, in the pages of *Playboy* and *Playgirl*, advisors have long discussed the phenomena of feigned orgasms as have Dr. Ruth Westheimer and numerous other "sexologists." Hollywood has long toyed with the disillusionment of feigned orgasms in its productions, probably nowhere more humorously, more vividly and in such rare good taste as in the movie *When Harry Met Sally*. In the movie, the female star simulates the facial gestures and sounds of orgasmic delight while sitting in a restaurant with her friend Harry. What does Harry know about Sally after her act? Very little. It was after all just an act. On the other hand, Sally could presumably not put on such a convincing act without Harry in mind as her sole audience. Her act called on resources available only with Harry in mind.

To suggest all intercourse results in the reciprocal revelation of individual secrets and vulnerabilities would be unforgivably naive. *Successful sex* does involve such reciprocity, and all sex, no matter how casually initiated, carries the potential for this sort of experience.

A further brief digression on "faking it" during intercourse: "faking it" is usually regarded as a female propensity and there are rather obvious reasons why. The male's achievement of climax is evident a mere moment or so after the event. In addition, when it comes to bedroom performance, men seem more narcissistic regarding their "performance." As young men, they learn to use terms such as "homerun," "touchdown," "score," and so on to denote the completion of sex. Implicit in this rhetoric is the sense sexual climax is akin to a winning performance in sports. Since sports achievements are applauded, men often seek praise for their sexual accomplishments. They may prefer a lie to any truth incompatible with the way they want to see their performance. In any event, both in cases of "faking it" as well as in cases of "performing," successful sex in such encounters is impossible. There is no sharing of vulnerabilities and no receptiveness to the "secrets" displayed by the other's body. A prostitute I spoke with, familiar with the narcissistic efforts of both sexes, insisted that such ventures should not even count as sex.

Genuine sexual ecstasy is one of the most honest things a person does. There are no calculations governing the use of each word and movement. Rather each partner gives in to impulses beyond self-conscious understanding. Deep secrets are involuntarily divulged in seemingly open expression.

In successful sex, one experiences a unique feeling of freedom, free of inhibition and the fear of rejection. This freedom exists because each partner can be trusted to be protective and appreciative of one's daring. This extraordinary trust provokes further exhilaration far beyond the titillation of predisposing biological drives. The omniscient presence of rejection titillates further the participants' sense of adventure and danger. The potency of this experience is peerless. It involves a far greater repertoire of dispositions than can be accounted for by physiology. It requires, in point, a distinctive *social* maturity.

Social maturity comes with having substantial amounts of the right kind of experience. This experience doesn't come easily. For example, the closest adolescents come to successful sex is the shared secret each possesses of how the other's biological mechanics operate. This adolescent analogue to adult intimacy is little more than conspiracy. Out of sight from disapproving adults, teenagers experiment with their equipment. In doing so, they come to share a secret with one another about how the equipment works. As adolescents mature, the unexceptional discovery that one possesses sufficient biological apparatus for mating loses its appeal. At that point and not before, physical activity between the sexes evolves and becomes more truly sexual, more intimate.

The participants are no longer preoccupied with mere biological function. As each becomes more sexual, each becomes increasingly intrigued with the idea that in sex it is another *person* who is responding. The eyes and facial gestures, cries and gasps, the deliberateness of the other person's movements all constitute a potential source of greater exhilaration for socially mature people. Rejection is recognized as a matter of the beloved turning away from some aspect of the lover's person-hood (as opposed to body or, at least, mere body). For example, imagine moving toward climax and suddenly your partner exclaims, "I can't go through with this." It is unlikely you will feel your body is being rejected. After all your body got you this far! What you do feel is your inner self, your entire person-hood is being rejected. It feels as if once all the drapes are removed and you are wholly vulnerable and exposed, your lover finds you wanting. At no other time are you so acutely aware of the indivisibility of yourself and your body. Only the socially mature have had time to appreciate these subtle and profound feelings.

Sexual intimacy is achieved only to the extent the biological events are accompanied by specific psycho-social events. Principal among these are the following three. First, there is a reciprocal revelation of vulnerabilities. Each invites the other to know the secrets of his or her heart and mind. Second, there is a reciprocal bond of trust. Each trusts that neither will reject the other during the course of lovemaking. Third, there is the *reciprocal joy* each has in the knowledge the beloved wants to know him or her fully. With genuine sexual intimacy, the lovers enjoy greater (and privileged) knowledge of the other. Because this occurs only when each senses a bond of trust exists between them, each is duty bound to respect and protect that bond. To ignore these moralistic caveats defeats the purpose and ultimate thrill of sexual intimacy.

A philandering thirty-seven-year old management consultant, Bob, admits he likes the quick conquest. However, he wishes he could avoid the inevitable feeling of guilt when, hours later, he leaves knowing it was just a one night stand. "I don't understand it. I'm no different than the next guy. I just want a little fun with these gals. So why do I always feel guilty afterwards? Usually I don't even enjoy it that much while we are doing it."

Bob's idea of fun is getting his dates to feel vulnerable, trusting and so on, but he refuses to reciprocate. This has two effects on Bob. First, he is haunted by his own deceit, his own untrustworthiness. Second, the sex Bob so eagerly seeks is never fully satisfying. How could it be since he hedged his investment and failed to contribute to the exchange of intimacy?

Just as it would be a mistake to confuse each sexual encounter with sexual intimacy, so too, it would be a mistake to confuse sexual intimacy with erotic love. Sexual intimacy can be achieved even in the "two ships passing in the night" scenario. Even Bob could enjoy sexual intimacy on nearly any one of his one night stands if only he were willing to risk rejection and be prepared to trust in the good will of the other. He is not. For Bob, sex aims solely at physical gratification. Exploitation of others is fair game. And, since others may exploit him, Bob remains ever vigilant not to let this happen to him. In Bob's version of the world, sex is a dog-eat-dog affair. As long as things remain like this for Bob, sexual intimacy and satisfaction will always remain beyond his reach. Erotic love is out of the question.

People like Bob never experience sexual intimacy. For those who mature, sexual intimacy can lead to bigger and better things, perhaps to erotic love itself. Before sexual intimacy can evolve into erotic love, however, there must be a development of both emotional and intellectual intimacy.

Emotional Intimacy

It is not uncommon to encounter a couple who have been sexually intimate for weeks, even months but neither mistakes their relationship for love. They respect and trust each other (as far as sexual intimacy is concerned); still, that is not enough for erotic love to bloom. Far more potent than sexual intimacy is emotional intimacy. Consider, for example, the following account of Frank, a hospital chaplain who found himself smitten by a woman with whom he had never shared a bed (nay, even a kiss!).

> This was all very disturbing to me. I had been married for twenty-three years. I thought I was happy all along and at no point could I find fault with my wife. It just seemed I had fallen out of love with her.
>
> I counsel people who are dying, likely to die or have a family member who is dying. This is emotionally very draining. I used to come home and tell my wife about my day's strains. We would talk at dinner. Several years ago, we discontinued these dinner talks because we felt it was too much for our three pubescent children to deal with.
>
> I began running after work with a young nurse. For two years, we met three or four times a week and would run for six to nine miles together. During that time, we shared with each other all the emotional victories and defeats of working all day long with cancer patients. After about six months, I began developing very tender feelings toward this girl. I really didn't worry about it at first. I believed this to be a natural consequence of the deep friendship we had developed. I saw myself as a faithful and loyal husband so there was no problem. This girl was simply a dear friend who happened to be female. As time went on, I found myself looking at her more and more fondly. Sometimes our eyes would exchange glances that struck me as dangerous, frightening and, worst of all, very loving.
>
> I found I had less and less to tell my wife. She would ask why I never talked to her anymore. I'd shrug my shoulders and say "There's nothing to talk about—just the same old routine." I don't believe I was being deceitful. It just hadn't occurred to me that I had talked everything out during the hour and a half to two hours I had been with my running partner.
>
> My interest in conjugal relations with my wife also began to wane. This I took to be a sign of age and not a symptom of an imperiled relationship, that is, until I started dreaming about intercourse with my running partner. Suddenly, it seemed everything was becoming confused. I felt so intensely close to my running partner it only seemed right that we make love. Our conversations hinted ever more strongly that one day we should

become lovers, that we were in love and needed to consummate it. I began to contemplate leaving my wife. Our marriage was quite obviously a mere shell of what it had been.

My wife sensed that I had left her emotionally and spiritually. What was I to do? I felt sorry for her. I loved my kids. I saw myself as a pillar of the community, an exemplary father and husband. I was supposed to have strength of character and honor. I taught others about the importance of commitment. Now I seemed to be turning my back on all this. What was wrong? Was I to be excused? All that I had done was fall in love. It was innocent enough. I never set out to betray anyone. God must have intended my new love or it would have never occurred as it did. After almost two years, I told my wife all that I was feeling. She was distraught, and I knew I had to make one last try at putting it all together.

I sought out the resources of a scholar. Not a psychologist, psychiatrist or other social scientist, but rather a humanities type who studied the human expressions of passions of the heart. This person made me realize there are different types of intimacy. I realized that by sharing my deepest emotional experiences with my running partner and denying those same experiences to my wife, I had all but guaranteed my sense of "falling in love" with the former and "falling out of love" with the latter.

For three months, I discontinued all contact with the nurse. I ran each night in my neighborhood and shortly before bed told my wife of the trials and tribulations of the day. After a couple of months, I found myself rediscovering the special bond I had with the original love of my life. I suppose it had always been there and only seemed to disappear because I had innocently, but systematically, begun to suffocate it. Sexual desire returned to our relationship. I rarely think of the nurse now and when I do, I recall her as a nice person but not as anything more. Our once innocent friendship came close to destroying many lives, and I think we both know that now. She will find her own love one day. For my part, I have twenty-three years invested in my one shot at a forever marriage. I will never again take it for granted.

Fidelity should not be thought of simply in terms of restricted sexual behavior. My running partner and I never kissed and never even held hands. Our dangerous liaison consisted solely in giving each other privileged access to the secrets of our heart and soul. In the long run, I think the temptation to become physically intimate with another is much easier to avoid than is the temptation to continue a relationship with one who has shared your deepest emotions. The longer you are married, the deeper your love for one another becomes. Nevertheless, one can never forget to nourish that bond daily. One can never risk imperiling it by active neglect.

Frank's story is exquisitely told and very revealing. In the book *Private Lies*, psychiatrist Frank Pittman points out even after a sexual indiscretion by one spouse, a relationship can often be saved if the couple seeks counseling and embraces a policy of total honesty. Infidelity of the body is survivable. The infidelity of the heart is far more devastating to a relationship even when it involves no sexual activity!

Of the three intimacies bonding couples, emotional intimacy is by far the most potent because it's connected to the most important of human emotions, trust. The ability to share one's deepest emotion with another is a direct function of the trust each has in the other. This is why therapists devote most of their time in the first few sessions with a patient to establishing a bond of trust. Only after trust is established can the patient reveal to the therapist the labyrinth of his or her emotional life. Trust leads people to become friends and sexual partners to become lovers. As the sense of reciprocated trust between people deepens, usually as a result of sharing ever more revealing secrets with one another, so does the intensity of the emotional commitment the two share.

People can fail to see eye to eye on many issues and yet sustain a marriage or enjoy a spectacular sexual liaison. But no marriage can sustain chronic distrust and only the strongest can weather an episode of acute distrust. Similarly, friendships and romances are more readily destroyed by a lapse of trust than by any other event.

The more people trust one another, the more they tend to share secrets of the heart and soul with one another. The more they share secrets of the soul with one another the more they sense a growing bond of affection for each other. The more their affection grows, the more likely they are to fall in love. Indeed, the therapist-client relationship is instructive here. The *competent* therapist is trustworthy. The patient learns to sense this and opens up. As the therapy moves toward a successful conclusion, the client enjoys enhanced self-esteem and a sense that a special bonding has developed between one human being and another. This special bonding is often mistaken for love. The client and the conscientious therapist must be always vigilant to disabuse the patient of this misperception. The bond of trust and the sharing of secrets provokes the misplaced feelings of love in these cases. Trust inaugurates emotional intimacy; secrets serve as its currency.

Trust and its full blown realization, emotional intimacy, are so much a part of the experience of love few people can distinguish between the two in their daily lives. The two are different, however. Emotional intimacy is far more expansive, covering a vast range of reactions to the world. Trust is but the bedrock upon which expressions of emotional intimacy flourish.

Intellectual Intimacy

Whereas emotional intimacy is principally concerned with sharing affairs of heart and soul, intellectual intimacy is concerned with affairs of the mind. People who share intellectual intimacy think alike. This is not to say each understands the world in a way identical to the other. Rather, it means they share something of the same worldview and something of the same techniques for adding to or deleting from that picture. Consider for example, the following story.

Karen, a clinical psychologist, agreed to let a university intern work with her for a semester to gain some practical insight into clinical work in a hospital setting. The young intern was an eager and earnest disciple. Karen and Randy, her intern, each loved the world of clinical psychology. Each delighted in figuring out ways to help people negotiate the trauma of ill health. The two spent many long hours together discussing individual cases and speculating about general principles of psychology and physical illness. Before the semester was over, they began sharing information about the feelings each experienced when counseling patients. Eventually, they began looking to one another with feelings that seemed to beg for sexual attention. Karen reports:

> I was delighted with how serious he was about his work. His questions ignited in me a passion for my work that I had lost years ago. He was the first man I encountered, since my divorce two years earlier, who really wanted to understand the distorted world of traumatized patients. There was so much I could teach him and so many new insights he provided me. I don't know when we began developing romantic feelings for one another. For so long, it seemed we were friends and ideal workmates. I'm not quite sure when

romantic feelings entered the relationship. One day while having dinner after work, it suddenly became evident to us both that we would shortly make love to one another.

The romance continues even though he is younger than I and not yet established in his field. What we share seems so much more superior to what keeps more traditional relationships together. When he finishes his degree and finds a job, I suspect there is a good chance we will marry.

Karen and Randy began their relationship through sharing in a common interest. Neither at first was particularly interested in the physical appearance of the other and neither was particularly concerned about the emotional predisposition of the other. The gateway to this romance was a *shared* interest in a world of ideas.

Intellectual intimacy, like each of the other two intimacies, results from sharing. In this case, Karen shared with Randy her advanced knowledge and formidable experience. For his part, Randy listened and readily shared his fresh insights into a world Karen had long become accustomed to. Each gave to the other. Each joyously received from the other. This reciprocity is necessary for intimacy. In contrast, "give and take" relationships share interests in the way businesses barter trade agreements.

The sharing that builds intimacy occurs when people freely give to each other, with no expectation of return. What is given must be received without immediate calculation on either part of how the giver can then be repaid. Karen's ideas were treasured by Randy. Reciprocally, his fresh insights were treasured by Karen. The intellectual intimacy developed between Karen and Randy led to other intimacies. The sharing of intimacies continued to expand until they found themselves in the midst of something they believed to be erotic love.

No discussion of intellectual intimacy is complete without some mention of its occurrence in the academic world. The trek from intellectual intimacy to sexual intimacy has been a favorite topic for script writers and novelists. From *My Tutor* to *Notes on a Scandal*, romance between professor and student is projected as rather commonplace. Indeed, even the wholesome and money-grabbing character of Alex Keaton in the television sitcom *Family Ties* found his greatest love in a college class for which he was acting as a teaching assistant. Occasionally, one even reads newspaper accounts of high school students marrying a favorite teacher.

Having spent most of the past thirty-five years in the academic world, I must note the popular picture created by the media is grossly misleading. Romance between teacher and student is not particularly common. One reason is academics tend to be a puritan-minded, married group. Another reason is such affairs generally reflect a certain impropriety. There are a few promiscuous types who abuse the privilege of office, but for the most part academics are a trustworthy, conscientious and conservative lot. The temptation to be otherwise is, however, great.

Professors are attracted to anyone who displays an interest in what is typically the instructor's greatest passion, his or her discipline. Students who learn they have great passion for study in a certain field often revere the person who first awakened their passion. Professor and student, professor and professor, or student and student possessing two such complementary passions tend to seek each other's company. What begins as a common intellectual passion can lead to the development of other intimacies as well.

Pursuit of intellectual intimacy with another is not a bad thing. For example, it may lead the young student to match or surpass the accomplishments of a mentor. This was the case with Plato and his mentor Socrates and later Aristotle with his mentor Plato. It may lead to successful collaborations both productive and romantic as in the case of Marie and Pierre Curie. But it also leads to tragedy. The tragedy occurs when one person's love for a gift of intellect is confused with loving, in unreciprocated fashion, the entirety of the other *person*. Tragedy also results when the person with superior power exploits the intellectual intimacy shared with a junior for transient self-serving sexual pleasure. On more than one occasion, such acts of exploitation have led the junior partner to give up his or her intellectual interests when the sexual interest is abandoned.

Cases wherein intellectual intimacy leads to other intimacies must be distinguished from less romantic situations wherein have-nots are trying to become "haves." For example, a wealth of knowledge can be a powerful aphrodisiac to some people just as power and financial wealth is to others. But in each of these cases, the allure is not a quest for intimacy of any kind. It is a simple quest for power or to be in the presence of power. The bold and ugly truth is various sorts of wealth often distract from romance and love. They seldom serve to enhance it. Consider the following account of Brenda, a young student now floundering about searching for renewed purpose in life. At twenty-four, this statuesque woman works at a variety of modeling assignments and waitressing jobs. She dropped out of school just one semester from graduation three years ago. She recounts the following story:

> Professor Lyons was the most impressive man I ever met. In addition to possessing great knowledge of his own discipline, he knew about the sciences, history, literature and the arts. One could bring up almost any subject, common or esoteric, and somehow Dr. Lyons would conjure up the most profound insights in just a minute or two. I would pester him, asking him to recommend materials I might read. Initially, he seemed barely tolerant of my efforts to raid his mind. But as it became evident that I was reading all that he recommended, he became more patient with me. His respect for me grew to the point where he invited me to critique passages from manuscripts he was writing. I found this to be the most flattering experience of my life.
>
> Shortly thereafter, I fell in love with him. I think he sensed it because he seemed embarrassed by my continued persistence in seeking his counsel. As time passed, I sensed he was weakening. I became a huntress and this sometimes pompous and sometimes bashful genius was my prey. One night, we consummated our affection, and then, twice more the following week. Suddenly, he refused to see me. I sent him notes and phoned. Finally, he answered the phone one day when I called. I think he was expecting a call from someone else. I asked him why he was disappearing from my life. He explained that the age difference between us was great, too great, and that he had no business inviting himself into my heart. He apologized for taking advantage of my passion for learning and allowing me to think it was him that I loved and not the subject matter. I was heartbroken; I lost interest in school, the subject, even in reading for pleasure. I got involved with drugs for a while and just "hung out."
>
> I think I'm getting my life back together now, but I know I'll never have another love like him. Sometimes I get very angry at him still. I think he should have known what was happening to me and should have done something to stop it. I made all the advances, but if he knew all along that he couldn't love me in return, he should have ended our friendship before it became too complicated. He had been a bachelor for a number of years, and I'm sure affairs of the heart are not new to him.

This example is very revealing for several reasons. First, as Brenda admits, she proved to be the aggressor. Professor Lyons was pulled into the affair reluctantly, grudgingly and with much trepidation about Brenda's and his own motivations. It is easy to sympathize with Lyons since it does not appear he sought a liaison with Brenda but only acquiesced to her pursuit. Still his experience "as a bachelor for a number of years" and as a professor should have alerted him to the dangers of becoming too intimately involved with a student—*even on a strictly intellectual level*. The danger emerges from the fact the intimacies are intimately related to one another!

Sharing an intimacy of one sort with a potential soulmate leads, in compelling fashion, to sharing intimacies of another sort. This phenomenon is dramatically portrayed in the movie *Dangerous Liaisons* wherein a rogue, Valmont, romances an innocent noblewoman for no other reason than to add her to his list of sexual conquests. To become sexually intimate with her, Valmont begins by establishing an intellectual intimacy. As he pursues his prey, he finds himself becoming emotionally intimate with her as well. By the time he secures his sexual conquest, he discovers he has shared too much with her and is genuinely in love. Such a terrible state for a rascal to be in! In short, intellectual intimacy (as well as each of the other two intimacies) is entangled with the other complementary intimacies. Dynamic and potentially intense relationships exist among the three intimacies, and it is to those interrelationships I shall now turn.

The Interdependence of the Intimacies

The three intimacies are so tightly interwoven that experiences of one intimacy invites, indeed often compels, pursuit of each of the other intimacies. This intrigue of the intimacies may: (1) be threatening to individuals and (2) it may also be damaging to relationships. When properly understood and successfully exploited, it is also (3) the most powerful source of sharing people experience. The intrigue of the intimacies is immensely important in the development of erotic love. Consider first the situation in which intimacy is seen as a threat to the individual.

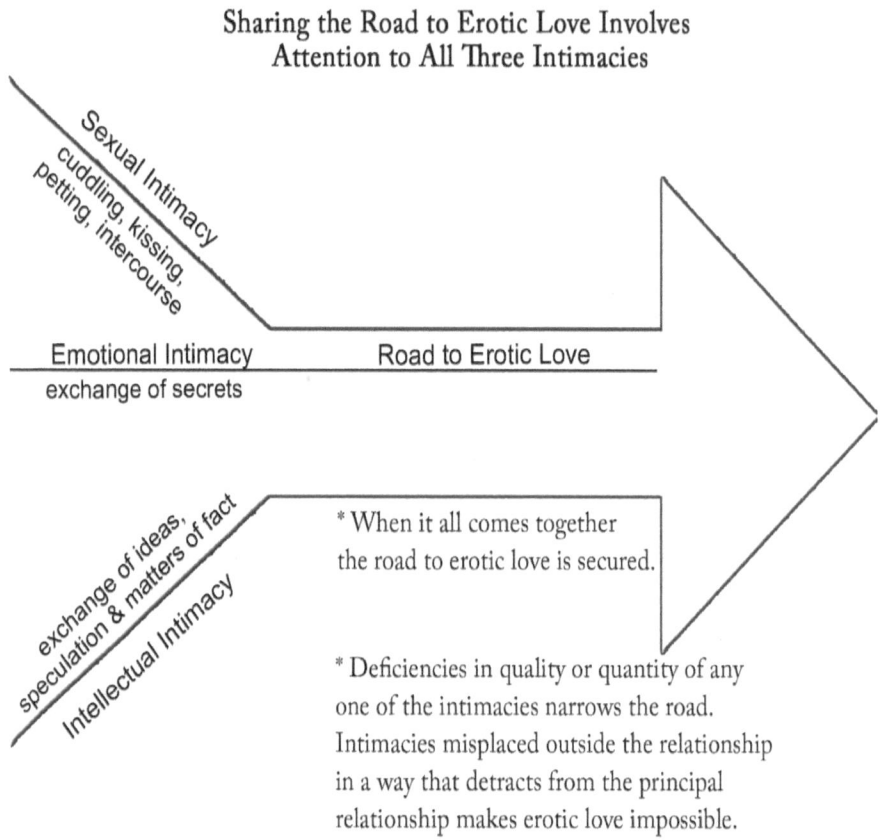

Intimacy: The Threat to Individuals

Prominent people are fully aware betrayal by a confidant can destroy their public image and career and, therefore, they weigh their words carefully when speaking publicly. To be candid is to risk betrayal. The only consideration warranting such risk is trust, which can only be extended to a special few and is a measure of intimacy. Once such an intimacy is established, emotional intimacy is always tempting and finally, with a sexually acceptable confidant, sexual intimacy becomes possible. As intimacy expands, so does personal vulnerability. Thus, for these people, simple intellectual candor can be foreboding of great personal harm. Best just to avoid such risks.

Ordinary people—men perhaps more than women—most fear the inappropriate sharing of emotional intimacy. Once a person shares his or her emotional secrets, he or she risks betrayal. When intimate relationships end on a sour note, it is not uncommon for a jilted lover or estranged friend to use previously held secrets to reap vengeance. Once betrayed, one is unlikely to divulge such personal secrets again.

Even when estranged friends and lovers act honorably, keeping each other's secrets, it is eerie to think so much of your private stock of treasures is carried about by someone who no longer values them. Betrayed lovers may never again want to share emotional insights with others. They may retreat from the dating world altogether or adopt a "love 'em and leave 'em" lifestyle. The one harms only themselves while the other harms other innocents.

Eventually, people who fear one of the intimacies in particular discover in order to avoid risk of the feared intimacy, one must avoid the other two intimacies as well. It is impossible to carry out this sterile approach to life in the long run. Consider the following account of David, a forty-three-year old land management account executive.

David was handsome and athletic. He had been divorced twice. In each case, his wife initiated the divorce. David saw himself as a good and loyal husband, but in each marriage his spendthrift ways brought him to the brink of bankruptcy. David admits each wife tried to rehabilitate his sense of financial responsibility, and yet David failed to change. In each case, he and his wife argued their way to divorce. David was very hurt by each divorce (the second even more than the first). He is again single and sought after by a number of attractive women. David's approach to dating is as follows:

> I'm not going to risk getting hurt again. I don't really blame my wives. Heck, they never knew from month to month whether it was going to be feast or famine. And given my proclivity for spending, even when I made a lot of money, things still turned out to be famine! Even so, when you are single, single women all sympathize with you, and they assure you they would never leave a man they loved just because he went broke. They say that when you're single. But just wait until you marry one and see what happens! As far as I'm concerned, I enjoy women's company and I love sex, but I'm not going to get involved with anyone ever again.

Three months later, I inquired into David's view of women, trust and so on. He replied:

I still feel the way I did before. In fact, I'm just about to break up with a girl who is perfectly wonderful and who wants to get married or at least live together. I've even told her I have no interest in getting attached to anyone and that I view our arrangement as principally sexual and a little bit of friendship. I have to admit, I really respect the girl and if I hadn't been stung twice before, I might risk marriage. But I've been there, and I never need to go back. In fact, I know I can't stay in this relationship. It's not fair to her, and besides, the longer you stay with something like this the more you feel you are supposed to be together. I just have to get out.

Seven months later, I again interviewed David.

Business has been great! I just bought a red BMW 325. I broke up with the girl I told you about before. I dated a few others, but things have a way of turning complicated. I just can't hack it anymore. I haven't had a date in over a month, and I haven't had sex in nearly three months.

You know sex is the problem. Once they get you in bed, they think they can start controlling you. Actually, the real problem is they are right. I've really lost interest in sex, and I've discovered I'm much better off as a result. I have unbelievable freedom. I enjoy being free of responsibilities and not having to answer to anyone else.

If business keeps going as it is, I may open a lodge somewhere in Wyoming and just opt out of this dating and city life altogether. There just isn't anything to be gained by getting your life tangled up with another.

David's assessment of dating is surprisingly common. Two other well-known bachelors I met have similarly disavowed further interest in sex, and this was after ten years or more of apparently successful Don Juanism. Each of these individuals believes himself to have greater independence as a result of dismissing sex from his life and, in that, each is indeed right. On the other hand, is the cost of such independence a good thing? Certainly not for the romantic. If one has a talent for sharing life with another, one cannot exercise that talent without risking intimacy. To suffocate a talent is to destroy a bit of one's life. David and others like him are engaged in a type of self-destruction. One is reminded of Janis Joplin's song "Me and Bobbie Magee" wherein she wails "Freedom is when you have nothing more to lose!"

Although in their mid-forties and well acquainted with the lifestyle of singles, David and the others do not recognize their treasured "freedom" is just the flip-side of their fear of intimacy. After years of admittedly unsatisfying sex free from emotional and intellectual risk, they refuse to recognize satisfactory sexual intimacy requires openness to the other two intimacies. The freedom they gain by avoiding sex is not solely freedom from a woman's controlling ways. It is also freedom from any opportunity to share with others emotionally and intellectually.

Sex is not merely a matter of biological responsiveness. It is a social phenomenon compelling us to trust, take risks, become vulnerable to rejection by others, and be responsible for how we treat others. From the earliest moments of sexual arousal to sexual satisfaction, people are compelled to confront their partners as emotional and intellectual equals. Each sexual partner is in a position to enhance the other's enjoyment and self-esteem or to attack and damage it.

Sexual intimacy, as much as emotional intimacy and intellectual intimacy, stands at the gateway to full-fledged intimacy, intimacy involving extensive sharing, love and commitment. More than anything else, these people fear repeated betrayal, rejection and abandonment. The interrelatedness of the three intimacies makes it impossible for them to play freely in one arena without risking exposure to the complications inherent in all the intimacies together.

Intimacy: The Threat to Relationships

Just as each intimacy is a threat to unmitigated individualism, new intimacies are ever a threat to pre-existing relationships. When intimacies are developed outside an intended relationship, the relationship is endangered. The intellectual intimacy of the student/mentor relationship, the emotional intimacy of good friends, work associates, and running partners can easily evolve into a full range of intimacies. When, for example, one of the intimates is already married or otherwise involved in a more or less permanent relationship, a burgeoning intimacy outside the relationship diminishes proportionally intimacy within the relationship. In like fashion, loyalty to a group may also threaten an individual member's capacity for intimacy with a beloved. Individuals can become intimately connected to a peer group and disconnected from a beloved. It takes time to invest in intimacy. If your time is misspent, your investment in an intimate relationship will cease bearing dividends. Thus, the nature of one's group affiliations can be as important to the flourishing of a relationship as one's affiliations with other individuals.

Sociologists have long noted the inclination to marry and divorce are a function of what others are doing in one's circle of friends. For example, a group of men may prize their friendship and the one for all and all for one spirit they maintained throughout law school and their early years of professional employment. Within a year's time, it is not surprising to find, say, five out of seven in a group marry. This is accounted for only in part by the fact these men may be of marrying age and this is the sort of thing twenty- to forty-year-old men do. The fact such a high percentage within that group marry is also indicative of the influence the group exerts over the individual. The same is true of divorce. The divorce of one friend seems to contaminate the marriages of all the friends. The appeal of divorce and return to single life moves through a group of friends almost like an infection. It is not surprising to find, say, six women working together, all married, and then, a year or two later, discover four have divorced and the other two believe their marriages are in trouble.

Friendship among members of the same sex or with someone of the opposite sex who is much older or much younger is a form of intimacy that by nature is limited. Either emotional or intellectual intimacy may be present in friendship and in the best of friendships, both are present. What is conspicuously absent is any inclination to expand one's reciprocal interests into the sexual domain. While distinctly limited, such friendships are demanding and may influence the unlimited intimacy of a marriage.

When the intrigues, world-views and feelings of friends contrast sharply with those of a spouse or a lover, an advance in intimacy on one side can only be at the cost of diminished intimacy on the other side. For example, if friends' counsel a specific protocol for money management contrary to the protocol advocated by a spouse, the resulting tension is resolved by abandoning not just the advice but also, to a degree, one or the other sources of intimacy. The longer one waits to resolve this tension, the more likely the person will be to experience a loss of self and sense of control. When sources of intimacy come into conflict, it is not that one source must be judged right and the other wrong; rather it is one's status as a trustworthy, predictable and reliable compatriot which is at issue. Friends expect their counsel to be respected. They may say that does not mean acquiescence to their advice, but after counsel is sought friends want to know why their recommendations were not acted upon. The person seeking advice must not only make a decision about which counsel to follow but also how to tell other advisors why their advice was ignored. This creates tension and anxiety. It may even diminish the strength of the bond between the person seeking advice and the advisors whose counsel was found wanting.

Intimacy demands trust. The individual balancing competing claims feels forced to present a false front to one or the other competing sources of advice. When this happens, the individual feels he or she is somehow less trustworthy in the eyes of the friend whose advice seemed inadequate. The individual may then begin to feel the only honorable thing to do is to end a previously rewarding intimacy.

In short, any intimacy *beyond the marriage* represents potential conflict *within the marriage*. This is not to say conflict is inevitable or one should avoid any form of intimacy outside the marriage. It is only to caution the potential for conflict exists, and people who care about all their intimate associations should remain ever vigilant to these possibilities. Even with such cautions in mind, do not forget there is a positive side to maintaining a network of intimacies. When various intimacies complement one another, each can serve to strengthen the other. Friends supportive of the institution of marriage can help an individual through many a difficult time with a spouse. On the other hand, when one's friends lack respect for marriage or any other relationship requiring unmitigated commitment, their lack of support can do much to further sever the relationship.

Intimacy: Successfully Exploited

When a person's most intimate friends support his or her commitment to marriage (or a similar relationship), the relationship is enriched. Intimate friends can nurture a couple's decision to grow together and to share even more with one another. Good friends can help the couple see there are two ways of sharing. The first involves bartering to distribute equitably the couple's common goods. Since this may be as important in dismantling a relationship as well as assembling one, it is hardly unique to healthy evolving relationships. The second sharing is more appropriate for marriage-minded types. It is helpful to think of this sharing as *intimate sharing* which involves giving of oneself emotionally, intellectually and physically with no expectation of immediate return. It requires each spouse to feel comfortable receiving goods from a mate while feeling no immediate need to compensate the other. Wholly intimate people give of their heart, mind and body without regard to calculation of an equitable return. Intimacy grows because intimates feel FREE TO TRUST each other. They feel protective of each other's interests and DUTY BOUND never to betray the other's trust. Good friends know the reciprocity of complete intimacy is a need of every married couple. Truly good friends try to nurture the couple, *as a couple*, without trying to extract anything in return from the couple or either spouse.

Intimacy is a powerful force. Many veterans of love trauma fear its power to destroy individual personhood. Others fear wayward intimacies can destroy relationships already properly in progress. There is a third group who understand the positive and productive power of the intimacies, knowing the most valuable thing the intimacies do is nourish promising and fulfilling marriages. All appreciate the peerless potency of human intimacy.

Just as good sex between lovers is enhanced by mutual trust, the temporary absence of sex is made more endurable by trusting the motives of the other. When trust is displayed as gracefully in the face of the spouse's declination as it is in his or her acceptance, intimacy flourishes. With or without intercourse, the manner in which spouses manage their sex life can always be turned into an asset when it comes to developing intimacy.

Trust and Patience

Trust not only forms the foundation for each intimacy it also *serves as the path from one intimacy to another*. And since it is *the collective sharing of the intimacies which makes erotic love possible*, trust is an essential bond for people to establish before they marry. Once marriage and erotic love are entered into, loving couples find nurturing trust ensures their bonding will be rewarding and eternal.

Trustworthiness is a very special virtue. A bond of trust between two trustworthy people makes intimacy possible. Trust requires each spouse to have the other's interest close to heart. This does not require each spouse to acquiesce in every request made by the other nor does it mean in every dispute compromises must be negotiated. When you truly have a spouse's interests close to heart, formal negotiation becomes unappealing and seldom necessary. Where trust and love abound, Romeo's interest in Juliet's well-being is very nearly equal to her own self-interest. Similarly, Juliet's self-interest is very nearly co-extensive with her interest in Romeo's well-being. When trusting, loving couples approach the threshold of dispute, a moment of patient reflection may avoid the anxiety of confrontation.

Patience is not part of the bond making a couple a couple. In other words, it is not the same as trust, intimacy or the eventual consequence, erotic love. Patience is always a valuable character trait for lovers and non-lovers alike. Patient people are not given to folly and are less likely to grieve over past mistakes. This is important in romance. For example, when lovers are patient with one another, the rate at which their love grows and their differences resolve is noticeably increased. Patience is a lubricant for greasing the wheels of a well-working relationship. Its absence, however, is not an insurmountable flaw.

Exercise for Nurturing Intimacy

While intimacies developing outside the bond of marriage may represent a threat to the union, attending to the evolving intimacies within the union is the surest guarantee of securing a successful common project.

When two people freely assume the responsibilities of forging a common life project, it becomes important for them to act in ways that *advances love in the direction they intend.* In the early stages of romance, it is all too easy to believe emotions just "happen," that they just drive one forward to action. Surely, there are times when people find themselves in the grip of an emotion so powerful it seems to hurl them forward without regard to consequence. Such is the case of the person who discovers his or her spouse in bed with another and in an uncontrollable rage murders one or both of the conspirators. The tyranny of the emotions is so dominant in such a scenario that most countries recognize it as a form of "temporary insanity" and excuse the murderer of wrongdoing. In less exotic circumstances, it is not the emotions which push and pull people toward the projects they undertake but rather *it is what people say and do,* which sustains, enhances or even creates the emotions they experience. For example, psychologists and family therapists often cite the disparate rate of divorce among adult children of alcoholics as evidence of the influence of what we say and do. The ACA often finds no matter how promising the conditions of the original marriage, he or she moves through the relationship with a little voice whispering, "This cannot last," "This will not work," or "I can't do this." Consequently, the marriage ultimately flounders, not because it was not made of the "right stuff" or because emotional vistas suddenly shifted. The marriage fails because the ACA repeatedly prophesied its failure. The continual prophesies producing emotional trauma accumulate and eventually rot away the sustaining foundations of intimacy. Following are recommendations for saying and doing the sorts of things which nourish trust and intimacy. As feelings of trust and intimacy intensify, they inspire transcendence to deeper experiences of erotic love. Trust and trust alone, affords fertile ground for developing intimacy. The exchange of the goods of intimacy accumulate without limit. The loving couple with twenty years of fruitful marriage possesses a treasure incomparable to that they possessed in the earliest years of their marriage.

The first and most important task for each seeker after erotic love is to strive for empathy with your mate. In the early days of romance, you may each be crazy about the other but there was little sense of what it means to *feel as the other feels* and to *think as the other thinks*. When this begins to occur, you may fancy you have already reached erotic love. This is certainly the right way to go about it, but in the months in which these feelings are first spawned you barely approach the threshold through which such feelings can turn into erotic love. To learn to empathize with your spouse requires you learn as much as possible about him or her. The longer your spouse has lived, the more richly textured his or her life, the more challenging (and rewarding) your task. Since personal knowledge of another is strictly privileged, access to that knowledge is both a function and a barometer of the trust existing between you. Reciprocated trust and knowledge of your spouse can proceed.

Empathy requires each try to imagine parts of the world as your spouse reports to see them and as he or she claims to feel them. Since you can never relive your mate's experiences *as* he or she lived them, the quest for empathy will never be complete. Still, the longer you are together and the longer you each attempt to learn what the other thinks, imagines and feels, the more nearly you each will "get it right." It is instructive to recount the experiences of others you know who failed to get it right, who failed to empathize with one another.

How often have you encountered a divorcee who, in a nostalgic moment, laments the destruction of a previous marriage? At thirty-four, Melinda, divorced from Rex after a seven-year marriage, complained:

> A mutual friend recently related to me how much Rex was surprised at the turn in my life since the divorce. A year after we married, I quit work and became a housewife. A year later, we had our first child and from that point on, Rex complained about how disorganized I was. At first, it seemed like a game. Something you kid each other about. After a few years, it became definitive of who I was or at least who I was supposed to be! The really irritating thing is that I really started acting the role.
>
> When Rex divorced me, he said he was exhausted from my scatter-brained approach to life. My first job after the divorce was as a truck dispatcher. A few months ago, I was named director of routing for the firm. The fact of the matter is that I am extremely well organized by nature. What started as a harmless joke turned my life and then our marriage into a joke.
>
> I understand from our mutual friend that Rex has said if I had been so organized while we were married, we would never have divorced and that he could easily love me as I am now. Can you believe this guy?!

A parallel story is recounted by Drew, a fifty-four-year old systems analyst:

> Liz and I had been married for twenty-three years. We were very much in love at first. But for the last ten years or more, Liz never stopped complaining about me. Principal among her complaints was the (supposed) fact that I was so insensitive. My girlfriend of the past two years has encouraged me in my painting and together we have been very active in raising money for Greenpeace. My ex-wife cannot believe I enjoy these things and thinks I am just doing them to impress my girlfriend.

> I was always interested in art. I've always had a social conscience. I could never find room to express these interests in the onslaught of her daily criticism. If she had only let me express myself, she would have found that there was much more to me than she ever allowed.
>
> Now that I'm free of her, I would never go back. She may think I've changed and am just what she always wanted, but the fact is that I haven't changed. I'm just enjoying the opportunity to be me. She'll never find a man she thinks is sensitive because she'll never pay attention to his efforts at self-expression.

In each case, the couples stopped listening, stopped being fully attentive towards the self-expression of their spouses. Melinda and Rex, and Drew and Liz sensed themselves "drifting apart," "growing in different directions" or, to employ one more well-worn cliché, "failing to grow apace of one another." The fact is, Melinda and Drew did possess the traits their spouses thought so important. How could their spouses be so blind? Simple. They just stopped trying to imagine what mattered in the hearts and minds of their beloved.

This problem of failing to notice the virtues of a mate is underscored by philosopher Richard Rorty in his book *Contingency Irony and Solidarity*. Rorty describes a passage from Nabokov's *Lolita* in which the character Humbert discovers only accidentally his beloved, Lolita, has a deep interest in death. Death is a very profound topic usually provoking conversation only among long-time intimates. But to the genuinely shallow and insensitive Humbert upon overhearing Lolita's ruminations, his only response is to snort, "I simply did not know a thing about my darling's mind," and "Quite possibly, behind the awful juvenile clichés, there was in her a garden and a twilight, and a palace gate—dim and adorable regions which happened to be lucidly and absolutely forbidden to me . . . "Humbert never got the romance he desired to have with Lolita because he never learned to listen, to empathize and to imagine the world from her perspective.

Divorcees often discover, after all is lost, erotic love had been within their grasp. Had they only attended to their ex's perspective and discovered how well it matched with their own, they may have found fertile soil for creating a durable marriage, and now, that promise is truly lost.

Building a Common Life Project — From Romance to Erotic Love

Stage 0. **Engagement** — Two people are fascinated by one another and want to build a common life project.

Stage 1. **Beginning a Successful Marriage** — Two people loosely affiliated with one another; addressing the world as a pair.

Stage 2. **Intersecting Interests** — As the marriage proceeds, the couple share more interests together, far more so than as friends or business partners. For example, they assume legal liabilities for one another, make major purchases together, develop shared eating habits, engage other couples AS couples AND, perhaps, start a family or assume genuine interests in children the other brought to the marriage.

Stage 3. **Eroding Boundaries I** — Not only does each spouse have an interest common to the other but the identity of interests as his, hers and "his and hers" begins to erode and become "ours." At this stage, the fear of losing one's identity by blending with and extending common horizons with another diminishes.

Stage 4. **Advanced Erosion of Boundaries** — The blending of self-interest evolves to a point at which each trusts the other's self-interest is identified in large part with that of the spouse.

Stage 5. **Erotic Love** — At this stage, the common life project becomes more encompassing than each individual life project alone even when the two are added together. Fear of individual loss of identity is absent and boundaries between the two are minimal. Each individual feels he or she is made "bigger" because of the richness the marriage extends to both.

It is tragic to hear divorcees bewail the fact that had they known of an ex's "latent" interest or feelings while they were married the two would " . . . probably still be married." The tragedy is interests or feelings remain "latent" only when spouses stop querying one another about them. Maybe a husband and wife stop talking because each thinks the terrain of conversation has already been well traversed. But just as repeated reading of a good book produces new insights, so repeated conversations with a beloved reveal more and more about the unfolding of his or her life narrative.

The moral here is learning to empathize is a never ending task. The more you attempt it, the better you'll get. Empathy is the product of continuing the dialogue and dialogue is a two-way street. You'll rarely get more from a lover than you're willing to reveal about yourself.

Psychiatrist Frank Pittman warns he has seen no truth as destructive to a marriage as the smallest deliberate lie. Lies corrupt the couple's quest for shared empathy. You can only empathize with someone you trust. Lies are a direct assault on trust itself. Lying does not make trust difficult; it makes it impossible. Without trust, there can be no empathy. Without empathy, there are no grounds for shared imagination. Without shared imaginations, there are no grounds for intimacy and erotic love.

Do individuals in a common life project lose all rights to individual privacy where a soulmate is concerned? No. Such a demand would require more than most are willing to give and would deprive the relationship of the gift of one person freely sharing his or her secrets with the other. As your relationship proceeds, maybe not in years, perhaps not for several decades, but eventually, you and your spouse will gradually extend to each other privileged access to all "secrets." The rate at which this occurs is a matter of each person's choosing. The sharing of a secret is itself an act of lovemaking. A secret's effect on a spouse is a function of its timeliness as well as its content. In one way or another, the sharing of secrets will nearly always advance the cause of erotic love. Share what you can, when you can, but never deceive your mate about that which you want to keep secret.

Sharing secrets is the most important way couples have for nourishing emotional intimacy. People need to trust, to really trust, in order to share their most sacred secrets. Trust evolves; it does not burst on the scene. There is no way to hasten the pace. Refusal to lie, even when seemingly entrapped by a lover, displays personal integrity. There is no greater inducement to trust than the bold display of integrity. The greater your show of personal integrity, the more your spouse will trust you.

The conscientious pursuit of a virtue such as personal integrity reflects reliability. The more reliable you are, the more comfortable your spouse will feel his or her trust is appropriately placed. Since success is now defined in terms of the couples' progress, rather than the individual's, it is important you each have an accurate sense of just how much you can count on one other in the broadest range of eventualities.

Martha and Robert, both divorcees, seemed to be perfectly suited for one another. Each was intelligent, successful, attractive, honest, and of relatively high personal integrity when compared to the population at large. To everyone around them their relationship seemed like the one heaven ordained for all others to model. Yet at the end of their third year of marriage, they divorced. In Martha's words:

> Robert is completely unpredictable. I love him dearly, and I have no reason to believe he has ever been unfaithful to me. But he never seems that far away from a dalliance. He has always been there when I needed him, but he always manages to do so in a way that keeps me guessing: will he be there the next time? Finally, the doubt became too much. I still love him, and I have no idea how I can manage without him. On the other hand, I have no idea how I can manage with him and, at this point, it seems he is perfectly prepared to go on without me.

For his part Robert protested:

> I never did feel she wanted to be part of me. She liked the idea of "us" and how we appeared together, but I was never sure she would be there if those around us no longer seemed so impressed with how we appeared. I really don't want this divorce, but in the end I suppose it is the best thing.

Robert and Martha seemingly began with all the "right stuff." Each was a good catch and each was committed to the other. Neither knew how to move beyond the point of romance. Neither knew how to build a common life project with the other even though each very much desired to do so. This marriage continued as a romance with each apparently maneuvering to arouse or sustain the emotional interest of the other. Throughout all this, the unpredictability such behaviors foster prevented Robert and Martha from passing through the threshold from romance to the adventure of building a common life project.

Just as the exchange of rings and the making of vows serve to protect a young marriage from outside intrusion so the very drab habit of being reliable serves to shelter a young marriage as it progresses towards erotic love.

Summary

This chapter has covered a great deal of territory. If one chooses to pursue erotic love, the above represents but a few of the more prominent considerations worth keeping in mind. *Say* things to your lover expressing affection and indicating your hopes for your collective future. *Say* things to yourself reinforcing all you hope the two of you will achieve together. *Avoid saying things derogatory* of either your lover or your relationship. *Do* things to assure your lover how much he or she means to you. *Do* things to make yourself feel more comfortable with the relationship. *Do* things to make your lover more comfortable with the union you are building. *Do nothing to detract* from your lover's self-esteem or respect for the union itself. *Never neglect saying or doing all you can to make the relationship all you hope it will become.* Do all these things and your emotions are sure to show sustained enthusiasm for the life the two of you will share. And still there is more.

Say things that reflect your hopes for the future. Each time you *exchange* even the most loosely construed thoughts about your future together, the more you reinforce the prospect that whatever future you in fact experience, you will experience it in common with your lover. *Do* think about your partner often throughout the day. Try to *empathize* with his or her current experience of the world. Try to *imagine* what his or her plans are for your collective future. In doing these things, you develop your skills of empathy and you reinforce your commitment to the relationship.

Do show affection to your mate through appropriate demonstrative acts. Touching, hand-holding, kissing, and caressing all show you care in tender and important ways. Tenderness is experienced only by those who have learned to see beyond their own self-interest. Do you feel tender towards your beloved? Does your beloved feel tenderness towards you? Tenderness is so sophisticated even erotic lovers are unlikely to sustain the experience throughout all contact with one another. Nevertheless, the more entrenched a couple's erotic love, the more frequent physical contact will excite tenderness in them both. Without something approaching tenderness, there is no erotic love, no prospect for a life of sharing.

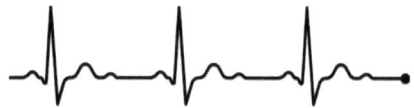

In Conclusion

This last set of chapters has been full of fun, excitement and a prescription for living happily ever after in marital bliss. These last chapters alert you to what the other sex wants in a companion. The chapters also advise you to present yourself honestly. It also cautions you about the categories of dating prospects each gender suspects (perhaps "fears" is the more appropriate word) is available for them. Remember everyone wants "something else"! Finally, do not seek marriage. For those to whom marriage has genuine appeal, every effort is made to detail the contributions partners must make to keep a relationship together.

Marriage and "enduring relationships" should not be a goal for everyone. But for those divorcees who look forward to a marriage that works, it is important to pause and consider at length what sort of relationship is required to sustain marriage.

As long as you are a carefree single, you may often find yourself referring to advice in the early chapters of this section. Should you get caught up in the throes of a hot and heavy romance, you may find yourself referring to the chapters on marriage and sharing since the prospects of impending union may be considerable. Finally, should you marry again, you will no doubt find married life full of peaks and valleys, euphoria and anxiety. In traversing the valleys, the way can be made easier if each spouse reads again the chapter entitled "Sharing." You should each dwell then on those passages which explain the nature of intimacy and how it culminates in the sharing of one life project. Together, the two of you should talk about those passages most relevant to whatever challenge is at hand. Finally, if your marriage seems to have settled so deeply into a valley that the prospects for regaining former heights seem all but lost, turn to my previous book *Love Trauma*. In this case, the point in doing so is not to prepare for divorce but rather to recall how ugly it is. With this ugliness in mind, you and your spouse may discover good reason for returning to the challenge of intimacy and marriage.

Beyond Love Trauma truly is a handbook. The reader should learn to read it very slowly and very carefully. Each section is about a different chapter in an adult's life narrative. It is one book the astute reader can benefit from again and again throughout the hereafter.

Reminders for Those Pursuing Erotic Love

1. Sharing is the foundation of erotic love.

2. Sharing leads to intimacy; intimacy fuels further sharing.

3. Intimacy is comprised of at least three separate and distinctly private experiences:

4. Sexual intimacy: This involves *risking vulnerability* to another's rejection and respecting he or she is at similar risk. Sexual intimacy concludes in a bonding of trust. It also makes available especially *privileged knowledge* to each lover.

5. Emotional intimacy: This occurs when you each serve as a *safe haven* for the expression of the other's emotional needs. This forms and strengthens trust.

6. Intellectual intimacy: This involves *respecting* the ideas of a beloved. Trust is the end product of this experience just as it is with the other two intimacies.

7. Intimacy requires trust as well as generates new conditions for the extension of trust.

8. Trust and intimacy together make erotic love possible.

9. Exercises for generating intimacy:

    i. Become as empathetic as possible toward your lover. This requires constant attention to learning more about him or her. It also requires a willingness to take leaps of imagination in order for you to vicariously experience the world as your lover experiences it.

    ii. Do not lie (or deliberately attempt to deceive)!

    iii. Secrets are not conducive to building a relationship.

10. Some secrets are even destructive and morally offensive.

11. Some secrets are wisely kept until a proper time and place is reached when the telling of the secret can be done without discomfort on anyone's part.

12. Personal integrity not only makes you a better person in the eyes of others it increases your prospects for achieving erotic love. People are less hesitant to marry or remain married to someone they know to be a person of his or her word.

13. Reliability is a trait illustrating you are sincere about your commitment. You demonstrate reliability by showing you are no longer maneuvering to score points in the dating game.

14. In general, your emotions follow the lead set by your words and actions. Happiness and the other emotions are largely a by-product of actions you directly control. Seldom do emotions pull you into action.

15. *Do* the things which show respect for you both.

16. *Say* things your lover needs to hear in his or her quest for happiness.

17. *Say* things that anticipate your shared future together. Do think about your partner throughout the day. Try briefly to empathize with what he or she may be experiencing at the moment.

18. *Do* touch one another often. This display of affection, along with mutual trust, sustains the bond of sexual intimacy between times of more intensive contact.

19. *Be* tender toward one another as often as possible. A gift, a touch, a comment, or a compliment are all rendered so much more powerful when expressive of tenderness.

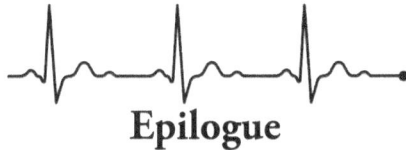

Epilogue

Remember there are many types of love. The love of a spouse is quite different from the love of a parent. Each of these in turn is different from that of a parent for a child or a child for a parent. Furthermore, in each type of love, there exists a singularly unique variant within each pair of lovers. For example, if a mother has two daughters, Sarah and Martha, the mother's love for Sarah will be different from her love for Martha. This is not to say she will love one more than the other, it just means she will love each one differently.

Love of any kind is the most intimate of human relationships. The uniqueness of each individual is a fundamental determinant in the course a love relationship takes. Sarah and Martha must be supposed to differ from one another in important ways; consequently, the relationship of love between Sarah and her mother will differ significantly from that between Martha and her mother.

Context is equally important for the expression of parental love. A child's love for a parent is affected by any hostility that exists between the parents. Assignment of custody affects future relationships between parent and child. Variance between the home environments offered by each parent influences the child's sense of belongingness and the parent's sense of responsibility. The dating activities of each parent also tend to confuse the child as to the nature of love and the enduringness of their own relationship to a given parent.

Social scientists have carried out numerous studies in recent years showing divorce is devastating to children. And divorce profoundly imperils the parent/child relationship. Parents have become increasingly aware of this fact and are taking the consequences of divorce on family life far more seriously than they did in the past. While there is much concern about these issues and much opinionated advice, there is little in the way of good, solid information. What information is available has not been collected and made available to consumers in a one easy to read volume. The need for such a volume is great.

If you are a divorced parent who has read this far, you can take comfort in the idea that at least now you have one very important area of your life under control. Having achieved this, even without additional advice on divorce-parenting, you may find you are parenting better as an indirect consequence of doing better in your social life.

As you bring each area of your life under control, your ability to negotiate the remaining problematic areas increases. As you come to understand the perplexities of a piece of life, you subsequently learn to manage it. This frees your deliberative resources for issues which continue to confuse and confound you. And the more you experience success in one domain, the self-esteem it creates often carries over to other areas as well giving you the confidence to address problems you previously feared were insurmountable.

APPENDICES

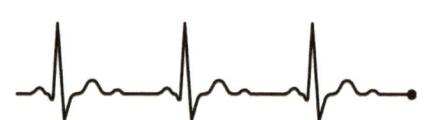

About the Author

Paul A. Wagner is a Ph.D., University of Missouri. He has taught courses in psychology, business management, philosophy, and education. He has held a number of senior level positions in national academic and scholarly organizations. He has also held positions on a number of Boards of Director in various organizations within the city of Houston and as Vice Chair of the City of Columbia's Human Rights Commission. He is a specialist in practical and applied ethics and moral theory. He himself has been a divorcee. He also has a long period of dating experiences going back to his class president days in college. He has written popular pieces on romance in the Austin American Statesman and the Dallas Morning News. He is the author of five books and over 100 publications ranging from philosophy and religion to the business of healthcare, probability, cognition, organizational development, learning theory, and the conditions for being a moral person. Once, as a result of volunteering by pushing a book cart around M.D. Anderson Cancer Center in Houston, he wrote a piece describing the romantic moments some patients experience as they cope with cancer while others realize they have no reliable companion at the end. He has had the opportunity to avail himself of the resources of a variety of social circles and in each he learned what he could about people's attitude towards marriage, divorce, dating, and responsibilities regarding child-rearing.

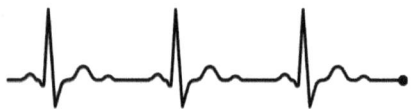

Appendix A

No one comes to the world versed in the art of sharing. Evolution ensured humans would cooperate as a species in order to survive but people learn how to share. Some learn sharing better than do others. Good marriages occur between people who share a common life project. Failed marriages occur most commonly among couples wherein one or both spouses never fully learned the art and craft of sharing.

The chapter on sharing suggests three ways a person can learn about sharing. First, and most importantly, a person can role-model others who are successful in sharing. Second, by reading or listening to thoughtful exposition, a person's attention to the details of sharing can be stimulated. While sharing is about a general attitude and disposition to act, it is through attention to detail sharing becomes most vividly evident. These are matters deserving considerable personal study, hence the third suggestion. A person must carefully think about the "experts" recommendations and about his or her attempts to role-model others.

This appendix gives you an opportunity to think about the details of sharing. In answering the questions which follow, you will learn something about your own optimal fulfillment and, I hope, that of your spouse. The questions treat concepts (many of which were adapted for this purpose from Robert Nozick's discussion of reality in his book, *The Examined Life*), which can illuminate the respondent's intended destiny.

Destiny sounds so other-worldly. Actually, it is not. Destiny identifies a destination, a place one wants to go. In undertaking a common life project with another there is a purpose at hand. The purpose is not just to go where the fates direct but, to go where *the couple* feels most complete. The purpose is not achievable by pursuing a list of activities or by designating a set of activities that can be assigned cost/benefit values and placed in a "management-by-objectives" plan.

The purpose of a couple's common life project should not be so ethereal no one can identify with it or so mundane it reduces to a mere job description. Successful couples want personal fulfillment. The only way this can be achieved is by incorporating each person's fulfillment into the couples' common sense of destiny.

The respondent to the items below should think carefully about the distinctive concept each query considers. Once completed, the couple can appreciate more fully what it takes for each spouse to be fulfilled. No deals need to be struck, no negotiations entered. With both sets of responses clearly in mind the task is to fulfill all goals as much as possible and in a mutually prioritized order where necessary.

The responses to these questions commit no one to becoming a tycoon, a marathoner or staying healthy and wrinkle-free. Rather they INFORM the parties of what it takes for each to be fulfilled. Please deliberate on the meaning of each italicized term before answering. Try not to give the same answer to more than one question. Different words are intended to mean different thoughts in this exercise. Of course, it is possible the same event produces the most meaning *and* exhibits the greatest value. Still, meaning and value are NOT synonyms. Try to identify 30 different answers for the 30 different questions.

1. When do you feel most *focused*?
2. When is your experience most *vivid*?
3. What *acts* have the most meaning for you?
4. What acts have the most *meaning for the two of you*?
5. What makes experience most *attractive* to you?
6. When do you *value your lover* most?
7. When does *your lover value you* most?
8. When do you feel most *physically intimate* with your lover?
9. What do you *value most about your relationship*?

10. When do you feel most at *harmony* in your relationship?
11. When do you feel most *serene* in your relationship?
12. When do *you feel most important* in your relationship?
13. When is *your lover most important* to you?
14. What is the most *important aspect of your relationship*?
15. When do you feel most *intellectually intimate* with your lover?
16. When do you feel most *complete*?
17. When do you feel most *intense*?
18. When do you feel most *virtuous*?
19. When do you feel most *creative*?
20. When do you most feel a common sense of *purpose* with the lover?
21. When are the two of you most likely to share a common sense of *purpose*?
22. When do you feel most fully *integrated* in the relationship?
23. When do you feel most *emotionally intimate* with your lover?
24. When do you feel your relationship gives you the greatest scope of experience?
25. When do you feel your experience has the greatest depth?
26. When do you feel the most *authentic*?
27. When do you feel most in *communion* with your lover?
28. When do you feel most *vulnerable* to your lover?
29. When do you feel most *cooperative* with your lover?
30. When do you feel most *understanding* of your lover?

When you have completed this survey, prioritize your responses in order of importance to you. Share your responses with your partner. There are no right or wrong answers. Your responses do not need to match one another's in any way. This is not an exercise aimed at measuring your compatibility. This exercise reveals what it takes for each of you to enjoy an optimal richness of life. The goal now is to work together. Develop a plan that will secure the most richness of experience for each of you. You are co-author of two interdependent life-narratives.

Appendix B

Emotional intimacy is the most potent of all the intimacies. It is crucial to couples bent on sharing a common life project.

The principal token of emotional intimacy is the secret. By sharing secrets, people bond with one another, joining a couple in a union that at the same time sets them apart from the rest of the social world.

It is necessary to energize periodically a relationship through the sharing of secrets. In the exercise which follows, a number of questions are asked that force you to dispose of boundaries separating you and your spouse. It also forces you to trust one another if the exercise is to be successful. The questions reach deeply into the mutual privacy of you and your spouse. It is necessary if the two of you are to create an enduring bond.

A couple is a new social unit. This new social unit strives to free itself from conflicting personal agendas. Ideally, *as a couple,* the two of you are becoming protective of, and coconspirators in, a single, co-extensive set of "secrets." Each of you is becoming for the other a reservoir of hidden and personal moments.

The exchange of secrets is a very delicate matter. There must be strict rules adhered to when you engage in this exercise. If you abandon the rules, you risk harming your relationship rather than enriching it. Betrayal will breed contempt. Read the rules below carefully. Begin this exchange at a moment when the two of you feel safe in the thought you can each depend on the other's unrelenting discretion.

Rules for Playing the Secret Exchange

1. Everyone has a right to privacy. No one gives up that right because they marry. No one should be coerced into answering any one of the following questions.

2. Before either of you begins answering a given question, both parties must review the question and agree to answer it with complete candor.

3. Attempt to be as detailed as possible in your answer. This is no time for being cagey or hedging your bets.

4. Do not attempt to answer any more than three of the following questions at any one sitting. To attempt too much can be exhausting. When people become exhausted they become easily agitated. Overkill can also lead the respondents to become glib with their responses. Since your goal here is to develop emotional intimacy, there is nothing to be gained by creating shortcuts and risk misunderstanding through either deceit or omission.

The Secret Exchange

1. As a child, when were you most *frightened*?

2. As a child, what is the *meanest* thing you ever did?

3. As a teenager, on what one occasion did you feel you looked the *ugliest*?

4. As a child, what is the most *charitable* thing you ever did (and very few people know about)?

5. As an adult, what is the *cruelest* thing you ever did?
6. As a child, what is the *sneakiest* thing you ever did?
7. As a child, what is the most *heroic* thing you did (and very few people know about)?
8. As an adult, what is the most *noble* thing you did (and very few people know about)?
9. As an adult, what is the *gentlest* thing you have ever done?
10. As an adult, when did you most *fear* that you didn't have "the right stuff?"
11. What was the *kindest* thing anyone ever did for you?
12. When were you most *humiliated* by an adult member of the other sex?
13. What was the *kindest* thing a stranger ever did for you?
14. What *sexual* event do you most regret?
15. When were you most *proud* of either parent?
16. As an adult what is the most *dangerous* thing you experienced?
17. What is your most secret *phobic* reaction?
18. What do you *fear most about growing old*?
19. What is the most *sensitive* thing you have ever done?
20. When were you most *ashamed* of your own actions?
21. When were you most *shamed* by another?
22. What was the *luckiest* thing that ever happened to you?
23. Describe the most *spiritual/mystical* moment in your life.
24. On what single moment did you experience the most grief?
25. Describe the one social occasion in which you felt the most awkward.

26. Describe a moment in which you felt terribly boastful but remained silent because it would have been in bad taste to do otherwise.

27. Describe one day in which you felt most loved as a child.

28. Describe the most embarrassing event of your teenage life.

29. Describe the time in your life when you felt most hopeless.

30. Describe the time in your life when you felt most hopeful.

31. When do you feel most *complete*?

32. When do you feel most *intense*?

33. When do you feel most *virtuous*?

34. When do you feel most *creative*?

35. When do you most feel a common sense of *purpose* with the lover?

36. When are the two of you most likely to share a common sense of *purpose*?

37. When do you feel most fully *integrated* in the relationship?

38. When do you feel most *emotionally intimate* with your lover?

39. When do you feel your relationship gives you the greatest *scope* of experience?

40. When do you feel your experience has the greatest *depth*?

41. When do you feel the most *authentic*?

42. When do you feel most in *communion* with your lover?

43. When do you feel most *vulnerable* to your lover?

44. When do you feel most *cooperative* with your lover?

45. When do you feel most *understanding* of your lover?

www.ingramcontent.com/pod-product-compliance
Lightning Source LLC
Chambersburg PA
CBHW030148100526
44592CB00009B/173